Foreword by *Dr. Shefali*

THE PERFECTLY IMPERFECT FAMILY

Real Solutions *for* Mindful Parents
Navigating *Today's* Biggest Challenges

CECILIA & JASON HILKEY
and other leading voices

SUMMIT PRESS

Disclaimer:

The information in this book is provided for educational and informational purposes only. The parenting tips and conflict resolution strategies reflect the authors' personal experiences and opinions. What has worked for the authors may not be suitable for every family or situation.

Names, identifying details, and certain scenarios have been changed to protect the privacy of individuals involved in the stories shared throughout this book.

For serious family conflicts or behavioral issues, readers are encouraged to seek guidance from qualified professionals. The authors and publisher do not provide psychological or legal services and assume no responsibility for how this information is applied.

Summit Press Publishers
PO Box 1356
Intervale, New Hampshire 03845

First Edition: May 2025

ISBN: 979-8-9852063-5-7

For information about special discounts available for bulk purchase, workshops, retreats, and webinars associated with this book, please contact us at support@HappilyFamily.com.

The Perfectly Imperfect Family is a real, practical, and relatable guide that reminds parents it's not about getting it all right—it's about building strong, connected relationships with your kids. Packed with insights from a multitude of experts and parents who get it, this book gives you the tools to handle parenting challenges with more confidence, clarity, and calm. A must-read for parents who want real solutions without the pressure of perfection.

—**Dr. Ann-Louise Lockhart**, PsyD, ABPP, *pediatric psychologist & parent coach*

In *The Perfectly Imperfect Family*, a collective wisdom emerges from the diverse range of expert voices. This wisdom emphasizes the importance of listening inward to discover our own healing and growth. By making this intentional investment, we can become models of mindful living, recognizing that our actions teach far more than our words. In a world focused on achievement and social comparison, these voices of care, love, and the acceptance of imperfection are not only welcome but also desperately needed.

—**Jennifer Miller, M.Ed.,** author of *Confident Parents, Confident Kids; Raising Emotional Intelligence In Ourselves and Our Kids — From Toddlers to Teenagers*

This book feels like sitting with a wise friend who gets it. *The Perfectly Imperfect Family* isn't full of fluff. It's filled with real stories, raw truths, and tools that meet parents right where they are. If you've ever thought, "I've read all the advice, and I'm still stuck," this book helps you breathe, reset, and remember that you're not broken—and neither is your family."

—**Dayna Abraham,** author of *Calm the Chaos: A Fail-Proof Roadmap for Parenting Even the Most Challenging Kids*

TABLE OF CONTENTS

Section Two:
Managing Stress and Finding Calm

Section Three:
Authentic Communication for Deeper Family Connections

Section Four:
Navigating Power Struggles with Wisdom and Grace

Section Five:

Understanding and Supporting Neurodivergent Children

FOREWORD

It is with deep joy and admiration that I write this foreword for the powerful and timely book *The Perfectly Imperfect Family*. As a pioneer (and eternal student) of conscious parenting, I know firsthand the courage it takes to redefine what it means to raise children in today's world. This book not only takes that bold step but also offers parents everywhere a compassionate, practical, and transformational roadmap for parenting from the inside out—a roadmap we all deeply crave.

Conscious parenting, in its truest essence, is not a set of techniques. It is not about following checklists, obeying scripts, reading the right books, or mimicking those who appear to have it all together. At its core, it is a sacred journey of self-awareness and self-discovery. It is a mirror—a relentless, unfiltered mirror—that reflects the parent's deepest beliefs, wounds, and conditioned patterns. This is why I was immediately drawn to the heart of this book: its unwavering commitment to self-awareness and growth as the foundation of parenting.

This practical and insightful book begins where all conscious parenting must begin—within the parent. The inside-out approach to raising children challenges the cultural paradigm that tells us we must first fix our children's behavior. Instead, the authors invite us to pause and ask the more profound question: Who am I, and how am I showing up in this relationship? These questions alone can shift the entire trajectory of our parenting path.

As parents, we often look outward for solutions. We are bombarded with advice, overwhelmed by expectations, and conditioned by generational norms that tell us to control, discipline, and mold our children into socially acceptable forms. But this book reminds us—gently yet firmly—that our ability to parent effectively begins with our ability to be present with ourselves. In truth, our children don't need perfect parents. They need parents who are present, attuned, and willing to do the deep inner work.

Self-awareness, as this book articulates so beautifully, is not a luxury in parenting—it is a necessity. It allows us to break free from reactive cycles and show up with compassion and clarity. When we recognize how our own upbringing, fears, and unconscious beliefs influence the way we respond to our children, we open the door to transformation. We begin to see our children not as problems to be fixed, but as sovereign individuals to be understood and empowered—for who they are, not who we wish them to be.

This wonderful book offers readers powerful tools for making the shift from reaction to response. This is no small feat. We all know what it feels like to lose our temper, to be overwhelmed by the chaos of daily life, to feel helpless in the face of a tantrum or power struggle. But in these very moments, we are given the opportunity to choose presence over reactivity. These pages guide us with wisdom and grace toward regulation, mindfulness, and emotional attunement—skills that not only change how we parent, but who we become as human beings.

One of the most impactful themes in this book is the emphasis on authentic communication. As a psychologist, I have seen how breakdowns in communication erode relationships—not only between parent and child but within the family as a whole. The lessons in these pages teach us that connection is built not through control, but through listening, validation, and openness. When we learn to hear our children without judgment, to sit with their emotions rather than fix them, we lay the foundation for lifelong trust.

Perhaps even more powerful is the reminder that conflict is not the enemy—disconnection is. In advocating for relationship-centered approaches to conflict, the authors dismantle the outdated notion that parents must dominate to lead. Instead, they show us how to lead through connection, cooperation, and mutual respect. It is here that true authority arises—not from fear, but from relational presence.

I was especially moved by this book's attention to the needs of neurodivergent children. In a world that often pathologizes difference, the authors offer a refreshing and compassionate lens—one that sees strengths instead of deficits, potential instead of problems. This perspective is crucial not only for parents of neurodivergent children but for all of us. It calls us to expand our understanding of what it means to thrive and to meet each child where they are, rather than where we think they should be.

At the core of the book is the understanding that the parent-child relationship is primary. Techniques, strategies, and routines matter far less than the energy we bring into the room. Our children feel us. They sense our stress, our disconnection, our love, and our presence. When we focus on the relationship—nurturing it with honesty, vulnerability, and attunement—we give our children the greatest gift of all: the experience of being seen, heard, and loved for who they truly are.

This book also courageously explores the terrain of intergenerational patterns. So many of us carry the weight of family dynamics that were never questioned—only repeated. This book empowers parents to become conscious cycle-breakers. It is both healing and hopeful to see how the authors blend storytelling, research, and practical guidance to help readers liberate themselves from inherited scripts and author new narratives for their families.

And perhaps the most heartening message of all is this: there is no such thing as a perfect parent. In celebrating perfectly imperfect parenting, these pages free us from the impossible standards that so often plague the modern parent. Instead of striving for an unattainable ideal, we are invited to embrace authenticity, repair, and growth. Mistakes are no longer failures—they become opportunities to model resilience, humility, and the courage to begin again.

The Perfectly Imperfect Family is more than a parenting book—it is a guide for living with intention, vulnerability, and love. It reminds us that while parenting may be the hardest job in the world, it is also the most meaningful. Each moment with our children is an invitation to awaken—to grow in consciousness, to choose love over fear, presence over control.

As I turned the pages of this book, I felt not only informed but inspired. I saw reflections of my own journey—my own missteps and breakthroughs. I felt a kinship with the authors as fellow seekers: parents who are willing to stand in the messy, beautiful reality of raising children while raising themselves.

To every parent who picks up this book: you are not alone. You are not broken. You do not need to be perfect. What you need is the willingness to show up—with honesty, compassion, and presence. This book will meet you there.

With deepest respect and love,
Dr. Shefali
NYT Bestselling Author of *The Parenting Map*

SECTION ONE:
HEALING, GROWING, AND FINDING BALANCE IN PARENTHOOD

1

THE WAKE-UP CALL I NEEDED TO FIND BALANCE IN MY LIFE AND MY PARENTING

Susan Notis

D o you approach parenting like an academic thesis paper? Researching every philosophy, reading every book, and scrolling late into the night for the "right" way to raise your kids? Do you feel inauthentic following a parenting model that seemed good on paper, or like a failure when it doesn't yield the expected results? I know this struggle well.

I embraced my hardworking parents' mindset—"Educate yourself, give it your all, and you can achieve anything"—and applied it to every area of my life. However, when it came to parenting, that approach didn't work for me. I tried to do it all: preparing meals from scratch, limiting screen time, filling every day with activities, creating a community of like-minded families, and crafting a nurturing environment for my children. I applied techniques I learned as a teacher and constantly strived to check off each item on my mental list of what it meant to be the "perfect mom."

But after four years and the arrival of my second child, I hit a wall. I was overwhelmed, exhausted, and my body was sending me clear signals that something needed to change. That's when, at 36, I received a cancer diagnosis.

During the week I spent in isolation for radiation treatment, I experienced my first real break from the kids in four years of motherhood. As strange as it sounds, it felt like a vacation. That realization hit me hard: I had been pushing myself to the limit and was running on empty. It was a wake-up call. I began my journey of self-reflection. I had to let go of the need for perfection and focus on what truly mattered: being present for my kids and finding joy in the beautifully messy, imperfect reality of life and motherhood.

The path to wholeness and balance was long and will be a lifelong journey for me. It required reevaluating all the areas and relationships in my life. I now parent from a regulated nervous system and practice balance each day. My health, my family, and my students have reaped the rewards. I now coach other families on their journey toward wellness.

Here's what I've learned along the way:

Create Balance Across All Areas of Life

A balance between mental, physical, emotional, and spiritual energies is key to nurturing a healthy, thriving family. When I work with parents to map out these different areas of their lives, we can identify aspects that are being neglected. These systems are deeply interconnected, and when they're in harmony, we feel whole, centered, and regulated. This, in turn, flows to your child, creating a space for co-regulation. Your calmness provides a model for your child to mirror, fostering a harmonious, centered family.

Act With Compassion

Parenting is challenging, and it's easy to say and do things you regret. Practice pausing and responding with empathy, both toward your children and yourself. When we can stay grounded through the highs and lows of parenting, we can respond intentionally rather than reactively in challenging moments.

Look For Gratitude in the Simple Things

In the hustle and bustle of everyday life, it's easy to overlook the little moments. Whether it's a quiet morning spent reading a poem, stepping outside to listen to the birds sing, or letting the sound of your child's laughter fill your heart, slowing down to appreciate life's nuances often leads to moments of true joy.

Align With Your Inner Wisdom

Parenting is an evolving journey. While it's important to explore new strategies and techniques, don't forget to trust your own instincts. You know your child best. The wisdom to know what's best for your family in any situation is already within you. Parenting is more of an art than a science. Flexibility and adaptability are key. Trust your intuition because it's your most powerful tool.

Nurture Knowledge of Your Child's Developmental Stage

By tuning into your child's specific growth and developmental stage, rather than applying a one-size-fits-all solution, you create your own parenting style rooted in understanding, not rigid rules. This creates more meaningful guidance that evolves as your children grow.

Commit to Self-Care

This was a tough one for me, especially while teaching full-time. Taking time for yourself can feel like taking time away from your kids. Ask yourself what you want to model. The answer for me was clear: I wanted my kids to see that self-care is essential.

Taking care of myself meant I was showing up better for them. This involved creating a strong support system of family and fellow parents who wanted to trade childcare—doing things like taking my kids to the playground after school to free up time for me.

Develop a Well-Planned Chore List

When a family works together to manage household tasks, your schedule suddenly becomes more open for time away from home. See below for a chore list that can be utilized for children as young as two.

Eliminate the Unnecessary

Take a step back and assess what truly matters to your family. The goal is to simplify. Focus on tasks that align with your values and let go of everything else that doesn't serve a bigger purpose.

Discover the Freedom in Imperfection

True success doesn't look like a pristine home or picture-perfect family life. It's about fostering a space where love and laughter fill the rooms, even if things are a little messy. The dream isn't about perfection—it's about connection. Rather than stressing over mistakes, see them as opportunities to teach resilience and adaptability when life throws a curveball.

Conclusion

How did I reach a place where I coach parents toward creating harmony in their families? I've always been drawn to a holistic perspective. As a holistic health chef and someone who spent many years teaching in a school based on a holistic model, I knew there had to be a healing approach that addressed the whole person.

The real transformation happened for me when I added an integrative wellness coach to complement my regular therapy sessions. When I stopped chasing the idea of perfect parenting and started prioritizing my own balance, I discovered a sense of inner peace. I saw something incredible happen: the energy in our home shifted. The anxious, chaotic vibrations gave way to a calm, centered space.

While I offer a variety of tools to clients for tackling challenging parenting moments, I find that when parents are guided to find balance within themselves, it naturally leads to the peaceful, harmonious family we all desire and deserve.

Susan Notis is a certified integrative wellness coach and the founder of *In Balance Life and Parent Coaching*. With a passion for helping parents navigate the challenges of raising children, she offers coaching programs designed to alleviate overwhelm, release perfectionism, foster balance, and empower parents to lead with compassion. Drawing from her experience as an award-winning teacher in both public and holistic schools, as well as her role as an educator for parents and teachers, Notis combines personal insights with professional expertise to empower families. A proud mom of two teenagers, she is dedicated to supporting parents on their journey. Visit www.inbalancelifeandparentcoaching.com for her free guide, *Creating Age-Appropriate Chores for the Entire Family*, and to schedule a free consultation to explore her coaching services.

2

HEALING YOURSELF IS LOVING YOUR CHILD: WHY WE HAVE TO RECONNECT TO OURSELVES TO MEET OUR CHILDREN'S NEEDS

Anita Stewart

———

W hen my oldest child was almost three, I woke up to a painful truth. We were preparing to visit my parents overseas. Despite having ample time, I felt the pressure of leaving. However, my daughter didn't cooperate; she became increasingly upset until she had a full-on meltdown. For a moment, I, too, got upset, thinking, *This isn't normal* and *This is unfair.* Then I looked at my crying daughter, clearly unhappy and stressed. I realized that it was *me, my* own inner state, that had led to her reaction. I wasn't the victim here; I was the cause.

At the time, I had been working as a parenting coach for quite a while, held a PhD in Psychology, and had a solid understanding of how evolution has shaped child nature and how to raise confident, competent, kind, and happy children. I understood much of it conceptually but not in spirit.

Children are highly attuned to their caregivers' experiences, taking on their fear and pain.[1] Both our outer *and inner* states matter. When we were preparing to leave, I was stressed and full of fear: fear of not making it to the airport on time, fear of missing our connecting flight, and fear that the flight itself would be challenging. It has been a painful but deeply healing journey to realize those fears stemmed from my own trauma. As a child, leaving was always stressful and chaotic. My nervous system reacted to the past, not the present.

In that moment, my daughter was communicating something through her unhappiness. On one level, she was expressing her fear (of me), and on a deeper level, she was indicating that her needs weren't being met.

Children's Behavior, Emotions, and Needs

We often focus on children's behavior and ways to "fix" it. But children's behavior isn't the real problem; it's a symptom revealing how they feel. A happy child may jump or sing; a scared child may cry or hide. Behavior reflects deeper emotions and, beneath those, core needs. When children's needs are met, they feel joy; when unmet, they feel fear or anger.

All children share the same needs for safety and autonomy because meeting these needs has been crucial for survival throughout our evolutionary history—just as a plant needs water and sun to thrive.

Let me explain.

Safety

There are two aspects to the need for safety.

1. Physical Closeness

Children rely on us for safety. For most of human history, we lived among predators, which meant leaving a child alone could be fatal. This shaped children's psychology to associate physical closeness with safety. Today, children aren't in danger when alone in their room at night, but their nervous system doesn't understand this. It has been shaped by the very situations that posed real threats throughout our history.[2]

2. Emotional Closeness

Children depend on us for protection, so they need to feel reassured that we are invested in their safety. Our unconditional love and acceptance provide this reassurance.[3] They feel emotionally close when spending time with us, learning to become competent and confident members of their group by mimicking our behavior.[4] Pushing children away or showing annoyance makes them feel threatened.

Autonomy

Children have an innate drive for autonomy, evident in toddlers' desire to do everything themselves. This drive helps them grow into competent, confident adults. Constant interference, correction, and control can disconnect them from their intuition, leading them to become people pleasers or rebels. This outward focus, while not immediately life-threatening, can have detrimental effects on mental and physical health over time.[5]

Meeting children's needs comes down to being connected and attuned, allowing them to feel loved and free, secure enough to stand up for their boundaries, and naturally willing to cooperate.

From this framework that views children's needs as the root cause of their emotions and behavior, we can understand why mainstream parenting approaches often backfire:

- **Focusing (solely) on behavior**

    When children "misbehave," they are expressing uncomfortable emotions and unmet needs. Focusing on behavior without addressing the root cause makes children feel unheard and can lead them to act out how they feel even more strongly.

- **Focusing mainly on emotions**

    Validating children's uncomfortable emotions while simultaneously causing them—by undermining their autonomy or withholding closeness—leaves children feeling betrayed and confused, worsening their behavior over time.

- **Focusing (solely) on the child rather than ourselves**

   I realized during our trip to the airport how often *my* own fear or stress triggers my children's distress. Children depend on us for survival; when we're anxious, the world feels unsafe to them. As Gabor Maté demonstrates in *The Myth of Normal*, most of us carry childhood trauma. When our needs went unmet, our nervous systems learned to be in constant fear, making it hard to provide children with physical or emotional closeness or sufficient freedom. While this may be common in our culture, it's not inevitable.

To break the cycle of intergenerational trauma, we need to confront our own pain and heal.

How to Break Intergenerational Trauma

1. **Identify underlying emotions and needs.**

   Ask: "Which emotion is driving this behavior? Which unmet need might be causing that emotion?"

2. **Reframe your child's behavior.**

   Instead of "Why are they making my life so difficult?" shift to "My child is asking for my help." This simple change can alter how you feel and respond.

3. **Notice your own internal state.**

   Is there anger, fear, stomach pain, or shoulder tension? Simply be with these emotions and sensations without thinking, judging, or justifying. Becoming aware of and accepting them reduces their influence, allowing you to respond flexibly and meet your child's needs. This is the essence of healing ourselves.

As with all healing, this is easier said than done, and there are additional steps and tools to help us heal and meet our children's needs (see my bio for more resources). Roadblocks may arise. When children feel safer, they often express suppressed pain more intensely at first. If we can hold space for that, it can be profoundly healing. Another key element is compassion for ourselves. It's difficult to accept our role in our children's distress. Many parents feel shame and either deny it or blame themselves. I still sometimes struggle with this. But the only way to truly heal and offer unconditional love is to cultivate compassion for ourselves, recognizing that it wasn't our fault our own needs weren't met (nor our parents'). Although challenging, this offers a beautiful opportunity to create a harmonious, joyful family life.

I still have areas to work on in healing my own trauma and in better meeting my children's needs. However, now when we go on a trip, it's easy and fun—no stress from me. No meltdowns.

Anita Stewart has a PhD in Psychology from the University of British Columbia and is the founder of Growing Up Connected. She helps parents and caregivers understand and heal their own trauma and unresolved pain, reconnect to their intuition, and understand and meet their children's needs so that their children can grow up happy, confident, competent, and kind. Anita approaches her work through an evolutionary and trauma-informed perspective. She offers families support through one-on-one sessions, workshops, and online courses. Anita lives with her two children, husband, and parents-in-law in a multi-generational home on Vancouver Island off the West Coast of Canada. She enjoys spending time with her family and friends, engaging in outdoor activities, gardening, and music. Her vision is that all children feel at home in the world and that families flourish and grow together, as humans did (and still do in many cultures) for most of our history. Download free resources that dive deeper into the topic of this chapter and help address challenging behaviors at https://www.growingupconnected.com/book.

3

YOU ARE PART OF THE EQUATION

Sandy King

When I was only four years old, I learned a tried-and-tested way of relating to and responding to others. I have used this approach to face life and its challenges for almost 50 years.

I used my small voice boldly to contribute an idea to a game among family friends. It was a fabulous idea, bound for glory in the annals of childhood fun and creativity. It reflected my desires, strong sense of self, wants, brilliance, and wisdom at such a young age. That idea was perfect, whole, complete, creative, resourceful, and wise. This is what kids are.

And yet, as that four-year-old, the youngest in the group of kids that day, I learned that my ideas were not valued and that I should "shut up." That four-year-old me learned to tone down my voice, my ideas, and my wanting for me.

Fast forward 43 years.

As a parent of, at one point, five kids under the age of five—two sets of twins and one in the middle—I continued my tried-and-tested way of relating. Without conscious awareness and with accolades for my "selfless" parenting, I maintained the belief that others' ideas were probably better than mine, that my needs and wants were less important, and that it was okay to be great but not too great at what you do. Don't stand out.

I developed the habit of putting myself last, holding back my ideas, forgetting fun, and working hard to make it okay for others.

This worked well for my kids and husband at the receiving end. However, 20+ years into parenting and partnering, resentment began to build, and I realized that I had lost part of who I was. I lost touch with my strong sense of self, drive, and deep wanting.

Don't get me wrong; I am a strong-willed individual, a devoted mum, a passionate life coach, community-minded, and nature-loving. I'm in a respectful and loving relationship with my husband, I identify as a feminist, and I have a sharp and clever mind. I don't act like a four-year-old now—not really—or do I?

The truth is, we can never know the meanings our kids will assign to their experiences. I didn't realize what an impact those and subsequent events had on me until recent years. This points to a fundamental truth about parenting. Ultimately, *we cannot control or know the meanings our children will take from the lives they have with us.*

So, if we ultimately can't control how our kids make meaning of life, what *are* the most foundational things we can work on as great parents?

It is as simple and yet as complex as:

1. **Learning to hold our own energetic sense of self** (so our kids can learn to hold themselves in the world),

2. **Calming our nervous systems** (so our kids can learn to manage their anxiety or emotional upsets), and ...

3. **Knowing that it is okay and important to want what we want** (so our kids can feel the deep motivation to strive towards something they value).

We are people, too.

When others always come first, especially in early parenting (and they must at times), and we begin to suppress our own needs and desires habitually, this can become a breeding ground for resentment and disappointment—essentially creating an inner conflict of dissatisfaction and depletion that spills over into our parenting and partnering relationships over time.

Some Context

In the parenting world, we have been conditioned to believe that it is not okay to want for ourselves. I am here to say that listening to our deeper sense of self and expressing our wants is essential for healthy parenting in the long run. It's also important to note that we will not always be able to fulfill our wants and desires; it may not be appropriate or viable at the time. However, it is a dangerous thing to suppress our wants altogether.

By "wants," I mean our deepest desires—to be seen, heard, and feel significant in the world. I don't mean wanting a new car, time for meditation, or a house cleaner; while these are valid and real wants, I am talking about the psychological need to feel seen, heard, and validated, the fundamental need to express who we truly are. This is the gold that becomes a beacon for our children.

As the author Terry Real says, "Great relationships (as a parent or partner) start with your relationship to self."

So, we must begin with ourselves. First, see, hear, and speak your needs and wants to yourself, then the outer world. Get real with yourself.

Welcome to Soul Parenting

Soul Parenting looks beyond how we attempt to parent our kids on the outside and recognizes our inner parenting patterns and our relationship with our deepest desires to be seen and heard. This is where we learn to hold our power and make ourselves part of the picture. Soul Parenting has the intergenerational ripple effect of freeing those who came before us and those who flow from us.

Soul Parenting; Inside Out Parenting, Partnering, and Personal Power support you to:

1. **Reclaim the ability to fully manage your fight-or-flight response when triggered**. This requires that we be aware of what is happening to our energy in the moment. This is an important early step. We must learn how to call our energy home and, from that place, make our decisions (see downloadable meditation below).

2. **Learn how to release the strong emotions** that cloud our judgment and drop into our inner intuitive knowing, freeing us to be fully present as parents.

3. **Hold empowering beliefs** such as "I trust and know that I am responsible for myself, and I hold space for others," which is infinitely more resourceful than believing "I am responsible for everyone and everything."

Please know that the inner shifts in how we hold ourselves have outer impacts. Have you ever noticed that when you and your partner argue, the conflict between kids increases?

Neuroscience now confirms that it takes just 0.07 seconds for a person to sense and respond to the energy in a room.[6] When this is unconscious, it is often adding fuel to the fire.

In the words of a client, "I don't want my kids to have the same issues; I want to break the cycle for them. I needed control for so long, and now I'm trusting myself to know what is needed in the moment, which changes who I am as a parent. My kids don't have to inherit my old struggles anymore."

It is important to recognize that as we soul-parent ourselves and tend to our nervous systems, we leave a lasting legacy for our children because our energy is deeply connected. Doing this work at any age frees both our children and ourselves. By clearing the static in our lives, we can be more present for our families, heal the past, and heal moving forward. Your children and your present self will thank you.

Sandy King has been a Whole Connections Coach for over eleven years, working with hundreds of families. She is a Master NLP Practitioner and an ICF-certified coach and trainer specializing in Kids Coaching Connection and The Empowerment Dynamic. Through her groundbreaking program, *Soul Parenting: Inside-Out Parenting, Partnering, and Personal Power*, she guides parents to transform their relationships with their children by addressing intergenerational patterns and inner parenting dynamics both practically and emotionally. Sandy is married to Christos and is a parent of five young adults. She has redesigned her life from the inside out, putting herself back in the picture and reinvigorating all her relationships and her vitality for life in the process.

When not coaching, Sandy loves bushwalking, spending time with family and friends, and cold plunges.

Access her free "Calling My Energy Home" meditation and "Emotions Across the Ages" PDF at https://sandykingcoaching.com.au/calling-your-energy-home.

4

GROWING TOGETHER: LESSONS LEARNED THROUGH SELF-REFLECTIVE PARENTING

Cathy Milwidsky

During the expectant parents' tour of the maternity ward, where we would welcome our child, Midwife Flo asked us to raise our hands to show who had read any books for new parents. We all raised our hands with confidence and pride, feeling well-prepared. She smiled kindly, "I'm glad you've done some reading. However, remember: your baby has not read a single one of those books." Some parents chuckled; others went silent. I heard her words deeply and recognized how profoundly her wisdom would shape my parenting journey.

Soon, I discovered that babies are born with their own wisdom and a reliable means of connecting and communicating.

I learned that listening to my inner voice was the most powerful way to foster a secure and loving relationship with my baby. I quieted external voices, turned inward to discover my authentic self, and embraced my strengths and vulnerabilities.

My two daughters became my most profound teachers, holding us accountable and challenging us to be their most dependable support. They taught me that to be the nurturing, intuitive parent I aspired to be, I needed to embark on a journey of deep self-understanding.

My parenting experience was enriched by my years working in early childhood leadership with talented educators and dedicated parents. The hundreds of children who entered my world, sharing their unique stories, reinforced my belief that when we show up for our children, hear what they have to say, and genuinely understand their communications, we give them the best chance to feel secure. Creating a space where children feel truly seen, held, and safe becomes the foundation for their growth and ability to thrive.

These are the four transformative life lessons I learned while navigating the complex responsibilities of raising young children:

The Legacy of Genetic Inheritance

Parents carry a profound responsibility to nurture not just their children's physical being but their entire essence. Each new person is born into a unique family with their genetic signature. Scientific research reveals how early experiences can deeply influence genetic expression, with impacts that may extend beyond our immediate generation.[7] Our experiences and emotional landscapes weave themselves into the genetic tapestry of our children and future generations.

This understanding of epigenetics can feel overwhelming, but it also empowers us to make intentional choices that support both our children's and our own holistic development.

Cultivating Curiosity: The Bridge of Connection

Babies are born with an innate drive to connect with their primary caregivers. They are completely dependent on this connection, and their understanding of the world is shaped by their caregivers' responses.

Parenthood unveiled the profound wonder of human connection through my baby's subtle, persistent efforts to engage. With each new stage, a new curiosity emerged. Engaging deeply with my child's developmental journey became a path of personal growth and increasing parental confidence. My learning was personal and profound. My genuine interest and loving gaze made my child feel seen and loved and inspired her own curiosity about the world.

Curiosity is one of our most profound human attributes, enriching our collective experience. Parenting often brings uncertainty about engagement and decision-making. It is helpful in these moments to be curious and to ask a question I discovered deep in my parenting experience: "Am I helping or hurting my child?"—a transformative question that invited me to draw upon my life experiences, personal values, and deepest understanding of my child's needs.

The Power of Presence

Children illuminate the complexity of human experience, revealing how our rich emotional landscape can challenge our daily routines.

Rushing, suppressing, or dismissing our emotions erodes our fundamental human experience. Children rely on us to guide them and provide a safe space for all their emotions to be felt, named, understood, processed, embraced, and received.

Navigating this emotional terrain can feel overwhelming for parents. I gradually understood three crucial insights: first, pausing before reacting; second, recognizing my choice in response; and third, taking a moment to consider how I was experiencing often revealed my child's emotional state and the support they required. This self-awareness became my compass for supporting my child's emotional journey. A tired child might need quiet rest, while an anxious child finds comfort in a structured approach. The results were transformative!

Hands as Vessels of Love

Holding hands represents a profound connection, a silent language of love shared with those closest to us. Each gentle touch—guiding a child across a street, soothing them to sleep, or wiping away tears—communicates a fundamental message of safety and unconditional love.

Children observe our hands with remarkable attentiveness. We write, type, fix, chop, and plant; we clap, open, close, and hold. We paint, knit, hammer, and cut. Inviting children to participate in our activities sparks their joy and supports their developmental growth. Our hands express our heart's intentions, while children's hands are powerful tools for exploration and learning. Our children look to us to learn how to be in the world; they follow the details and feel the rewards. The more they practice, the more confident they become.

Their growing confidence becomes the foundation of their sense of belonging.

Conclusion

The human experience remains beautifully complex, with each generation facing unique challenges. Nurturing independent, thoughtful children requires a profound commitment to intentional parenting. We can do this if we trust ourselves and care for our well-being. We can do this when we know ourselves better and when we understand we are part of a larger community of parents. This self-awareness parent with authenticity and love.

Cathy Milwidsky is both a high school and early childhood educator and a registered counselor. Cathy held the position of Head of Early Learning and Development at a large school (ELC to Year 12) for 18 years; she is a steadfast advocate for young children, their families, and educators, understanding and promoting the importance of these foundational years. Prior to this, Cathy worked as part of a Family Support Team in a communal organization, providing counseling and guidance to vulnerable families. More recently, Cathy has harnessed her skills and experience to establish an educational consultancy, Loving Well, designed for parents and educators of young children.

Cathy's first children's book, *Why Is Baby Joe Crying, Papa?* which explores the importance of crying as an integral part of the healing process across generations, was published in 2024 under the pen name Anna Mills.

Cathy was born in Johannesburg, South Africa, and in 1997, she immigrated to live in Sydney, Australia, with her husband and two daughters. They all feel fortunate to belong to a large, extended, and loving family.

5

THE PLEASER'S PARENTING DILEMMA: HOW TO PARENT WITHOUT LOSING YOURSELF

Michelle Godfrey

"Fists clenched, I screamed at the top of my lungs, completely out of control. My two kids, the most adorable little beings I love more than life itself, cowered in disbelief, petrified of the monster their gentle, loving mummy had suddenly become. The click of the front door opening pierced 'The Wheels on the Bus', and I reeled around, our chaos interrupted.

"On autopilot, my body launched toward the hallway. My feet pounded through the kitchen, my arm outstretched, my finger thrust forward. I don't remember what I shouted—only the exhaustion, frustration, resentment, despair, and anger.

"Suddenly, my husband's equally enraged face was pressed against mine.

"Time froze. Shocked, my pulse pounded like war drums. As if pierced by a jolt of clarity, I noticed our children. Their tiny, wide-eyed faces mirrored the damage I was causing—not just the fear at the moment but a threat to the safe, loving environment I'd worked so hard to create.

"My face pushed into his. Transforming my voice into a slow, articulate weapon, I coldly stated, 'We better take this upstairs, away from the kids,' thinking, *I'm not going to be ignored anymore. I'm not going to keep letting him get away with this.*"

Janice had kept her eyes fixed on the floor as she shared this story with me over Zoom. The scene she described couldn't have been more polarized from the mum, wife, and person she strived to be. It contradicted every family and personal value she held. So, what had happened?

The Pleaser Saboteur

In my coaching practice, I've encountered many clients who sabotage themselves. In my quest to understand this phenomenon, I discovered Shirzad Chamine's work (founder of Positive Intelligence). His research identifies ten negative autopilot responses, or "saboteurs," that undermine us.

These include the Judge (universal to everyone), Avoider, Controller, Hyper-Achiever, Hyper-Rational, Hyper-Vigilant, Pleaser, Stickler, Restless, and Victim.

While everyone has the Judge, the other saboteurs appear in different combinations depending on our personality traits and life experiences.

Our innate personality traits help us navigate childhood challenges, but they can become saboteurs when overused. For example, empathy, love, and a giving nature—qualities that create connection—can morph into the Pleaser saboteur. People with this pattern strive to make others happy to gain approval and avoid rejection, frequently neglecting their own needs; this is often referred to as people-pleasing.

This pattern leads to exhaustion, resentment, and a loss of self. The effects on family life can be devastating, for example:

- Parents experience burnout and emotional depletion from neglecting self-care, leading to increased impatience and emotional absenteeism.

- Families suffer from reduced quality time together as parents struggle with exhaustion and overwhelming schedules.

- Family boundaries become inconsistent, undermining the security that all family members need to feel safe.

- Children develop patterns of prioritizing others' needs over their own, fostering fear of conflict and rejection that impacts their future relationships and self-esteem.

- Family members struggle with emotional regulation as suppressed feelings lead to withdrawal or unexpected outbursts.

- Parents and children lose authentic connection with each other as genuine interactions are replaced by functional exchanges.

- Family members turn to overindulgence in food, screens, or other activities as coping mechanisms for unaddressed emotional needs.

The Pleaser had pushed Janice to the breaking point, damaging her health and family life and causing her to lose her cool that day.

Recognizing her Pleaser was the first step to reclaiming her power.

This is Me

Here's how we worked together to restore balance using a process I call "This is Me."

1. Rediscover values.

People often lose sight of their identity and values when influenced by the Pleaser saboteur. Rediscovering them is crucial. Using guided exercises, Janice clarified what truly mattered to her. Values became her compass for decision-making and boundary-setting.

2. Recognize and label the Pleaser.

Awareness is key, as saboteurs thrive on automatic reactions. Janice learned to notice when the Pleaser took over by paying attention to her emotions, body sensations, and triggers.

Initially, this was difficult; she had suppressed her emotions for years. We used tools like a body chart, an emotions wheel, and five-minute meditations to help her tune in. Once she recognized the telltale signs of the Pleaser, she labeled it: "Ah, there's the Pleaser again." This simple act created distance between her and the sabotaging pattern and enabled her to anticipate when she might be hijacked and plan accordingly.

3. Practice grounding techniques.

Grounding exercises interrupted the Pleaser's automatic responses. Slow, deep breaths, focusing intently on the five senses, and letting all thoughts go (PQ reps from Positive Intelligence) helped shift her brain from stress mode to clarity and calmness.

4. Set and maintain boundaries.

We used her values and triggers to identify areas where her needs weren't being met. Together, we created a clear plan for communicating boundaries and practiced visualization techniques to reinforce them.

Reframing boundary-setting as a way to model self-respect and emotional health for her children helped ease her guilt. She was giving her family a gift.

5. Reframe negative thoughts.

Those influenced by the Pleaser often feel guilt when prioritizing their needs. Instead of avoiding it, Janice learned to embrace it as a sign of growth. She reframed her thoughts, repeating, "I am modeling self-respect and emotional health for my children."

6. Communicate effectively.

When boundaries were crossed, Janice practiced addressing the issue calmly and assertively. Using "I" statements—such as, "When I do the housework alone, I feel overwhelmed"—fostered understanding and collaboration.

7. Build self-acceptance.

At the heart of the Pleaser saboteur is a fear of rejection or disapproval, so working on self-acceptance was crucial. Confidence grows when you embrace your worth and stand firm in your values. Janice began asking herself, "What would please me?"—a powerful question that reconnected her with her true self. We frequently played the song *This is Me* for inspiration.

Through these steps, Janice transformed her life. She intercepted and labeled the Pleaser saboteur, began to anticipate and plan for when she would be hijacked, practiced grounding exercises, and learned to pause before reacting. Recognizing and communicating her needs assertively created a more equal partnership with her husband. The effects were profound and beautiful to witness.

Janice shared that by using the skills and tools we'd explored, she finally approached her husband about an ongoing battle regarding housework: "For the first time, I felt truly seen and heard. It meant the world to me." To her surprise, he confided, "I'm sorry. I know I bury my head in the sand when there's a problem. I do the same at work."

Well, hello, Avoider saboteur!

The result? A family dynamic that now reflects Janice's true values of love, respect, and connection ... and the chores are shared!

Janice's final words: "It's been quite a journey, but worth every step. I feel closer to my husband than ever before. I feel he's supporting me, like he gets me now. I love him so much, and ... we're even having sex again."

You, too, can create a life of deeper connections, restored balance, and renewed self-worth. Reclaim your power one step at a time.

Michelle Godfrey has over 25 years of combined experience in holistic health and wellness. After years in hands-on therapies, she transitioned to coaching, founding Let's Blossom in 2021, where she has since helped hundreds of families improve their health and thrive. Michelle's journey is deeply personal. Struggling with her own Pleaser saboteur, she discovered the power of Positive Intelligence, reducing its grip from 9.8 out of 10 to a place of freedom and understanding. This transformation fuels her passion for guiding parents to strengthen their mental fitness and model resilience for their children.

As a Certified WILDFIT® Coach, Adventures in Wisdom® Coach, Mind, Body, Eating Coach, and Positive Intelligence Coach, Michelle helps families build their mental fitness, develop a healthy relationship with food, and gain confidence in their bodies. She believes that a child's relationship with food and their body begins at home, and she is on a mission to help parents create a foundation of lifelong wellness, both mentally and physically, by nurturing the mind, body, and soul.

Scan to get 6 Simple Scripts for setting boundaries, why they work, plus a bonus video on The Pleaser.

6

THROUGH THE UPS AND DOWNS OF FAMILY LIFE

Kathleen Blackmore

Many moons ago, when I brought my first newborn for daily walks in the neighborhood, older women often stopped to congratulate me. Their parting words were usually a reminder to "Enjoy your baby!" At the time, I thought they must have forgotten the huge responsibility of raising a child. Enjoying my baby felt less like a priority and more like a bonus to be experienced in the small moments when he fell asleep or gave me a smile. My default parenting modes were protective and alert. Worrying felt necessary to keep me attentive to my child's needs.

So, I ignored the older neighbors' advice and stuck to my anxious, perfectionist parenting style. It worked out for a while, but as our family grew, so did my worries, and my parenting style felt less sustainable. I often felt overwhelmed and ineffective as a mom. There were many happy moments, too, but I often felt like the family's Chief Worry Officer.

Some difficult events led me to reflect on my parenting style. My son began refusing to go to school during grade two. It was a daily battle getting him ready in the mornings, and by the time we left the house, we both felt frustrated and angry with each other. It was unclear to me what was causing him distress, leaving me confused and helpless.

Then, unexpectedly, my beloved father died. The grief of losing him reminded me of the importance of relationships. As I reflected on my childhood with him, I thought of the small moments of connection, like when he made me tiny sandwiches for a doll's tea party or comforted me after a nightmare. One of my child's last memories of him is when he called over with new kites and took them kite-flying in the park. His death taught me that no amount of worry will stop bad things from happening and that life, though often hard, is also a gift to be enjoyed with our loved ones. I began to wonder if my son's distress about school was partly connected to my anxious parenting, and I decided to do something about it.

I started counseling to reflect on my childhood, my parenting, and how I wanted to parent going forward. As I grew in self-awareness and learned new skills, I became more compassionate with myself and my son. On school mornings, I spent more time connecting with him and less time correcting him. If he became upset, I listened and then talked with him about what might help. I observed that school was draining for him, so I made fewer plans after school and left more time for unstructured play. Over the following months, my once-anxious child became more outgoing and confident. He began to enjoy school, and much to my delight, our relationship became more loving and playful.

My parenting journey led me to train as a clinical social worker, where I now support families in reducing stress and experiencing more joy in their daily lives. I focus on helping parents develop skills in four key areas: connection, observation, delight, and empowerment. These four areas provide a helpful framework tailored to each family's values, culture, personalities, and challenges.

The Method in Action

One family I worked with was Amy and John, whose ten-year-old daughter, Molly, had been recently diagnosed with ADHD. Molly often became angry when asked to do homework or chores. She fought daily with her older sister, with whom she shared a bedroom. Amy and John often yelled at Molly in frustration. They worried things would get worse as she entered her teenage years. We explored ways the family could develop their skills in connection, observation, delight, and empowerment.

1. Create connection with one-on-one time.

For connection, I encouraged Amy and John to prioritize one-on-one time with Molly, even on days when she was particularly challenging. John began playing video games with Molly after dinner. At the same time, Amy connected with a friend whose child also has ADHD for emotional support. To enhance social connections for Molly, they signed her up for a soccer team with her best friend.

2. Observe your thoughts and feelings.

The parents strengthened their observation skills by learning to notice their thoughts and feelings about parenting Molly. They recognized that most communication with her had become focused on her problem behaviors. Amy and John helped Molly notice and articulate the thoughts and body sensations that indicated she was starting to feel stressed. This information enabled them to step in earlier to support her.

3. Notice the qualities you value and what you enjoy.

To increase their capacity for delight, Amy and John began paying attention to the qualities they valued in Molly and sharing these observations with her. The family also started going for weekly walks outdoors in nature with their dog, fostering shared enjoyment. Since the parents enjoyed movies, they began going to the theater regularly with friends.

4. Communicate and collaborate.

Finally, we worked on empowering the whole family to communicate more openly, listen to each other, and problem-solve together. Amy and John became less reactive to conflicts between Molly and her sister. Instead, they focused on supporting their daughters to find solutions that met both their needs.

As the family implemented these changes, Amy and John felt more confident in their parenting and more connected with Molly. There were still stressful moments and times when they got off track, but they were confident they could handle whatever challenges came their way in the years ahead.

Now You

You can start right now if you want to move from worried and overwhelmed to confident and fulfilling parenting.

The first step is becoming more self-aware of the experiences and beliefs that shape your parenting. Reflecting on your childhood, what enjoyable moments do you remember with your parents? What made them enjoyable? Do you remember a time when your parents appeared stressed or found you challenging? What did you appreciate in their response? What do you wish they had done differently? How did your parents look after their own needs? What do you want to bring forward into your parenting from these experiences?

Now, reflect on your role as a parent. What values and beliefs guide your parenting? What positive qualities do you see in how you connect with your children? What challenges make it hard for you to enjoy parenting? How do you meet your own need for fun and connection?

From these reflections, what could you do today, this week, or this month to make parenting and family life more enjoyable? Why not start today?

Kathleen Blackmore, MSW, RCSW, is a clinical social worker with thirty years of experience supporting parents and their children in Ireland and Canada. She has worked across the full range of parent support, providing early intervention to prevent problems and helping families navigate mental health challenges, neurodiversity, and stressful home environments. Kathleen has supported parents at every stage, from expectant and new parents to those raising children, teens, and young adults. As a mom of four (in their late teens and twenties), she has been on her own journey from anxious to confident parenting. Her personal and professional experiences in Europe and North America have given her a unique perspective on what helps families thrive and how to get things back on track when parenting feels overwhelming.

Based in Vancouver, Canada, Kathleen works as a child and family therapist and offers online parent coaching locally and internationally. She loves helping parents build confidence in themselves and strengthen their connection with their children, even in the hard moments. If you want more joy and less struggle in parenting, download Kathleen's free guide to Enjoyable Parenting at https://www.kathleenblackmorecounselling.com/free-guide.

7

THE RIVER AND THE ARROW: PARENTING DESPITE A DYSFUNCTIONAL FAMILY OF ORIGIN

Jennifer Lytle

I was born to teenage parents. I was raised through multiple marriages, interim partners, and siblings with no two shared parents. At the age of four, stepdad #2 became my primary caregiver. At some point, I knew exactly what I would never do.

The River Perfected

Parenting is intended to move us—an invitation to grow and deliver. It is an unparalleled greenhouse for maturation and development. As parents, we tend to think we're the deliverers—the ones bearing the birth and life of our children. While that can be accurate, the journey bears us anew when we flow in it.

The River Restricted

As a counselor, I've worked with hundreds of families and parents. The pattern is undeniable for parents from intergenerationally dysfunctional family systems that yield adverse childhood experiences (ACEs). A restricted river yields conflicted parenting: you don't want to replicate the pain of your past and feel unsure about the *right* next step. You're overly sensitive to, and sometimes suspicious of, innocuous events while being intentional not to overlook, dismiss, or deny them. The rapids are real.

The Rapids

Jim grew up with an alcoholic dad and a codependent mom. As a dad, Jim was passionate about prioritizing being a good father. He was desperate to avoid some of the mistakes his parents made and was overly sensitive to his son's social status. Peer relationships could become the target of Jim's unresolved past. While Jim intended to protect and care for his son, he occasionally interpreted situations through a lens of trauma and projected issues of powerlessness or concerns of inferiority.

Daniel had behavioral concerns about the daughter he and Danielle co-parented. The power struggle was rooted in Daniel's fear of his childhood regrets being replayed. He resisted Danielle's instinct that their daughter would benefit from transferring schools. He also resisted initiating other changes. Instead of informing his decision-making, his past pain restricted options for his daughter. While his actions were well-intentioned, his inability to compromise may have exposed his daughter to vulnerabilities and ultimately fractured his relationship with her.

Clinically speaking, these behaviors could be referred to as intergenerational transmission within a revictimization cycle from wounded parent to child. You are here because you want to sidestep this common parent trap.

The Arrow

How can you enjoy the passage of parenthood without being towed under, wiped out, or beached? One Psalm likens children to arrows in the hand of a warrior. As parents, we can do more than *overcome* past pain. Informed by the past, we can recalibrate and position ourselves to advance our children like arrows. Independently, children are designed to go far beyond us. This is what the healthy parent wants to see: successes for their children in ways unimaginable for them personally.

After observing this pattern in families like Jim's and Daniel's, I developed the ARROW method. Are you ready to row toward intergenerational development? The ARROW method offers proverbial oars to move beyond the bay's limited inlet. This method is a nod to the Psalm that gave me hope. My children will never be where I once was. It's an admonition to be courageous and strong as I guide them. The steps for the ARROW method are not sequential and can be returned to at any point in the parenting journey. They include:

A: Acknowledge and Accept

Acknowledge, then accept, pain from the past. For many with ACEs and intergenerationally dysfunctional families, this will involve the cycle of grief. Get support. Celebrate Recovery or other community-based support groups, professional mental health services, and pastoral care are all legitimate ways to do soul care. You may find multiple sources are needed during some periods of acknowledgment and acceptance. This is normal. You may find that you go through a journey of healing, only to need more again later. Recovery often flows in such a rhythm.

Some parents engage in discovery, documenting, sourcing documentation, researching, and interviewing to understand the timeline and facts of *what* happened. When you have support, this process *may* be biopsychosocially safe. It is not without risk. Support is key. Many prefer to accept that the past was painful. Bypass research if you are not personally motivated (or emotionally equipped) to face whatever you discover.

R: Redirect

You are not your past. You are not bound to repeat your parents' missteps. Even if you have had a rocky run in the river with your children thus far, you can pivot. Redirect your flow. Redirect your time and attention, and aim beyond the pain. Recognize changes you are empowered to establish and work to produce tangible action steps. Change is often manageable when small steps are specific and oriented to your action. Again, formal support may be the best route for redirecting habitual behaviors.

This may look like the following:

- I can have fun with my kids.

- I can navigate emotions.

- I can talk with my kids about emotions.

R: Refine and Release

As a parent, you have the privilege to discover what works well with and for your children. The discovery is generally followed by a realization that your son or daughter has developed beyond your most recent discovery. The best way to parent is to understand your child's heart and lean into their natural bent. Refine your proverbial aim by releasing the ideal parent-child relationship and allowing your child to teach you what they want and need. Embrace your son's or daughter's distinct preferences.

O: Own Your Ownership

This is your voyage! Navigate the river to your liking. Own this journey. Find joy and beauty. If you cannot find it—make it. You've got this.

Sometimes, we find our children moody, sad, or even temporarily depressed. When you have tried your best to engage, communicate, and leave the door open for connection, it's time to ensure you have cared for yourself and pursued separate passions and goals. You are a model to your children. They may care for themselves one day as much as you do for yourself.

Questions to consider:

- Am I feeding myself well throughout each day?
- Have I gone to my annual and regular health/physical appointments?
- Do I have something outside of my family that nurtures me?

W: We-lease

W: We-lease, as in a collective, unified, team-oriented release of external expectations and imposed or perceived norms. While navigating what you want for your children in various settings, it is okay to side-step explaining yourself to those outside the home. Your children will likely appreciate communication around decisions affecting them and their freedom to interact with others.

W: We-leasing may sound like the following:

- We sleep at home.
- We sit in a chair (not in a lap).
- It's okay to say no.
- No is the answer. We can talk about it after dinner.
- It's okay to walk away and take a break.

The River and the Arrow

Children were never intended to remain in the pit of an unresolved, painful past. As evidenced by your possession of this book, they will naturally stand on your shoulders. Intentional, present parents create a stable base. Row on, warrior.

Jennifer Lytle is a licensed marriage and family therapist in Texas and the founder of Joyful Journeys Counseling. In everyday life, she has been married to Michael for over fifteen years. Together, they are raising three children at home, with the younger two being homeschooled. They also have an adult son. Jennifer has worked with hundreds of children and parents since graduate school, when she provided parenting courses at a community center before working as a school counselor. Her specialization is parent education and providing evidence-based treatment for children and teens with anxiety. Currently serving as the Austin Chapter President of Christian Counselors of Texas, Jennifer annually organizes and hosts eight to ten continuing education events. She has been published in several online magazines, including Scary Mommy, Austin Fit Magazine, Choosing Therapy, and Care.com. Download her accessible family communication model, "Apples of Gold," for free at joyfuljourneyscounseling.com/parenting.

8

CAN YOU USE YOUR CUTE VOICE?

Sarah Hayes-Hawkins

———

Kids are like mirrors of our inner selves.

When my son was in kindergarten, the day before winter break, he told me, "They wasted school time watching a movie." Was I doing something really right or wrong? Adorable as that was, I didn't see a kindergarten version of myself; I saw a version of myself today. When did I stop enjoying the breaks and little moments in life, and when did he?

I looked back.

My kiddo had a rough start. He was born with an autoimmune disease, which made eating very difficult. On top of that, he had weekly physical and occupational therapy and was eventually diagnosed with a neurological speech disorder. For years, on paper, he was labeled "failure to thrive," but in reality, he walked and ran early—very early. I was told there was a chance he might never be fully verbal, but now he speaks like a poet with a scientist's vocabulary. His autoimmune issues can still cause pain, and he struggles with eating, but he exudes pure joy. He is my definition of strength and resilience.

This is a lot for a small human to process in the first few years of life. When I look back at his story, it's easy to forget I was in the fight with him, too. When he started to medically "thrive," and my fears calmed down, I found us both in a constant state of fight or flight.

That's when I dove into a storm of parenting videos, books, and webinars, yet I was still sinking in the mud and becoming an information hoarder. I felt inspired, but when my adrenaline spiked and my family was in free fall, I couldn't remember what to do. I hadn't internalized it yet.

At this point, my health spiraled. I was on a demanding after-hours regimen of studying how to fix my immune system when I found a common thread between parenting and healthy living. A single point where both worlds met: mindfulness.

Mindfulness became my means of regulation. It helped me grab the end of the flailing water hose, allowing me to absorb all the techniques I had learned—a bridge to find calm so I could remember what the experts said.

Sensory-Minded Tricks That Worked for Me

1. Touch

My baby step into remembering to regulate was tapping into the sense of touch. I literally wrote "regulate" on a small rock. Every morning, I put it in my pocket. When I blew up, I would grab it, feel ashamed, and redirect my efforts. Eventually, the shame faded away, and I found calm more quickly. After a while, I added, "Perfect doesn't exist." It was crucial to remember not to expect it from myself or my son.

You don't have to be quirky and put a rock in your pocket. It can be a note or anything you can keep handy to ground yourself. Even just placing your hand on your heart for a moment while you breathe.

A hand-sized squeezy toy can work wonders for kids. I often used chew necklaces for my son when he was agitated or unfocused. Giving them to him reminded me that he wasn't in a regulated state, allowing me to give him more grace.

2. Sound

Auditory input is very impactful; find your song or use mantras. I would think, "He's still a kid; he'll be okay." I needed to remember that I was not looking at the future person but the present one. Dance party moments also helped us reset.

My son developed his own saying during tough times: "Can you use your cute voice?" Hearing that instantly reminded me that we are not enemies, like a verbal white flag. He needed me to be softer with him. Often, I'd tell him, "I'm on your team."

3. Visual

The next big hitter for me was visualizations. I like to imagine a tiger-stone-looking rock in my belly that represents my core and strength. When I am upset, it goes on fire; I close my eyes and cool it back down to a smooth rock. I like this because our calm is at the core of all of us; it just helps to see it.

Sometimes, seeing a baby picture on my phone helps me remember that the sweet kid is still in there. He has words but not the skills to operate in this world.

Visualizations are great for kids, too. I taught at a hands-on science education center, and physical or imaginary visuals were great mood-changing tools. I'd have the kids hold out their arms to show how big their anger was; then, together, we'd squeeze it dramatically until it became a manageable ball.

Modeling is the best way to teach kids of all ages, even resistant teens. The next time you step on a Lego while trying not to curse, squeeze the pain down and kick it to outer space. A little laughter can help us all find our cool. Kids tend to respond better to us when we're not angry, but it doesn't have to be all comedy. Sometimes, I have my son focus on a color in his head when he's struggling to fall asleep or visualize anything calming when he feels his emotions are unmanageable.

4. Smell

Now, on to the sense of smell. I love having lavender flowers around. Our local grocer carries them in the spring, and I stock up for the year. Recently, I had a biopsy (everything's fine), but it was terrifying, and I struggled to center myself. So, I grabbed a few lavender buds and kept them with me to sniff when I felt my breathing getting rapid. I may have looked a little nutty, but it helped me calm down and breathe.

My son loved the ritual of plucking lavender flowers off the stem and putting them in a bowl to prepare for a massage. Rituals like this are delightful ways to strengthen bonds. Oils and lotions are also great to have on hand to improve mood.

5. Space

My last piece of advice is to allow space in your mind. Listen to the available guidance, but when you start to feel overwhelmed by the sea of information, turn to your top heroes for direction. For me, those are Dr. Becky Kennedy, Mr. Chazz, Dr. Daniel Siegel, Dr. Gabor Maté, and Happily Family. I've encountered many other great voices but had to limit my focus for my sanity. Lastly, don't try to do it on your own. I'm incredibly grateful for my son's physical therapists and SLPs.

I want us to find joy again—every day. I understand what it's like to have your nervous system on fire, your child's sensory system over-loaded, and your house resembling *The Hunger Games*. If we slow down and take a breath, we can return to the time when we were expecting our little ones and live each day with excitement. It takes practice because failure is part of the process. I believe that even in the most challenging moments, we can strive for joy. Our kids are our life and air. You've got this.

Sarah Hayes-Hawkins lives in St. Petersburg, Florida, where she spends as much time as possible with her family, enjoying nature, volunteering, and playing in an orchestra. As the oldest of a herd of cousins and a brother, she felt a spark for caregiving very early in life. Sarah has worked extensively in the animal care and behavior field for over 18 years and has loved her time teaching at a hands-on science education center. She has a passion for learning every day, as well as for embracing a sense of community, especially in the complicated realm of parenting.

9

EMOTIONAL GROWTH IN FAMILIES

Leonora Found

I fell in love in my early teens. The boy who lived down the road consumed my thoughts, and I was hopelessly caught up in the magic of my first romance.

One evening, after walking me home, he leaned in and kissed me goodnight. It was so perfect that if the earth had opened and swallowed me, I would have gone willingly.

But the story doesn't end there. What I didn't realize was that, at that exact moment, my father was out watering the garden. As "love" disappeared home, he emerged from the darkness with a disapproving look that sliced through my happiness. "Go inside," he said. His tone had a familiar finality, and I knew there would be no chance for discussion. A mix of guilt, fear, and shame crept in, quickly followed by anger and frustration at not being able to express what felt like the most significant moment of my life.

Looking back, I don't blame him. Like many others, he was a product of his generation and lacked the tools to deal with emotions.

As a result, neither did I.

I was a loud and expressive child, not the type to conceal emotions. "Calm down" and "Not so loud" were phrases I heard regularly. Over time, those repeated commands made me feel like I needed fixing, leaving me unsure of how to express myself authentically.

As a teen, my emotions were wild and woolly, and I had no idea how to manage them. I tried suppressing them, which only left me feeling miserable. When I tried expressing them, it was at the "wrong time" or in the "wrong place," leading to many misunderstandings and frustration. "She's such a drama queen," I'd often hear, prompting me to try being someone I wasn't. The truth was, I didn't want to create chaos; I just wanted to understand my emotions and express them.

Breaking Patterns, Building Bonds

As a parent, I thought breaking the patterns of the past would be simple. It wasn't.

My philosophy was that no emotion would be too big, messy, or inconvenient, encouraging our children to express themselves freely.

But here's the problem: without structure or guidance, this approach led to chaos.

Misunderstandings flourished, often becoming a game of "who could shout loudest" in hopes of being heard. Feelings were hurt, and sometimes, running away seemed easier.

My six-year-old son once took this literally and, to my daughter's horror, packed a bag and announced he was leaving. Of course, he didn't make it beyond the front gate, but my response was one of award-winning maturity: "Fine," I said, "but don't forget your water bottle."

At the height of emotional exhaustion, many parents, including me, have found themselves behaving like a two-year-old. Take heart; you are not alone. When emotions run high, it's easy to feel lost and unsure of whether you are doing the right thing.

For us, change came when I stumbled upon Nancy Kline's book *Time to Think*. She focuses on deep listening and creating an environment where individuals feel heard and valued. Those words "heard" and "valued" touched me deeply. Isn't this something we all deserve? Could I honestly say I was giving my five-year-old that kind of attention? Or my precocious eight-year-old? Was I offering them the nurture and care in navigating their emotions that I had craved? And if not, why?

I realized we needed to create an environment that allowed emotions to grow.

Implementing Change

We began making feelings part of our everyday conversations—in the car, over dinner, or during bedtime routines. This step was about fostering connection—no judgment, no interruption, no immediate solutions—just a shared space to process and grow together.

We began asking open-ended questions:

- "What are you feeling right now? Can you describe it?"
- "What do you think triggered that feeling?"

For those less expressive, we used prompts like:

- "Let's share one thing you liked about today and something you found difficult."
- "I noticed you crossed your arms as if you were angry. Can you tell me more about that?"

Knowing that I didn't have to have all the answers was freeing. Being present and listening attentively was what they needed most.

Next, we focused on expanding our emotional vocabulary. There's so much more to emotions than simply being happy, sad, or mad, and it takes effort to explore the full range. Discovering new words to describe feelings helped us uncover the root of emotions and gave us clarity about what to do next.

To make this practical, we used the Feelings Wheel, a simple yet powerful tool that helped us peel back the layers of emotion. Instead of stopping at "angry," it guided us to more specific feelings, like frustration or resentment. Once we could name the feeling more precisely, it became much easier to understand and respond to it effectively.

For example:

- "I thought I was angry, but I'm frustrated because I feel stuck."
- "I feel disappointed, not sad, because I was hoping for a different outcome."

These small but consistent steps changed how we related as a family. More importantly, we saw visible changes in our children. There was far less frustration and anguish when things didn't go according to plan because they had the tools to work things out. It benefited us all, me included. Drawing alongside them and showing my own vulnerability only strengthened our bond.

Real-Life Challenges

Of course, on paper, this all sounds great. Yes, we've absolutely experienced the benefits of this work as a family. There's more understanding, stronger connections, and fewer shouting matches. But let's be honest—emotions are messy, unpredictable, and rarely convenient. While we've made progress, there are moments that feel like we're right back where we started.

I've often had to resist the urge to jump in with advice when my children are upset—and I'd be lying if I said I've always succeeded. There are still times when I dive in boots and all, determined to "fix" things. And then there are nights when a peaceful family dinner of "what went well today" spirals into chaos because the kids have turned it into a competition. Parenting is full of these unplanned dramas.

But the truth is, these obstacles and challenges are just part of the growth process. Honestly, there's nothing that a heartfelt "sorry" can't smooth over. It makes moving forward so much easier.

When I think back over 25 years of parenting, I am grateful for the knowledge and resources we have today. Sometimes, I wonder how different things might have been for my parents if they'd had this kind of support. They did their best with what they had, and I respect that. It's a reminder that every generation is figuring it out as they go.

So, here's to the courage to stay curious about emotions, the strength to show up even when it's hard, and the grace to grow together as a family—one moment at a time.

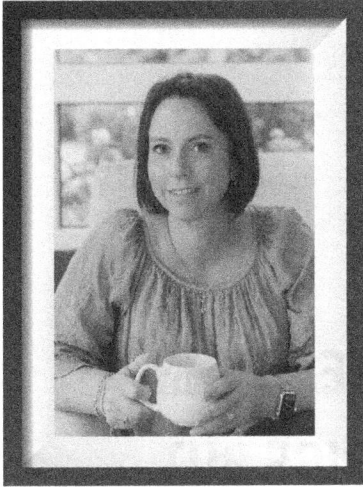

Leonora Found is an accredited life coach with a background in industrial psychology and communications. Drawing from her professional training and real-life experience, she is passionate about helping families build strong and healthy emotional connections while supporting mothers in reclaiming their sense of self and prioritizing their own growth and well-being.

A natural storyteller, Leonora blends humor, honesty, and decades of lived experience into her writing and coaching, making her insights engaging and deeply relatable for anyone navigating the unpredictable journey of parenthood. She demonstrates that fostering emotional awareness in your family is not about perfection but progress, learning, and connection.

To connect with Leonora and explore more of her work, visit her website at www.leonorafound.com.

As a supplement to this chapter, she is offering a free resource of practical tools, real-life examples, and actionable strategies for cultivating an emotionally present family. Scan the QR code to gain access and begin building stronger family connections today.

10

WHEN YOU'VE READ THE PARENTING ADVICE BUT IT'S STILL NOT WORKING

Sarah George

S omeone once said that we can all parent well when we're on form. It's when things are tough that it gets harder. This was certainly true for me. Once the stress hit big time, I lost my way and all the good parenting techniques I'd learned from books and courses. Even though I knew how well they worked and saw how my children responded, I couldn't get back on track. I was left with a nagging voice and a memory of when things were different. This went on for months, then turned into years.

In the end, I found my way through, and it wasn't what I expected. It was like a little piece of magic and deceptively simple: look after yourself first.

It's tempting to view self-care as an indulgence, a nice treat that we can do without. But we really can't. The longer we neglect our needs, the poorer our parenting becomes. We all know what it's like to run out of patience when we're frazzled.

Looking after yourself doesn't mean being selfish and abandoning your children to a life of neglect—quite the opposite; but it does mean putting your oxygen mask on first (as airlines always advise) so that you have enough resources left to care for those who are relying on you—your children.

We can't parent our children unless we parent ourselves first. We all have gaps of different shapes and sizes from our own childhoods. We fill in those gaps when we stop and look after our needs. When we practice self-care, extending that care to our children becomes easier.

How do we go about parenting ourselves? Here are two things I've found most helpful:

1. Check in with yourself regularly.

It's easy to forget to look after ourselves when we get caught up in day-to-day life, and this can lead to problems. Allocate a time to check in with yourself, however briefly. Do it once a day, several times a day, or whenever you're feeling stressed or irritable.

While we can't always change everything, checking in is an act of self-care itself, and a lot of subtle changes can happen by simply noticing how we feel. I practiced this recently when rushing through tasks. The time pressures didn't change, but noticing how I was feeling helped me ease up a little and made me a nicer person to be around.

Sometimes, we need to listen to ourselves the most. We can always return to this whenever we find ourselves slipping back into bad habits or feeling utterly overwhelmed. It helps us reset things—like returning a fallen object to the shelf.

2. Be kind and compassionate to yourself.

For example, find ways to ease the pressure—allow yourself to ask for help or find ways to give yourself a break, whether it's a weekend away or just five minutes hiding in the toilet for a breather.

Avoid words like "should," "need to," or "have to." When I dropped these (I want my son to do X, Y, and Z), I focused more on my son and what he was enjoying. I realized I'd been holding on to so many things that really didn't matter—not as much as our relationship.

Kindness also means allowing ourselves to mess up and get things wrong and forgiving ourselves when we do. Remember that we're humans stumbling through life, doing the best we can. Let's also celebrate those overlooked moments when we do get it right, when we mean well, and the things we do on autopilot day after day.

Putting It into Practice

All that came together recently when my son and I had a tough morning. I knew I hadn't gotten it right and risked falling into a pit of doom and gloom, but instead, I shared with a friend and felt understood and supported enough to come back, apologize, and set clear expectations. I also found time to give myself a brief rest. This gave me the space to reflect on how best to manage things and the energy to get through the rest of the day without being grumpy.

Looking back, I saw that it had been rumbling for a few days, and I didn't know how to deal with it. Taking care of myself freed me up to work out some solutions and ultimately reframe it as one of those sticky parenting challenges we often encounter; I'd gotten stuck, I took care of my needs, I found a solution, and came out the other end with a successful result, having learned a bit in the process.

It's a lovely truth that when we look after ourselves, we automatically do the same for our children. Children model our behavior. When we forgive ourselves for messing up, take the pressure off, look after ourselves, and set fair boundaries, what wonderful lessons we teach them.

It's like alchemy. By doing less, we give our children more. Things change without us even trying. A subtle shift in our mindset can lead to an avalanche of changes. Things we might have been stubbornly stuck on for months suddenly find a way of lifting. New perspectives help us solve problems that once seemed impossible.

For me, discovering all this was the key to change, like suddenly walking into a bright summer day after a long winter. Things improved when someone pointed out how burnt out I was and recommended some dramatic steps to look after myself. Looking back, that was all it took. I just needed to give myself permission to look after myself. Remarkably, before I even put anything in place, all the good parenting I'd learned in the past came flooding back, and I found myself being the best parent I'd been in years.

Now, when I feel grumpy, the alarm bells go off, and I know it's time out for me—permission granted, no questions asked.

Life is more fun now, and I enjoy my children more. I've had moments when they've made me double over and cry with laughter, as well as moments when I recognize what delightful people they are that make me proud to be part of the human race.

I talk differently with them now. I listen more, and I respect their wisdom and contributions. I have greater confidence in my abilities to step out of my comfort zone or to push back when a boundary is needed. I show more trust and confidence in them. I worry less and enjoy them more.

Sometimes, I still make a complete mess of it. Sometimes, it all falls apart, and I forget all the good stuff, but I know the way out now—I have a map, and I'll always have that. The best part of all is that looking after yourself first is really nice. It's something that doesn't depend on time or money. I hope it works for you, too—it'll always be there to come back to, no matter how lost you get along the way.

Sarah George has been passionate about connection parenting since her children were young. She has tested it through the highs and lows of raising them and has found it invaluable. It was when the stresses of life knocked her off track and she had to find a way back that she learned the most. She rediscovered the joy of connection parenting, which was made richer by embracing her own needs. Sarah knew she wasn't the only one who had found things hard sometimes, so she wanted to help other struggling parents feel less alone. She understands that parenting can be tough and that parents don't always get the appreciation they deserve.

Sarah is passionate about child development. She has a background in psychology and has worked as a teacher and trainer with children and adults. Her other enthusiasm is the natural world; she regularly helps at a local farm. She lives in the UK with her husband and two children.

To read more from Sarah on parenting and other topics, visit her blog at oakandacorn.blog.

SECTION TWO: MANAGING STRESS AND FINDING CALM

11

TRIGGERED

Amy Lynch

A m I being triggered too much while parenting, and what does that say about me?

My middle son recently told me, through a mouthful of cereal, that I am becoming a "master at knowing what to do when the kids get sad." This is the same kid who has driven me to scream so loudly and with such bravado that a passing neighbor paused to see if I was being murdered. He continued on to make his point: "You used to be really bad at it, and now you are really good at it."

He's not wrong, and I took this precious opportunity to repair, as I have done many times before.

During the early years of my three children's lives, I was overwhelmed, underskilled, under-strategized, and constantly triggered (and shocker, I am a trained trauma therapist, yet I was unprepared for the pokes and prods to my nervous system that came with child-rearing).

I am not alone; here in the U.S., 48% of parents report that their daily stress is completely overwhelming—a number so high that the U.S. government issued a call to action to support those of us raising small humans.[8]

Being responsible for children has always carried tremendous weight, and we know that parents of color, parents with complex trauma of their own, and parents who face low resources like access to childcare, healthcare, and community support report even higher levels of stress and overwhelm.

The Inevitability of Being Triggered

How do we determine if we are being triggered too often? Fellow caregiver, I compassionately commend you for being here; trying to do better is a gem of wisdom and practice that can be passed along not only to your children but to the other tired and overwhelmed caregivers around you. I can assure you that you do not travel this road alone.

Triggers happen, and they serve a function. There is no earthly relationship in which we will not be triggered. It is not a matter of if you will be triggered while parenting but when.

You are meant to get overwhelmed, built to be stressed, and primed to have a myriad of experiences in your life and in the relationship between parent and child.

This biology is necessary, and we do better to work smarter with its function instead of against it.

To be stressed is very different from being triggered. To be triggered is to pour too much, too soon, or for too long into an attachment system that reads in simple analog: am I safe, or am I in danger?

Stress is activating (think driving, writing an email that required several drafts so you don't get yourself in trouble, moving money around to ensure that the bills get paid) and is meant to help us function in a flexible way, meaning you have a hand on the so-called wheel of the situation; you are still present in the process of finding a solution.

To be triggered is to experience your flexible adult self moving to the back as another part of you emerges, signaling and ringing alarm bells that quickly notify your nervous system that this situation is life or death, making connective parenting difficult in those moments.

Are You Being Triggered Too Often?

How do we know if it is happening too often and is problematic? I usually ask parents in my office two questions when they give me the "If you only knew some of the things I have said (done, thought, wanted to do) to my kid, you would know that I'm an awful person."

I inquire: "How does being triggered disrupt your connection with your kids?" and "What does it say about you as a parent today?"

If there is any sense of shame (shame being any resemblance of I AM bad) in the answers—"I'm a bad mother/father/parent; everyone is better at this than me; I'm not good for my kids"—I know that we have entered some hurtful territory.

What to Do When You're Triggered

What can we do about it today?

1. Let your kiddos know it is not about them.

If you feel triggered too often, let your kids know it is not about them. It is okay for them to see you angry, frustrated, and overwhelmed; it only becomes damaging when they begin to believe it is something they have done.

When that neighbor heard me screaming and asked me if I was essentially dying, it was a lightbulb moment for me to stop hiding the fact that my children triggered me often and that I did not know what to do about it. I began simply. I used age-appropriate language, but it basically sounded like this: "I'm sorry I reacted that way. Mommy got hurt when she was little, and that is not your fault; it's up to me to deal with it." My kids were amazingly gentle with me, visibly relieved that their adult parent could take away some of the blame that was beginning to blossom in their chests.

2. Share with others.

Share. Share with a partner, a friend, or a therapist if you are privileged enough to have one. There are community groups and forums, and there are other parents in the pickup line. Shame cannot live in the light; it can't grip us as tightly and incapacitate us if we allow another human being to tell us we are not alone and that we are not broken. I often tell other parents that they are not a problem to be fixed; the triggers and the reactions are the problems to be worked on.

If you are like me, you cannot learn parenting skills and strategies to reduce your triggers alone. I needed professional help, and even more importantly, I needed the support of my friends and community to remind me that it is not my fault that I am triggered, but it is my responsibility to learn from it and to try to do it differently.

3. Believe your nervous system.

Your nervous system plays a key role in being triggered. If you find yourself constantly triggered, start by believing in yourself as a trigger detective.

Write down what triggers you. Is it sensory? Is it the screaming of a baby and a toddler? Is it multitasking? Is it the overstimulation of being touched or rapidly changing plans? Write this down like you are a detective. Now, if there is anything you can do to relieve yourself, do it. I would get triggered taking my kids to storytime because they could not sit still, and we had gotten scolded for being loud several times. It took me years to figure out that I shouldn't go.

Where are we now?

I'd like to say that I don't get triggered anymore and that my house is full of soft voices and responses, but that would not be genuine to this human experience of raising children. Even so, despite the ups and downs and occasional reactions over responses, my son still reaches for me, telling me I am good at this thing called caregiving because, in the end, gentle parent, it is about trying for the connection over and over again.

Amy Lynch, LCSW, is a joyful survivor of childhood trauma and finds it a deep pleasure and joy to serve other parents who are trying to leave this world better than they found it. Amy owns and runs her own private therapy and coaching practice in Littleton, Colorado, and combines trauma-focused therapy, parts work, psychospiritual therapy, and storytelling to support others in their healing journey. Amy deeply believes that parenting and partnering in a skilled and secure way changes the world! She is both challenged and honored to be a parent of three kiddos and is constantly learning from having a neurodivergent, sensitive, and very humorous household. Amy believes that your healing impacts her healing and impacts the world! Please sign up for monthly inspiration and upcoming workshops at https://wildopenjoy.com/.

12

MANAGE YOUR FEARS FIRST

Annmarie Chereso

How often do you hem and haw over whether you've made the "right decision" regarding your child's upbringing? From agonizing over toddler tantrums to navigating college applications, you've probably worried that you're not doing it "right." A 2023 American Psychological Association study found that 68% of parents cite uncertainty about their parenting decisions as a significant source of stress, while 72% worry about repeating their parents' mistakes.[9]

Every parent wants their children to be happy, healthy, and successful. Yet, there's one thing that blocks every parent from raising happy, healthy, and successful children: fear.

Fear is the leading cause of stress, anxiety, and drama in your life—and your family's. Until you become aware of the conscious and unconscious fears influencing you, this emotion will interfere with your ability to parent from a place of unconditional love. Fear wreaks havoc if left unchecked. Without realizing it, we often pass down fears of failure, scarcity, rejection, judgment, and unworthiness.

But what if you could trust every decision you made? What if you never again doubted what was best for your child and your family?

There is a way out of the fear cycle.

The antidote to fear is trust. But what happens when trust feels scarier than fear?

As a baby, my youngest had colic. She would cry twelve hours a day. I tried everything to stop her, only to be told she'd grow out of it. This was not true. Her "colic" grew with her, and she became an angry, anxious, out-of-control kid.

Despite consulting teachers, therapists, and experts, nothing seemed to help manage her violent tantrums. I tried every recommendation—rewards, positive reinforcement, even punishment—desperate to control her behavior. Each failed attempt left me feeling more hopeless.

Finally, when she was seven years old, I woke up.

It was a bright sunny day when all hell broke loose in the kitchen over an after-school snack. I didn't cut the apple just right, and it set her off again. My sweet, lovable, toothless daughter transformed into a raging tornado of emotions, screaming and thrashing just two feet from the knife block.

I was terrified. My mind raced: Is this normal? Will she ever learn to regulate her emotions? What will the neighbors think? As my anxiety rose, I felt my body bracing fiercely against the storm approaching me. I fell into my familiar panic, overwhelmed by the voices of my mother, grandmother, and inner judges: "Stop her! She's out of control! This is insane—it's just an apple! What is wrong with her? She's upsetting the other kids! She needs to learn to behave!"

Somehow, I managed a few deep breaths. Suddenly, a new voice spoke—louder than the judgment inside me: "Show her the rage in you." I balked. I was the parent; I was supposed to be in control. But the truth was, I was not in control at all. My daughter was showing me how I was feeling inside my body; I could feel how she was feeling inside her body. We were one another's mirrors.

If I wanted a new reflection, I knew I needed to create it.

I "mimicked" her. I began to stomp, scream, and pound my fists like she was. It didn't make logical sense—it just felt right. That's when something magical happened. My daughter stopped, stared at me like I was crazy (let's be honest, I looked crazy), and began to laugh. And so did I.

As our laughter subsided, our bodies and minds relaxed. In that moment of heart-to-heart connection, my daughter became my teacher, showing me how to move through big emotions instead of trying to control them.

Looking in the mirror, I saw that my fears were the real problem, not her tantrums, her anger, or her anxiety. She was a seven-year-old processing emotions messily, needing a model for healthier expression. I was afraid she was damaged by our "broken" home, afraid of public judgment during her tantrums, and afraid I wasn't good enough for my children. I feared I would never remarry; I worried my other children would suffer from a lack of attention. My fears were interfering with my ability to parent from love.

That day in the kitchen, I realized that love naturally guides the way when I parent from intuition and trust rather than my ego's need for control. If my own fears were disrupting my parenting, then it was time to examine how I let those fears control me.

That's how I discovered my true power: radical self-awareness. It's summed up in a straightforward question: "Where am I?"

In that chaotic moment with my daughter, asking, "Where am I?" helped me acknowledge my triggered part rather than resisting or judging my feelings. The question invited me to offer myself awareness, acceptance, love, and grace. (I was parenting myself!) When I could show love for my triggered self, I could also show love for my daughter's triggered self.

"Where am I?" is a tool like your GPS; it serves as the roadmap to self-awareness. As adults, we're conditioned to ignore our bodies' fear-based signals in service of our logical minds. We talk ourselves out of what's actually happening. We override intuition, our deeper knowing.

This question lets you pause to determine if you're feeling threatened. It turns the spotlight back onto you, where you have control and can examine the energy you're bringing and inviting. Remember: our kids energetically entrain to us. If we want them to experience love, we have to be the presence of love.

Answering this question honestly helps you see yourself more clearly, enabling you to make authentically empowered choices. Through life's inevitable challenges—marriages ending, struggles with addiction, academic difficulties, abuse, and health scares—this question will help you parent from love rather than fear.

This gift of radical self-awareness has allowed me to become more connected to myself and my kids, giving me the chance to embrace my messy, imperfect humanity.

Like all parents, I still want my kids to be happy, healthy, and successful; now, with this one question, I get to teach them to love their messy human imperfections, too.

Explore the "Where Am I?" approach to conscious parenting for more guidance on moving from fear to trust in your parenting journey.

Author, meditation teacher, and transformational coach **Annmarie Chereso** empowers parents, children, and families to discover authentic happiness and true success. Through her playful, heart-centered approach, Annmarie combines mindfulness mastery with practical tools. She helps clients cultivate self-awareness, harness their innate power, and overcome limiting beliefs to embrace their most empowered selves. With over two decades of expertise, Annmarie has trained educators, students, and parents globally through online courses, coaching, speaking engagements, workshops, and retreats. She has collaborated with renowned leaders, including Dr. Shefali Tsabary and The Conscious Leadership Group, and has worked with institutions such as the University of Chicago Laboratory Schools, Francis W. Parker, KIPP, and the Chicago Public Schools.

Based in downtown Chicago, Annmarie and her husband co-parent their blended family of nine children and three grandchildren.

Ready to transform your parenting journey from fear to trust? Download your free guide: "Where Am I? Your Roadmap from Fear to Conscious Parenting."

13

FROM REACTING TO RESPONDING: HOW I TRANSFORMED MY PARENTING THROUGH AWARENESS

Barby Jimenez

I'm standing in the hallway, overwhelmed by uncomfortable emotions as I yell. My outburst is directed at my seven-year-old son for something I can't even remember—which says a lot. Given my past patterns, it was likely something he said or did that I perceived as "wrong" or "disrespectful."

Later, I cried myself to sleep—again—promising that I would finally be the present and connected parent I had dreamed of being tomorrow.

Despite my best intentions, I rarely made it through the day without something setting me off. I was trapped in a vicious cycle, with no idea how to break free.

The Wake-Up Call That Changed Everything

One day, in the middle of my yelling, my son turned to me, locked eyes with mine, and said, "You are trying to control me. Stop!"

For the first time, I didn't react. Instead of snapping back about "disrespect," I became curious. What if he was right?

I realized that if I wanted a connected relationship with my son and my daughter (who is two years older), I had to be the one to change. This led me to discover Dr. Shefali's work. I devoured her books, took every class, and became certified as a conscious parenting coach. Even with my years of experience as an educator working with young children, nothing had prepared me for parenting my own.

Why We React Instead of Respond

As I applied conscious parenting principles, I discovered a truth that changed everything: our reactions to our children are not about them at all.

When my son expressed anger, I felt an irrational fear about his future. My mind would fast-forward to an imagined scenario where he was yelling at a stranger in a bar, getting into a fight, and ending up in jail. He was only seven, but my fears were overwhelming.

When I looked deeper, I realized where that fear came from—my own childhood. I had never learned how to process emotions in a healthy way.

Moreover, a family member had spent a night in jail, causing distress to my family. That unresolved experience had been sitting in my nervous system for years.

As a result, when my son displayed anger, my body interpreted it as a threat. I wasn't reacting to him but to my own past.

The Pause and Reframe Framework

This realization fueled my passion for helping parents realize that parenting is not just about raising children—it's about healing ourselves.

The following framework helped me break free from my reactivity and transformed my parenting. This is the same process I have used with hundreds of clients to help them shift their own parenting:

Step 1: Practice Awareness

Identify the thoughts and feelings behind your reactions. Our thoughts shape our emotions, which drive our behavior—yet most of our thoughts are inaccurate.

When I believe my child is being "disrespectful," it triggers frustration and a sense of threat, leading me to react. But what if that belief isn't true?

Understanding the brain helps: The part responsible for self-regulation isn't fully developed until about age 25. If emotional control is challenging for us as adults, imagine how hard it is for our kids!

As we become aware of our inner dialogue, we take back control. We stop reacting unconsciously and start responding intentionally.

Step 2: Strengthen the Pause

Create space between trigger and response. Awareness is powerful, but without pausing, we'll still default to old habits.

Pausing requires inner spaciousness, which means tending to our own needs. Yes, we've been conditioned to put our children first. But if we're running on empty, we don't have the internal resources to stay calm.

Building spaciousness can be simple:

- Take a deep breath before responding.
- Schedule small moments of joy throughout the day.
- Repeat a grounding mantra like, "I am safe," or "I can do hard things."

As we practice pausing, we gain space to see our child in the moment—not through the lens of our fears or frustrations.

Step 3: Reframe Your Thoughts

After we pause, we can reframe our perspective. Instead of thinking, *My child is being disrespectful*, think, *My child is having difficulty regulating emotions and needs my help.*

That shift changes the emotional state inside us, helping us respond with compassion instead of reacting from fear.

What If You Still Struggle?

Even with awareness, pausing, and reframing, challenges will arise. Here's how to handle common struggles:

1. **"I don't have time to pause!"**

   Start small. Even a two-second inhale before responding can make a difference.

2. **"My child's behavior is unacceptable!"**

   Acknowledging emotions doesn't mean excusing behavior. You can hold boundaries while remaining calm.

3. **"This feels unnatural."**

   You're undoing years (or generations) of conditioning. Give yourself grace.

Healing Through Reflection

One of the most powerful aspects of conscious parenting is that it allows us to heal our own childhood wounds.

After a tough moment with your child, take time to reflect:

- What are you believing about your child, yourself, and the world in this situation?
- When was the first time you held that belief in your life?
- Where do you feel this belief in your body?
- Can you hold steady and allow those sensations to move through you?
- What does this part of you need to hear to feel safe and seen?
- Processing our emotions in this way helps us stop passing them down to our children.

Final Thoughts

Parenting challenges don't mean you're failing—they mean you're growing.

After months of practice to react less often and stay more present—not just with my children, but in all my relationships—I saw the results. I became more aware and more centered, and I no longer gave my power away to each situation.

This shift created safety and trust with my children. They became more authentic, knowing I wouldn't fly off the handle. I'm not perfect—no one is—but when I do react, I repair. I take responsibility and let my children know my reaction was about me, not them. Imagine if all humans learned that skill.

Practical Tools for the Moment

While working on your inner transformation, here are quick mindset shifts and skills to use when your child is struggling:

1. **Pause.**

    Anything you do when triggered won't be helpful. Focus on calming yourself first.

2. **See Behavior as Communication.**

    Ask: What is my child's behavior trying to tell me they need? It's usually one or a combination of these:

    -   More connection (your presence)

    -   Learning a skill (expressing emotions, sharing, problem-solving)

    -   A compassionate limit ("I won't let you hit. Let's go to another room to calm down.")

Every trigger is an invitation to heal. Every pause is an opportunity to choose connection over control.

Ready to learn more? Connect with me for additional tools and support on your parenting journey.

Barby Jimenez is a Conscious Parenting Coach, educator, and facilitator dedicated to helping parents shift from control to connection. With a background in elementary education, reading instruction, and early childhood development, she spent nearly a decade teaching before founding Natural Beginnings Homeschool, a play-based, nature-focused early childhood program that she operated for eight years. When traditional discipline methods strained her relationship with her children, Barby sought a new approach.

She trained under Dr. Shefali Tsabary and became a certified Conscious Parenting Coach. She also facilitates parenting workshops and support groups through The Parent Club at Florida International University, equipping families with practical tools for greater cooperation and connection.

Barby's private coaching integrates Compassionate Inquiry, Polyvagal Theory, trauma-informed practices, and mindfulness, offering parents a holistic approach to emotional regulation and relationship-building.

Scan the QR code for free resources you can start using right away to bring more connection and calm to your parenting.

14

A MIRROR OF INHERITED PAIN

Arleen Tyndall

His eyes swell with angry tears, and his face flushes red with frustration. He finally lets go of the iPad and punches me as hard as he can. Reeling from the sting, I feel the urge to hit him back. Seething, I spit, "You're just like my mother!" My eight-year-old son, feeling the scorn, winds up to hit me again. I grab his wrist and push him away, fleeing to the bathroom.

Slamming the door, I slump to the floor, sobbing. My hot anger morphs into shame, overwhelming me with guilt and self-rejection. *What kind of mother am I?*

Time stands still as I hide in the locked bathroom, just as I did in my childhood, running from my abusive mother. A knock rouses me. "Mom? I'm sorry. Please come out." When I open the door, I see my shame and guilt reflected in him.

I've studied conscious parenting for years, but the podcasts, webinars, and books fail me. Therapy, yoga, meditation—none of this self-care seems enough. *What am I doing wrong?*

Goal-oriented, overly competent, and a perfectionist, I find making mistakes unbearable. As a clinical pharmacist, I thrived on solving problems—each fix giving me a dopamine hit that validated my worth. This addiction spilled into my parenting. When my four-year-old son began asserting his will against mine, I diagnosed it as a behavior problem and kicked my research skills into high gear to solve it.

Working with patients suffering from addictions, homelessness, mental health issues, and HIV in Vancouver's Downtown Eastside, I sought training in trauma-informed care and harm reduction. A colleague in the same community, Dr. Gabor Maté, developed his Compassionate Inquiry based on trauma research, which aligns with Dr. Shefali's Conscious Parenting methods. Yet, despite all my knowledge, the calm mother I aspired to be vanished when faced with my child's defiance. Instead, anger and yelling ensued. If I couldn't handle my big emotions, how could my child?

Failing in my "perfect mother" role, I spiraled into shame and guilt. Unaware of the buried childhood fears and anxiety that drove me to search for more answers, I created a never-ending cycle. All my constant DOING—studying, yoga, meditation, therapy—distracted me from BEING.

This emotional and spiritual bypassing kept me disconnected from myself, unaware of my feelings, needs, or worth. Lacking self-love, I sought validation externally, especially from my son. When he didn't meet my expectations, it triggered my childhood wound of not being "good enough," making me feel unworthy of love.

If I didn't break this cycle, I would continue to harm him by passing down this story. At only seven, he'd begun coming home from school saying, "I'm stupid. I'm a bad kid. I want to kill myself." I hired him an art therapist. Today, I understand that I must model self-love. My son became my mirror and greatest teacher.

With growing self-compassion, I learned that dissociation is a natural response to trauma: a disconnection from one's feelings, thoughts, behaviors, and authentic identity. This allowed me to cope as a child.

Reading Dr. Maté's *The Myth of Normal*, I recognized both capital-T and small-t traumas from childhood that led me to choose attachment over authenticity. Anxiety from constant uncertainty stayed with me into adulthood, suppressed beneath a busy, socially acceptable persona that protected me from the shame and rejection I grew up with—trapped in an endless search for belonging.

Hearing Dr. Shefali speak about Co-Creation was transformative. As the adult in the room, I had to be accountable for how I showed up. Instead of being present with my child, I pressured him to fulfill my fantasy of being the "perfect child" to reflect my "perfect parenting." Unsurprisingly, my sensitive son mirrored back disrespect, shame, and blame—messages I projected onto him. Focused on his behaviors, I couldn't address his unmet emotional needs because I didn't understand my own. I had to question my behavior.

Burned out from working at the hospital after COVID, we left Vancouver to live in Bali, my mother's birthplace. In paradise, I ironically learned I had brought my stress and anxiety with me. Surrounded by extended family, stories unfolded of my mother's traumatic upbringing and the effects of colonization on our ancestors. This brought understanding, empathy, and forgiveness for my childhood pain long after my parents' deaths.

Determined to break intergenerational trauma patterns, I delved into meditation, breathwork, family constellations, and psilocybin therapy. These experiences helped excavate the repressed emotional baggage I carried and projected onto my relationships. My therapist referred to it as my "Spiritual Awakening."

At 50, I quit my pharmacy career and trained in Conscious Parenting and Life Coaching with Dr. Shefali.

An e-scooter accident during our last month in Bali forced me into stillness. This time became a medium for healing, allowing me to reconnect with my body—a connection that had been severed since childhood. This accident marked a new chapter.

After moving back to Vancouver, Canada, and recovering from intensive surgery, I returned to Bali to train in somatic alignment and breathwork to strengthen my mind-body-spirit connection.

Through meditation, I have learned to give myself time to pause and observe thoughts that enter my mind without reacting. It was initially painful to sit in stillness, even for a minute; it has taken years of slowly learning to remain present and face the discomfort of my anxiety around not doing anything. The next step was to stop believing every thought and to question the judgments I created in these stories about my child and others. Looking deeper within, I discovered fears that ignited every reaction. By understanding these fears, I could change each narrative and not allow wounds from my past or fears of the future to blind me from experiencing the present. If fear did not stand in my way, how would I respond to my child with love in this moment?

Integrating this meditation practice of becoming aware of my thoughts and judgments was pivotal in releasing my expectations of my son and husband to meet my emotional needs. I had to meet my own, which allowed me to connect with them more deeply. Moment by moment, I practice understanding my needs by listening to my body, setting boundaries that I must respect, and showing self-compassion when I make mistakes. These acts of self-love enable me to parent authentically.

My pre-teen son has absorbed what I have modeled over the last few years. Now he can repair our relationship with a sincere apology when he is ready, openly share his feelings with affection, and contribute to our family dynamic with autonomy and enthusiasm on his terms. No matter how good my intentions are, it is vital that he feels my love in our interactions rather than my fear.

We can all break generational cycles and overcome limiting beliefs rooted in fear with an open mind. Empathy and compassion arise from understanding our shared human experiences, which, in turn, fosters love. The belonging I sought from others had to begin with understanding and accepting myself. Within a community of parents, I truly grew, realizing that it takes a supportive tribe to uplift each other toward our highest potential.

Arleen Tyndall is a mother dedicated to helping others break free from intergenerational cycles. She left her 27-year career as a clinical pharmacist to bring her trauma-informed care and harm reduction practices into her training with Dr. Shefali as a Conscious Parenting and Life Coach. Born in Toronto, Canada, to Indonesian immigrant parents, Arleen shares her lived experiences in her memoir, which fuses Western societal ideas with the Eastern spiritual guidance she discovered while returning to her mother's birthplace of Bali. As she navigates her identity and beliefs while assimilating into another culture, ancestral stories unfold within her extended family, igniting understanding and empathy for the dysfunction and pain of her upbringing. This healing journey deepens her connections to her present relationships, enabling her to be the mother her sensitive and strong-willed son needs. By sharing vulnerable stories and effective tools in her coaching and workshops, parents from all backgrounds have awakened to a new way of seeing their children and transformed their family dynamics.

15

RETURNING TO OUR SENSES: WHY TRYING HARDER DOESN'T WORK (AND WHAT TO DO INSTEAD)

Dawn Behm

———

My journey to understanding and healing my family relationships is deeply personal, shaped by years of hands-on experience, professional training, and the wisdom gained through success and failure. While many experts and researchers have explored parent-child relationships and family dynamics, I would like to share the unique insights and practical tools that emerged from my own path of discovery—ones that transformed my family and helped other parents I've worked with reconnect.

Simply by reading this, I know you care deeply about your children. You want to be a good mom. Oh, me too. Being a good mom can feel elusive no matter how hard we try.

Parenting feels high-stakes, where mistakes can be devastating. Frustrated with broken systems and contradictory advice for their children's well-being, moms like me watch helplessly as things fall apart. Life has become more complicated than we ever imagined. It can be paralyzing—in survival mode, we overreact, second-guess ourselves, and often feel we're failing those we love. Boy, have I lived this.

Twenty-five years ago, after years of infertility, my dream came true: I had a son. Armed with a decade of experience, a degree in early childhood education, and all the parenting books the library held, I was determined to be the best mom ever. How hard could it be?

My sweet son was born healthy and strong but not a sleeper. This was my first clue to the challenges that lay ahead. The books and all the advice from others held no answers—they were contradictory. For years, I stumbled along, doing my best. My quirky, intense children and their equally unique parents struggled as time passed. The harder I tried, the worse things got—until the unthinkable occurred.

At sixteen, my son texted us, requesting to move across the country. In his words, "I can no longer live in our home, and if you try to stop me, you will lose me forever."

While we appeared to be a happy family, inside, our home was plagued with painful interactions among highly sensitive, hurting individuals. Stunned, I felt like his request—and his legitimate pain—was the death of my dreams. In my heart, I knew I had to love him enough to let him go without knowing if I'd ever see him again. Devastated and humbled, I admitted defeat as a mom and surrendered.

That surrender was the beginning of our profound healing journey as a family. Before we dive in, let me jump ahead in my story to offer hope.

Months later, our son asked us to move back and fight with him, for him. Reunited, we traversed a long, winding road to uncover what we needed as humans. We created a new toolbox and established a new way of being together. Today, my son and I share a deep, loving connection and peace as he navigates his path at twenty-four, knowing we're here for him. There is hope.

The Foundational Human Piece—Start Here

We are human beings—with overwhelmed nervous systems in a chaotic world.

Did you know that fear states change our senses? When we're afraid, we develop tunnel vision and our hearing shifts. We are literally out of our minds and have lost our senses! In this state, the harder we try to fix our families, the more dysregulated and reactive we become. We REACT like cornered tigers (and so do they).

The Way Back

Pause, gently place one hand on your heart, and take a slow, deep breath through your nose. Let it out through your mouth with a sigh. Observe. Look up and around; name the colors, shapes, and textures around you. Listen. Hear birdsong, your heartbeat, or your breath. Notice that right now, just for this moment, you are okay.

That pause you just took—it's the antidote.

The most remarkable thing is that by allowing ourselves to pause and regulate, we see better, think more clearly, and make better choices. No longer reactive, we become responsABLE. What a shift and relief!

First, a clarification: long-term patterns don't disappear with one breath, and sometimes, medical and therapeutic support is needed. Many supportive resources are available to help us untangle trauma, beliefs, and responses and reawaken this marvelous inner guidance. Much of my work involves creating spaces and opportunities for women to experience and cultivate this. What I share here is a trailhead and place to begin.

This embodied, heart-centered state can only be accessed in the present moment through the nervous system's inputs and processes in the body. For some of us, it can be a long journey from an overthinking, worried mind to a centered, embodied heart.

That little pause you took a moment ago? That was returning to your senses. It's how you cultivate presence moment by moment.

Returning to Your Senses

These practices continue to guide me from reactivity with my family to responsiveness.

1. Breathe in support.

Breathing a calming scent deeply through the nose activates the parasympathetic nervous system—bringing back presence. Research shows that our sense of smell is the fastest way to disrupt a hijacked brain, calm the amygdala, and restore balance. In a moment, we're home.

Regular inhalation of a calming scent brings immediate relief and fosters a long-term shift out of reactivity toward recovery. Plus, diffusing oils support everyone around, enhancing co-regulation. When triggered, the smell of Frankincense brings me immediately back to myself, and my children relax as well. No essential oils? Simply breathe and imagine.

2. Orient in your world.

Remember how a stressed nervous system cannot effectively see or hear? Orienting uses our sense of sight and hearing to guide us home into our bodies. Look around and notice things without judgment. Research indicates that looking 20 feet away for 20 seconds or more signals safety to the body. That's much farther than our screens or rooms. Listen to the birds, the air, your breath. When we consciously give the body input that it is safe, we gain access to that well-regulated state.

3. Walk it out.

Emotion is energy in motion. When emotions run high, walk fast before responding. As you walk, you'll return to your senses. Insights will arise. Movement allows the body to safely release pressure. Many nights, I tried to calm myself by meditating, but it didn't work. When instead I shadow-boxed, danced, pushed against the wall, or stomped, my body completed the stress cycle and relaxed.

As we become skilled at navigating stress in our system, we can find peace in difficult times that helps us know what to do, who to listen to, and when to reach out. We discover our kids are not problems to fix but co-journeyers. As we breathe and look around, we realize the world still holds beauty and goodness. Our children need to see this in us—and we in them.

Bit by bit, we remember what is truer than all our trying: our inner source of guidance—a calm center within to navigate the challenging waters of our ever-changing world with those we love.

Dawn Behm's journey through a family crisis compelled her to look within and recognize the importance of her own well-being for her family. Her son recently said, "What helps you most [be a good mom] is getting in tune with yourself through meditation, oils, and things that make you happy." Her drive to heal for herself and her family led her through various professional programs. She describes it as her "long journey from an overthinking, worried mind to a centered, embodied heart." As a certified Wayfinder Life Coach (ACC, ICF), she enjoys creating safe, nurturing spaces where women can reconnect with their true selves, discover their inner wisdom, and rekindle joy. Through aromatherapy and a blend of holistic coaching tools, Dawn empowers women to uncover the resilience and guiding light already within them.

She lives in the foothills of the Cascades in the Pacific Northwest with her artistic husband, their daughter, and their dog, Ginger. In her free time, Dawn explores the woods, sings, photographs nature, or dives into brain/body research.

You're never alone. Download Dawn's free Returning to Your Senses Packet, which includes audio meditations and resources, at www.heartnature.life/breathe.

16

CULTIVATING CALM: A FAMILY GUIDE TO CONNECTION, NERVOUS SYSTEM, AND EMOTIONAL REGULATION

Layne Burkette, LPC, E-RYTE-RYT

I magine it's the end of another hectic day when the kids are finally in bed, and the house falls into a rare moment of silence. I remember it well: collapsing onto the pillow, feeling anything but calm. Instead of peace, my body would buzz with tension, my mind would race, and the weight of the day's emotional rollercoaster pressed heavily on my chest. You may relate to this feeling—overwhelmed, stressed, disconnected, and unsure how to meet the needs of yourself and your family.

As parents in a fast-paced culture, many of us are caught in a cycle of emotional and nervous system dysregulation. We react to our children's emotional needs without being able to recognize and manage our own. Our patience wears thin, our bodies are exhausted, and our hearts are heavy. We may think this is just part of parenting (a "phase," right?), but what if we rewrite this narrative and create a calmer, more connected family?

Let's explore how cultivating calm can allow you to parent from a place of inner peace, genuine attention, aligned actions, and an embodied presence—and then model this calm for your children. By connecting with yourself—body, mind, and heart—you can release your grip on managing their behaviors and parent from your most authentic, true, loving self.

As a mother of four and a counselor specializing in somatic therapies, I deeply understand parenting as an extraordinary, challenging, and transformative journey. I've seen firsthand how small, daily shifts in emotional regulation can create a more connected family dynamic, one rooted in peace and presence.

Your Nervous System: A Key to Emotional Balance

Our nervous system plays a vital role in emotional regulation. When it's overactive, we slip into "fight, flight, or freeze" mode (activating the sympathetic nervous system), which can bring on feelings of anxiety, irritability, overwhelm, and even physical pain or tension. This heightened state affects our mood and clouds our ability to think clearly and act in ways that align with our values—making it harder to respond calmly to our children. Our kids sense this tension and may act out, creating a cycle of heightened emotions and compounding stress.

We can shift this narrative. Somatic and embodiment practices— connecting with the body to process emotions—are key to emotional regulation and healing. Techniques like mindfulness, yoga, and meditation help foster awareness, clarity, and inner calm. By regulating our nervous system through such practices, we move from survival mode to connection mode—activating the "rest and digest" system (parasympathetic nervous system). This shift allows us to meet our emotional needs while slowing down and responding to our children with patience and presence. The whole family feels this transformation, opening up to joy, ease, and peace.

We create a new baseline of calm. The more you practice when you are calm, the easier it becomes to implement these techniques when you or your children are dysregulated. These practices rewrite the neural pathways in our brains.

Somatic Practices to Increase Connection

Here are some great ideas to get you started on your own practice and skills to use with your family:

1. **Breathwork**

   - Breathe in and exhale with a big sigh. Picture your breath rising from your feet to your head, then exhale any tension.

   - Hold up your hand and take 5 breaths. For each breath, put a finger down. Do this with your children and let them put a finger down each breath.

   - Take slow, even breaths, and ask your child to match you. Gently hold them so they can feel your breaths.

- Notice how your breath impacts your emotions.

2. Body Awareness

Notice tension and consciously release it. Ask yourself and your children, "How does your body feel? Where do you feel tension? Where do you feel calm?"

- Scan your body from head to toe, letting go of any tension.
- Offer a gentle massage, cuddle, or tap the rhythm of your child's heartbeat on their chest or back.

3. Moving

Enjoy a mindful walk, play outside, stretch, do yoga, or have a dance party (start with their favorite song, then yours!). Movement helps balance energy and release stress.

4. Grounding

Pause and ground yourself before reacting. Stand, feel the earth beneath you, inhale and rise onto your toes, then exhale and release onto your heels.

5. Mindfulness

Practice gratitude as a family. Ask your children what they are thankful for, and share your own. Try simple visualizations: imagine a positive outcome for the day, an event, or a moment of connection, and feel the associated emotions.

6. Affirmations

Create positive statements together, such as:

- "I am calm."

- "I am strong."

- "I am loved."

Repeat them morning and night to shape your mindset and feel the empowering connection they create.

7. **Meditation**

Sit quietly together for 2-5 minutes, focusing on your breath. This stillness can significantly impact how your family responds to stress. Start small and be consistent.

8. **Emotional Awareness**

Teach children to name, share, and allow their emotions. (Emotion wheels are great tools to help identify and understand feelings, increasing comfort with this practice.) Use somatic skills to nurture and follow up with a heartfelt "I love you" and a bonding interaction. As parents, begin with your own emotional regulation and model this for your children.

Implementation Tips

To implement these skills in your family, commit to setting aside 5-10 minutes each day for yourself and a short family practice. Be gentle and compassionate; these practices take time and consistency.

First, set an intention—a phrase that reflects the qualities you want to cultivate for yourself and your family. Examples include:

- "I create calm and peace within myself and my family."

- "I embrace connection."

- "I slow down for love, joy, and connection."

Next, incorporate simple somatic practices, like a few minutes of conscious breathing (with big, audible sighs on the exhale), a calming stretch, or just sitting in silence. When introducing these to yourself and your children, keep it light, fun, and enjoyable.

Acknowledging Challenges

Consistency can be difficult, especially when life is busy, but even a few minutes of practice before breakfast or bedtime each day can help regulate your nervous system and set a calming example for your children. If kids resist, keep it light and fun—short and sweet. Turn it into a game or use stories to help them understand.

Consistency and Resilience

Integrating somatic skills and emotional regulation practices can shift your family dynamic from stress to calm, connection, and resilience. The key isn't perfection or immediate results—it's consistency, patience, and self-compassion, creating a loving foundation for you and your children to navigate life's challenges with greater ease.

Whether it's a breathing practice, a grounding exercise, walking together, or pausing to breathe and repeat an affirmation, these tools will begin to rewire your nervous system. Over time, you'll notice shifts in how your family responds to stress and how you feel inside. The emotional rollercoaster will smooth out, and you will experience more peace and connection.

I still collapse into bed at night, but after years of practice, I do so feeling gratitude, peace, and compassion. My nervous system is regulated, my body is calm and at ease, and my heart is full. I bring my hand to my heart, take a deep breath, and offer myself a nurturing, "I love you."

As you lay your head down tonight, take a moment to reflect on the small moments of connection and the peace and calm that you are cultivating. Remember: you are worthy of calm. Your family is worthy of calm. And together, you have the power to create it.

Layne Burkette is a life-loving mother of four, Professional Counselor, and Yoga Psychology & Meditation Teacher dedicated to helping individuals and families transform their emotional well-being. With a passion for holistic healing, she specializes in guiding people toward emotional regulation, energy balance, and profound personal connection through an integrative approach combining Somatic Skills, Breathwork, Yoga, Meditation, and Counseling. Drawing from 20 years of professional experience, Layne empowers individuals to: reconnect with their authentic selves, regulate their nervous systems, rewire trauma responses, and cultivate deep self-compassion and love.

Beyond her counseling practice, Layne enjoys coordinating and coaching community running and triathlon events, bringing her holistic approach to physical and mental wellness.

She offers weekly live Somatic Skills sessions, along with a monthly membership that includes an on-demand video library and kid-friendly content. Individual and family sessions are available to address your unique needs.

Download her free 5-Day Breath, Yoga, and Affirmation EBook.

17

THE MOST UNDERRATED TOOL IN PARENTING—YOUR BREATH

Sonia Kamboj

———

Let me take you back to when I stood in my living room, and my son would not stop screaming and throwing his toys. I had asked him several times to stop, but he just kept going. Feeling overwhelmed and depleted, I threatened to take his toys away, yet he continued as if he hadn't heard a single word. At that moment, I could feel my anger taking over. I felt triggered because I wasn't being heard, and just like that, it happened again—I reacted and yelled at my son for what felt like the hundredth time that day. He looked at me, startled, as soon as I raised my voice, and I saw his big brown eyes welling up with tears. It felt like a gut punch. Cue the guilt and shame: Why do I keep yelling? Am I failing as a mom? Why do I react this way? As I watched the tears fall, I knew there had to be a better way than reacting with anger toward my then three-year-old.

You've probably had a similar experience because this seems to be a rite of passage.

Growing up being yelled at, I knew this feeling too well. I realized the last thing I wanted was to repeat my childhood for my son. Every atom in my body signaled that yelling wasn't the answer. My son was looking to me to guide him on communicating and behaving. In my desperate search for solutions, I dove into my inner child work, which led me to discover the practice of mindfulness. After years of practicing mindfulness and watching my son grow into a kind, confident, thoughtful, and determined tween, I'd like to share what has worked for me in hopes that it will help a fellow parent.

The High Cost of Yelling

Let us first examine the costs of regularly yelling as a parent. Children feel more scared and anxious when they are frequently yelled at, which contributes to low self-esteem. They may come to believe they are unworthy or unloved and often see fault in themselves. Children learn that yelling is the way to work through difficulties. Most importantly, the parent-child connection deteriorates over time as the unpredictable nature of yelling erodes their trust in you. An environment of regular yelling can lead to significant behavioral and emotional issues well into their teenage years.

Mindful Breathing to Quell Turmoil

Over the years of practicing mindfulness, I've learned it's not about controlling our thoughts or silencing our inner voice. It's about being present on purpose and connecting with what we are feeling and experiencing in our body in the moment. My journey began with mindful breathing, completely transforming my parenting approach into one that is more proactive.

I developed the PAUSE method to help me remember the key foundations and to remind myself to pause and breathe to regulate my nervous system.

P: Presence

Be alert in the moment and tune in to your internal atmosphere while also recognizing what you and your child need. Get out of your mind and into your body. When you find yourself in a familiar situation where you know you've yelled in the past, pause, and take a conscious breath, ensuring your exhale is longer than your inhale. The longer exhale will help reset your nervous system to its baseline.

A: Allow

Let the experience to be as it is, without judgment or expectation. Allow all feelings to arise and validate them. This may sound like, "I am feeling triggered, and that's okay," "I am feeling frustrated, and that makes sense," or "I'm allowed to feel angry, and I will choose to take deep breaths."

U: Understanding

Intentionally align with your heart and recognize that your connection with your child is pivotal. When I feel like I'm going to react, I say, "I need a minute to calm my heart by taking some deep breaths," or "Your body is showing me that you're feeling upset. I am going to sit here and take big belly breaths; you can join me when you're ready." Do not expect your child to join you initially; this is a practice your child will observe and eventually mirror over time. Once you've regulated your nervous system, you can proceed to co-regulate with your child.

S: Self-compassion

Nurture yourself with love and care, affirming your capability to handle any situation. This may sound like, "I know I can handle this," "Even though I feel this way, I am still a good parent," "This is out of my control, and that's okay," "He is not giving me a hard time; he is having a hard time," or "I can breathe through this." As you speak, place one hand on your heart and one on your belly as you connect with your breath.

E: Equanimity

Accept the emotions that arise without becoming attached to or reactive toward them. Let them come and go with time while giving yourself grace.

As you keep practicing this PAUSE, you will build unwavering calm in the face of emotional turmoil. It's essential to remember that the work occurs outside of the heated moments; this preparation allows you to respond effectively when the time comes.

I began my journey by taking deep, intentional breaths (every morning and night), which may look like inhaling through the nose for a count of four, holding it for four, and exhaling through your mouth for four counts. Note that you should not take shallow breaths in your chest. Belly breathing involves breathing in such that your belly extends outward. This activates your parasympathetic nervous system, calming your body and mind.

First You, Then Your Child

The result was that my son would watch me breathe and try to mirror me. I'd ask him to lie beside me, placing his favorite stuffed animal, Cocoa, on his belly. I would tell him that every time he breathed in, Cocoa should move up as his belly expanded outward. I turned this into a game we played every day. In the beginning, it felt like a roller coaster of emotions, and I would be lying if I said I didn't revert to yelling while my brain was still strengthening its mindful muscle. The important thing is to apologize for yelling and repair the moment with your child, so they know the yelling is not their fault.

The impact of mindful breathing is clear to me today when I see my eleven-year-old take deep breaths when he starts to feel big emotions or faces conflict. My connection with him now would not have been possible if, years ago, I had not made a conscious choice to find a better way than yelling and regulate my nervous system through a mindful approach. Continuously applying the PAUSE method has been a game-changer in my parenting experience.

Sonia Joshi Kamboj is a compassionate parent coach and mindfulness advocate who helps parents consciously cultivate calm and connection in their relationships with their children. As a mother who struggled with yelling, she has firsthand experience with the emotional toll of reactive parenting. Through years of exploring mindfulness and inner child work, she discovered the transformative power of mindful breathing, leading her to create the PAUSE method—a unique framework designed to guide parents toward emotional regulation, mindful communication, and deeper connections with their children.

Sonia's coaching approach is grounded in the belief that true change starts within, and she is committed to helping parents create peaceful, loving environments where both they and their children thrive.

In her downtime, she finds joy in practicing calligraphy, reading, meditating, and being in nature, all of which contribute to her own sense of peace and mindfulness. As a mother to a vibrant son, Sonia believes in the power of small, intentional moments to create lasting change for both parents and children.

Connect with her on Instagram @gratefulbeingspc for tips, resources, and a free guide on breathing exercises to do with your kids.

18

TAKE THE NEXT BEST STEP

Debbie Simmons

———

Parenting often feels like walking a tightrope—every step feels precarious, and the stakes seem impossibly high. As you strive to be the best parent you can be, one moment you're confident in your choices, and the next, doubt creeps in, making you question everything.

As a mother of nine adopted children with trauma backgrounds, I've been there. I've felt the crushing weight of not knowing how to handle a child screaming, throwing items, or trying to self-harm. I've walked alongside these children as they live with maladaptive behaviors that haunt them as they struggle to make sense of their world. Too many times, I've lost it while my child was losing it.

In these moments of uncertainty, a simple principle can be transformative: you don't have to figure it all out at once. Instead, focus on one thing—the next best step.

A Parent's Crossroads

It was a chaotic morning. My three high school students were struggling to get ready for school. They moaned as if life were just too much. My two middle schoolers were bickering, fighting over the bathroom. My youngest grade schooler was not interested in attending school that day and was melting down. The chores weren't done. I wasn't ready for my day as CEO and was already behind schedule. I'd be late for an important meeting if we didn't get our act together. I wanted to get back in bed, pull the covers over my head, and drown out the chaos.

Then I remembered something I had read: "Parenting isn't about being perfect. It is about being just good enough." These words offered clarity in the chaos. Instead of trying to solve everything, I focused on one small action—getting the high schoolers out the door. Once they were gone, I moved on to the middle schoolers and, lastly, my youngest. Slowly, the chaos began to feel manageable, and I started to breathe again.

That day, I learned a valuable lesson: progress in parenting doesn't come from perfection but from moving forward, one small step at a time. I gave myself permission to release the guilt I had been carrying—for the chores I hadn't done, the tantrums I couldn't prevent, and the moments I felt I had failed. Forgiving myself brought me peace and clarity to move on.

The BEST Strategy: A Roadmap to Building a Strong Family Legacy

Through the years with my children and my grandchildren, I developed the BEST strategy for helping parents work through overwhelming situations. Having worked for decades in ministry with literally thousands of overwhelmed parents, I refined this strategy so that it works in every situation imaginable—parenting or not. The BEST Strategy works in virtually any situation. Each letter represents a crucial element:

B: Breathe

If we can learn to breathe before making our next move, the action following the breath allows utilization of our prefrontal cortex (where rational thinking occurs). Our first thought before breathing is often an emotionally triggered response that typically does more damage than good. Take a moment to pause, calm yourself, and collect your thoughts.

E: Evaluate

Assess the situation with your child objectively. What's happening? Why might your child be acting this way? What do they need right now? This is your special private investigator moment to gather information. Jot down your thoughts but resist the urge to overanalyze.

S: Step Back.

Resist the urge to react impulsively. Step back, both physically and emotionally, to consider a thoughtful response. This space helps you focus on the bigger picture rather than a knee-jerk response.

T: Take Action

Choose your next best step that aligns with your values and supports your child's growth. Even small, intentional actions can lead to meaningful progress.

During one of our Pathway to Hope Camps, a dad learned to stop and breathe before doing anything. He realized that he would respond better if he took a moment for himself before engaging with his child. He discovered that if I'm OK, my child will be OK, and we will get through this. You can experience this same freedom, too.

Clarity Comes in Action

Parenting is full of moments when the path forward feels unclear. Should you enforce that boundary or let it slide? Should you encourage independence or offer more guidance? Clarity doesn't come from overthinking—it comes from action.

Consider the story of a mom who struggled with bedtime battles. Each night felt like a war zone, filled with tears and tantrums. Instead of trying to overhaul the entire bedtime routine at once, she focused on one small step: introducing a consistent bedtime story. That simple change created a comforting rhythm and transformed their evenings.

What's your "bedtime battle"? What small, actionable step can you take today to bring peace and progress to your parenting?

Practice Makes Perfect: Your BEST Strategy

To implement your BEST strategy in the heat of the moment, practice with these steps:

1. **Pause and Reflect**: Find a quiet place where you can practice this strategy. Breathe deeply and center yourself. Identify a parenting challenge that's weighing on you.

2. **Apply the BEST Model:**

   - B - Breathe
   - E - Evaluate
   - S - Step Back
   - T - Take Action

3. **Forgive Yourself**: Release any guilt or self-judgment. Remind yourself that progress, not perfection, is the goal.

Focus on the first step—breathing. The next time you feel overwhelmed, tell yourself to breathe. If you can do this, the rest of the steps will flow naturally because your prefrontal cortex is engaging. You can do this!

Closing Thought

Parenting is a journey of a thousand moments. It's not about perfection or having all the answers—it's about trust, intention, and the courage to take the next best step.

As you navigate your parenting journey, remember to extend grace to yourself. Celebrate the love and effort you bring to your family and let go of the unrealistic expectations. What small step will you take today to grow as a parent and build a deeper connection with your child?

Remember: even the smallest acts of love and intention can profoundly shape your child's future. You got this!

Debbie Simmons is a passionate leader, devoted mother, and expert parenting coach dedicated to empowering families and building lasting legacies. As the founder and CEO of Anchor Point, a nonprofit providing hope and resources for parents, Debbie has guided countless families with wisdom, faith, and practical strategies. As a mother of nine through adoption and a grandmother of fourteen, Debbie understands firsthand the challenges and rewards of parenting. She believes legacy isn't just about what we leave behind—it's about how we live today, shaping future generations with intentional love, faith, and guidance.

Through speaking, writing, and coaching, Debbie equips parents with actionable insights to help their families thrive. Her fearless approach to parenting and leadership encourages others to step boldly into their calling and raise children with resilience and purpose.

Want to strengthen your parenting strategy? Visit https://thedebbiesimmons.com/ for free resources and expert tips on building a focused, faithful, and fearless family legacy.

19

MANAGING STRESS TO MASTER CONNECTION

Dr. Elizabeth Joy Shaffer

———

S ome days, I handle ups and downs with ease and grace while continually stumbling over my feet on others. For parents of children with extra needs, however, daily challenges become a high-stakes game of chess while juggling flaming torches. The associated stress affects every family member.

The U.S. Surgeon General has recognized parent stress as a significant public health issue, emphasizing the importance of practical and effective stress management practices for parents.[10] Such management becomes even more critical for parents of children who need support with self-regulation.

I have worked with children and families worldwide for twenty years and witnessed firsthand how stress affects learning, skill development, decision-making, interactions, and behaviors. When I became a parent, I truly grasped the various factors influencing parental stress and the consequences that arise when it goes unmanaged. To raise awareness about how mindfulness-based practices can help, I conducted and published research and collaborated with other parents.

I discovered three key steps that can help reduce stress while also enhancing your connection with your children.

Step 1: Restore - Foster resilience and well-being.

Managing the day-to-day demands of parenting is challenging, especially when navigating raising a child with extra needs. This journey requires immense physical, emotional, and mental stamina. When your battery is running low, mindfully managing the challenges of the day is like attempting to herd cats in a room full of laser pointers. When parents do not restore and recharge their batteries, they are more likely to flip their lids instead of finding the best solution.

Well-being means making time for things that "restore and replenish" your energy and identifying those unconscious thoughts, habits, and behaviors that needlessly drain your energy and often impact parent-child connections. The challenges parents face are real, and certain unconscious patterns of thinking or behaviors can add to the complexity of parenting a child with extra needs. Are you aware of thought patterns or habits that drain your energy? To change, you must first become aware of the thoughts and behaviors that are not serving you or your child.

Transforming thought patterns can significantly improve your well-being and energy while fostering elevated emotional states like love and joy. Which emotional state would you like to be in more often with your child: love and joy or stress and fear? One way of consciously changing your emotional energy is to be more mindful of your thoughts and how they influence your emotional state. Are they energizing or draining? When we are aware of our thoughts, we can actively choose which to nurture and which to let go.

"Should haves" are disempowering thoughts that create guilt and make us feel inadequate or regretful about past actions. Guilt is a low-energy emotion that drains our emotional well-being. Should-have statements do not empower us to change but instead make us feel guilty about doing it wrong. Be mindful of your thoughts today. Are they empowering or disempowering? Do they make you feel good or bad?

Are you making time for the things that "feed your soul" and fill your bucket? When we "give from an empty bucket," our health suffers, our reactions result in regret, and our relationships become strained. Remember, giving time to restore your health and well-being is good for you and your family.

Step 2: Reconnect - Revitalize relationships and enhance emotional awareness.

Energy is contagious, and this realization can be transformative. Our emotional states impact those around us. Have you noticed how you feel when surrounded by optimistic individuals versus those who adopt a negative outlook? This phenomenon, known as co-regulation, occurs when one nervous system affects another. Too often, parents unknowingly engage with their children from a place of fear, anxiety, or stress, which can negatively impact the parent-child relationship.

Rita, one of my clients, found herself in a perpetual heightened state of stress and anxiety due to worries about her son with autism. As she became more mindful of her thoughts while with her son, she realized that most of her thinking was rooted in fears and anxieties regarding his challenges. She wanted to change this relationship dynamic. To achieve this, she began adjusting her thoughts to focus more on the positive, what he could do, while adopting mindfulness attitudes of acceptance, letting go, and non-judgment. This shift in thinking allowed her to enjoy her time with her son without the weight of emotional burdens such as stress, worry, and anxiety. To her surprise, when she changed her emotional state, his emotional state improved as well.

Your loving presence is what your child truly needs. Cultivating connections rooted in love and joy creates a positive, energetic balance between the heart, mind, and body. It establishes a solid foundation for calmness and safety, which is crucial for child development. It acts like a superhero cape, protecting both you and your child from life's stresses while strengthening your bond.

Step 3: Reinvent - New habits, new story.

To create a new story, examine and adjust your thoughts and beliefs about the situation. It's important to be mindful of the roles you and your child are playing. Do these align with the new story you want to create? Then, explore new habits and routines that can help you build this new narrative.

Sarah often felt stressed each morning as she rushed to get her kids ready for school on time. As she became more aware of her thoughts, she recognized the patterns that kept her stuck and hindered her ability to create a new story. She found herself frequently saying, "I should have," whether it was about waking up earlier or packing her bags in advance. This habitual use of "should have" kept her focused on what she didn't do.

When you say, "I should have," does it really lead to change, or does it merely evoke guilt for what you didn't accomplish? This thinking pattern often results in stagnation, where no changes occur.

Recognizing this, Sarah decided to shift her mindset. Instead of dwelling on "I should have," she began to say, "Tomorrow, I will set the alarm five minutes earlier so I can leave on time." This simple change brought new energy—a sense of empowerment. This thinking empowered her to take action and create new habits that support change.

The Best Gift

The greatest gift we can offer another person is our love. This involves being fully present in the moment, free of judgment, and connecting from a place of gratitude, joy, or love. Spending just five minutes a day interacting with your child can profoundly enhance your relationship while supporting both your health and well-being.

Creating a new parenting paradigm that aligns with your intentions will require your active participation in mindfully improving your health and well-being and adopting new mindsets to reconnect with your child positively.

Dr. Elizabeth Joy Shaffer, OTD, is the founder and visionary behind Therapeutic Innovations International, LLC. An experienced occupational therapist, educator, and mother, she mindfully manages neurodiversity. She delivers talks and training worldwide, following her passion for empowering parents, educators, and children with the knowledge and tools to foster child development and create calm, resilient homes and classrooms. Her research on mindfulness-based practices to reduce parental stress is integrated into her coaching practice, fostering co-regulation and deeper connections between children and their care-givers. Connect with her and her programs at www.therapyintl.com.

20

MANAGING STRESS AFTER A BIG INTERNATIONAL MOVE

Raquel Santos-Minarro

———

My youngest daughter didn't even look up from the puzzle she had spread out on the table as I entered the room. She was fully focused, carefully placing the pieces with her little hands, completely absorbed and ignoring me.

"Good morning! It's time to start the routine," I said, trying to convey my cheerful tone.

"Not now! Wait a moment," she replied sharply.

I turned toward my eldest daughter, who had just entered. Upon seeing me, she sighed and gave me that eye-roll that always puts me on alert. Clearly, I was the last person she wanted to see. "Ugh, Mom? Do you ever stop? You're always telling us what we have to do."

Her words stung, but I knew they weren't aimed at me. The routines, the expectations—to her, they felt like a burden, and I had become the face of that responsibility.

It wasn't how I had imagined our morning. I stood there, feeling a mix of sadness, confusion, and, honestly, disappointment. I woke up ready to start fresh, but my enthusiasm turned into frustration in just a few minutes.

Parenting is full of these moments—when your kids feel a million miles away, and even the simplest things turn into a battle.

But these mornings aren't about a simple routine or another activity; they are about something deeper. My youngest daughter, absorbed in her puzzle, was holding onto a moment of control in a life that feels uncertain to her, where she can't decide anything. My older daughter wasn't upset with me; she was overwhelmed by the weight of everything she felt she had to do.

Raising children is never as simple as we expect. There is no manual to navigate these moments when they resist, roll their eyes, face challenges, ignore us, or engage in battles without reason. And there is no manual for when life brings a drastic family change, like our recent move from California to Spain; everything I thought I knew about parenting vanished.

Moving to Another Country Ups Stress

Moving to another country has meant adapting to a new culture and new routines, leaving our social environment, and starting from scratch. It also involves managing my daughters' emotions as they adjust to their new world. My youngest, usually cheerful, began rejecting chores, homework, and even activities she once loved. My older daughter, who was already prone to feeling overwhelmed, became even more sensitive to expectations.

In those moments, I felt exhausted, disconnected, and very far from the kind of mother I wanted to be. But parenting isn't about being perfect. It's about learning how to rebuild the connection, even when I'm tired and don't know where to start.

I discovered that there are concrete steps I can take to improve the situation.

Step 1: Change my attitude.

The first step is focusing on myself: "What can I do to improve this situation?" Instead of attempting to fix my daughters' behavior, I concentrate on how I show up for them and take control of my own actions. Sometimes, this means choosing to see the humor in a frustrating moment, counting to one million, taking a deep breath, or simply asking myself: What kind of mother do I want to be right now?

It's not easy, especially during a chaotic international move with endless to-do lists and everything feeling urgent.

One evening, when my youngest was tired and cranky after a long day, instead of snapping back at her when she threw a tantrum over not wanting to do homework, I took a deep breath and found humor in the situation. "You know what? Let's pretend it's role-play time, and you need to teach your stuffed animals your homework!" To my relief, it worked!

If I get caught up in stress again, I remind myself not to be too hard on myself. I choose compassion, take a moment to reconnect, and start over. I focus on the mother I want to be and keep trying as many times as it takes.

Step 2: Focus on the cause, not the behavior.

I often catch myself reacting to the behaviors I observe—tantrums, defiance, or backtalk—but I've learned that these are usually signs of something deeper. Is my daughter feeling tired, overwhelmed, or simply needing connection? When I take a moment to look beyond the behavior and try to understand what's going on, I can address the root cause.

It's not always easy, but it helps me find lasting solutions instead of quick fixes. For example, during our move, my youngest daughter's "no" phase was her way of processing the loss of control in her life. She needed to assert that control, and understanding this allowed me to respond with empathy instead of frustration.

Step 3: Practice gratitude.

In the midst of daily chaos, it's common to focus on what's not going right. To shift that negative perspective, my family introduced a simple tradition: during dinner, each family member shares something they appreciate about someone else in the family. It's a simple act, but it's impactful. Gratitude fosters connection and reminds us that, even on tough days, we're part of something bigger: our family.

Step 4: Personalize time with my child

Spending undivided time with each of my daughters has been one of the most rewarding changes I've made. It's not about creating big plans or elaborate outings but rather about 10 to 15 minutes of focused attention, allowing my daughter to take the lead. During this special time, I set aside my agenda and follow her cues—playing, building, talking, or just sitting together. The key is to be fully present.

One evening, when we were both cranky from a long day, I sat down with her and let her take the lead in playing a game she loved. For those few minutes, everything else faded away as we laughed together. These moments allow my daughters to feel seen, heard, and valued.

Challenges I Face When Trying to Personalize Quality Time

- **"I'm busy or tired"**: Even five minutes of focused attention can make a difference. I set a timer, put distractions aside, and let that be enough.

- **Boundaries tested**: If my child pushes limits, I stay calm and redirect: "I know you love playing with slime, but not now. What else can we do?"

- **Upset or tears mean my child feels safe expressing emotions.** Instead of trying to fix it, I acknowledge: "You're upset, and that's okay. I'm here."

- **Don't enjoy it**: Sometimes, I don't love the activity but focus on my child's joy. Over time, I've started looking forward to these moments more than I expected.

Parenting is chaotic, and no strategy works perfectly all the time. I've learned that the key isn't perfection but consistency. Even when it's hard, showing up for my kids builds a foundation of trust and connection. When I shift my mindset, address the root causes of behavior, practice gratitude, and prioritize connection, I see real change in my kids and myself.

What if we chose not just to survive but to fully enjoy this journey? Raising children isn't about being perfect; it's about finding joy in the imperfections.

Raquel Santos Miñarro, M.Sc., M.A.Ed., is a Certified Positive Discipline Parent Educator and teacher based in Spain, having recently relocated from California. After dedicating her career to education, Raquel's perspective on parenting shifted when she became a mother, leading her to understand the importance of respectful, connected approaches to both parenting and education. Today, she combines her passion for teaching with her work as a parent educator, helping families create positive changes in their relationships and guiding them toward building stronger, more meaningful bonds. Raquel believes that true growth happens through moments of connection, not perfection, and is committed to supporting families in transforming their relationships for the better.

When she's not teaching, Raquel enjoys walking by the sea, reading a good book, and spending quality time with her family.

Ready to strengthen your family connections? Contact Raquel at rsantosminarro@gmail.com to receive your free guide and start building stronger bonds with your family.

SECTION THREE: AUTHENTIC COMMUNICATION FOR DEEPER FAMILY CONNECTIONS

21

ONE PARENTING TOOL THAT MAKES EVERYTHING BETTER

Cecilia and Jason Hilkey

———

Years ago, our child said, "I want a horse for my birthday." When I heard those words, I was flooded with feelings. (I use the singular because, despite Jason and me being on the same page, it was I who experienced this particular moment.) I felt annoyed. I grumbled, albeit in my head, that we had worked hard for years to help this child pursue their interest in horses. Wasn't that enough? I felt sadness knowing that we didn't have money for a horse. I felt irritated, thinking, *Kid, can't you be grateful for everything you have?* It took everything in me to stop myself from teaching about privilege, lecturing about gratitude, shaming, and giving our child advice.

Instead, I took a deep breath and said, "Tell me more."

We talked. I listened to our child's hopes and dreams, hearing why they wanted their own horse. I did my best to fully understand our child's perspective, even though I didn't necessarily share it. (Note: I'm referring to our child using "they/them" pronouns for privacy.)

In the end, our child knew that I had heard everything they said. I thanked them for sharing and said that, unfortunately, we couldn't buy them a horse.

This was clearly a major disappointment for our child. But what made it manageable was that we felt connected. Humans are social beings, and connection soothes.

Connection Makes Everything Better

After decades of raising our own kids, teaching preschool, and coaching parents, we believe that connection (being with our child's feelings, understanding them, and helping them make sense of it all) is one of the most important parts of parenting. To be clear, connection doesn't solve everything or make everything perfect; it just makes things better than they were before.

Connection is simple but sometimes complicated to enact in practice. In our work with parents, we've seen three main obstacles to connection. We'll list the problems first and then follow up with our recommended solutions.

Problem 1: You've "run out" of connection.

Sometimes, connecting with your kids is hard because you're emotionally empty. You feel exhausted, "done," or "tapped out." We can all run out of connection in about two seconds if we think our child is acting rude, entitled, ungrateful, dramatic, or selfish.

Solution: Start with self-connection.

If you connect with yourself, you build your capacity to connect with your child. Self-connection is best done silently in your head. It's free, and you can do it anywhere.

I have a few favorite self-connection statements that I rotate through as needed. You're welcome to use them too. When our child talked about wanting a horse, my self-connection sounded something like this:

"This is hard."

"This is not how I wanted my morning to go."

"I feel so [mad, sad, frustrated, irritated, disappointed, exhausted, etc.]."

"I'm only human. I make mistakes."

"I'll do my best until I know better. Then I'll do better."

"This is the most important thing I'll do all day."

"This is not an emergency."

Note: the last two phrases come from Dr Laura Markham.

Problem 2: Figuring out the best time to teach a child.

When a child behaves "poorly," it's tempting to jump in and start teaching and correcting them immediately. Parents don't want their child to think their misbehavior "is okay." But we suggest that you take a moment to connect with them instead of jumping in.

Solution: "Connect before you correct."

Like Dr. Daniel Siegel, we believe that connection is the first step in teaching kids. As humans, we tend to be most open to teaching and feedback when we feel understood, safe, and calm. Work on connecting with your child first before you teach, give advice, or offer a solution.

Here are some ways to connect with your child and fully understand their perspective so that they will be more open to your teaching and your perspective:

"Tell me more."

"Ah, it makes sense that you'd feel [upset, mad, sad, hurt, etc.]."

"It sounds like you felt X because you were trying to Y. Is that right?"

"Let me see if I've got this right. You feel ... "

"What is the most important thing you want me to hear?"

"Can I offer a different way to look at that?"

Problem 3: There's no time to connect.

You have a lot of demands on your time, energy, emotions, patience, and resources. That's one of the biggest sources of guilt most parents face. Of course, there are various reasons why you might not be able to fully connect "in the moment" with your kids, given the real-life limitations of modern parenting. We understand.

Solution: Circle back around.

If you believe you have somehow shortchanged your child because you've lacked time, resources, or patience, "circle back around" to your child outside the moment.

If you're ever wondering whether your child has any "leftovers" from a situation, the easiest thing to do is to ask. Find a time when you're already feeling connected. You might feel hesitant to bring up a potentially tricky topic with your child, but consider that conversations like these are healing; they build your relationship with your kids in the present and could make things easier in the future. Parents sometimes don't want to talk about hard feelings because they're afraid it'll make them bigger, but most often, talking about hard feelings makes them decrease rather than increase in size.

This is what circling back could sound like:

"Earlier today, X happened. How are you feeling about it now?"
"If we are in a similar situation in the future, is there anything that you want me to do differently?"
"Do you have any feelings that you want to make sure I've heard?"
"That makes sense to me."
"I believe you."

Connection Is the Bacon of Parenting

According to a chef we heard on the radio, bacon is an ingredient you can add to almost any dish to make it better. If bacon makes all meals better, then connection is the bacon of parenting. Connection makes everything better; not perfectly solved, but better.

Connecting with ourselves and our kids is one of the hardest things to do in parenting, yet connection is where the magic happens. Connection is a tool for understanding ourselves and other people.

We don't always have to agree with our kids' behavior, but we can relate to the feelings that underlie our child's actions; relating to their feelings is the foundation of connection. When we see that others are not that much different from ourselves and possess their own feelings and reasoning, we banish the divisions in our family and the world.

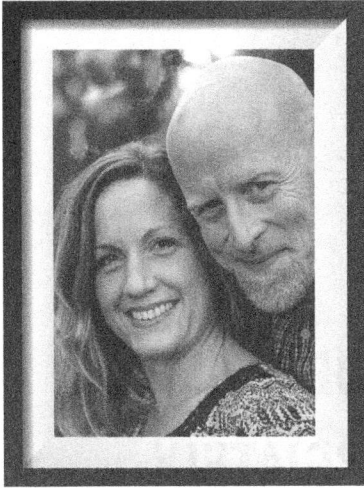

Cecilia and Jason Hilkey co-founded Happily Family, an online education company dedicated to giving parents the support and tools to understand how kids' brains work, address challenging behaviors, clear up communication, and create connection in families. Since 2012, they have interviewed over 250 parent experts and created online conferences and courses that reach a worldwide audience of over 100k families each week. Cecilia and Jason have worked as early childhood educators and with special needs children and have raised three kids of their own (two biological and one "adopted"). They have been featured in local and national media and regularly present at schools, businesses, and conferences locally and abroad. They live in Oregon with their family in a house shaded by an oak tree.

To find out more about Happily Family, scan the QR code below. As a thank you, you'll get a free worksheet to create a "Calming Plan," so that each member of your family has the tools to self-regulate when big feelings come up.

22

GETTING INTO YOUR CHILD'S WORLD, APPROPRIATELY

Denise Colpitts

—

"Do I have to go?" "We always go hiking. Can we do something else?"

Sound familiar? If so, you are likely facing what many parents do: You plan an activity for your family—something everyone will enjoy—and then ...

Your kids aren't as enthusiastic as you hoped. They try to wrangle their way out of joining, which makes you feel disappointed and unappreciated.

What are your children *really* telling you? You plan things you *think* they will enjoy but not experiences they would choose. Sometimes, this works; most times, it doesn't, resulting in frustration.

As a middle school teacher and school leader for over thirty years, I have worked with many parents trying to connect with their children. I have seen children who feel misunderstood by their parents. As a parent coach, I see these same concerns.

Let me help you build real connections with your children by meeting them where they are while avoiding the most common pitfall: trying to connect with your children by becoming their friends—dressing in similar clothing or hanging out with their friends. This is *not* getting into your child's world appropriately. Your child will likely react negatively to these efforts, often expressing embarrassment.

Well-Intended but Disconnected Efforts

Here's a secret: Parents often overlook their children's need for control. They create adult-directed situations—where to go to dinner, what vacations to take, and how to spend the weekend. Because children have little control over their lives, they react with disinterest and negativity.

Not connecting appropriately deprives you and your child of the opportunity to create authentic bonds. You will continue to plan activities that ignore their interests, creating resentment and a feeling of not being understood.

For example, one of my clients has a son and a daughter, both teens. Her husband travels during the week, so she considers the weekend family time. While the children usually enjoyed spending time outdoors, the son was becoming resentful.

My client and her daughter connected during the week through common interests, but she did not feel such a bond with her son, which was causing her concern. Through coaching, she had a great *Aha!* Moment: She was not engaging in anything her son liked to do, such as playing video games or watching movies. She'd expected that their bonding would come from weekend activities, which clearly, they did not.

The LEARN Approach: Getting into Your Child's World Appropriately

My client recognized that she "had not gotten into his world." Making efforts to understand her son's interests created a positive impact on their relationship and family dynamics.

I walked her through the LEARN approach I developed, one that will likely help you:

L = Lean into your children's interests

E = Engage genuinely

A = Ask questions

R = Reframe—provide opportunities for children's voice and choice

N = Name it!

Your children want to know they are important to you. The LEARN approach does that. It relies on finding joy in engaging with your child where they are. Genuinely show interest in your children's interests and how they spend their time.

Implementation

With younger children: Spend time together where they lead the way. Your child selects the activity, and you go along, getting into their world. Be sure not to direct.

Whether structured or unstructured, a few times a week empowers your child and builds strong bonds.

Two examples to borrow ideas from:

- Parents of preschool twins planned a time called "Daddy and Daughter" and "Mommy and Me." Naming made this time special, as the girls looked forward to it.

- A single mom called the twenty minutes set aside for her tween daughter "Just You and Me." She focused on her daughter and not the many other things she managed.

I experienced getting into my grandson's world when he asked if I wanted to watch him play a video game. I put down my phone and said, "I'd love to," giving him my full attention and asking a question or two, to which he responded. After a few minutes of silence, he said, "Nonna, I love you." Magic!

For middle-grade children and teens: Observe what your children like to do. Then casually ask a question—maybe why a video game is a favorite or about a movie, book, or craft.

"What do you like about that new game?" could be a starter question. Even asking why gaming is so popular can be a pathway to connection.

Involve kids in decisions. As my client realized, letting her son choose a family activity for the weekend helped empower him and changed his attitude. Sometimes, it can be as simple as shooting hoops in the backyard.

Benefits

Your children will feel seen and heard, and your efforts will show that you value who they are and what they like. Having choice fosters control and empowerment, which every child needs.

An added benefit? Research shows that parental involvement in their children's interests can improve academic achievement, social skills, and health.

Bumps Along the Way

Reactions will vary depending on your child's age and personality. Keep trying, and remember to be genuine. You should notice a difference in attitude and responsiveness over time.

You might think that teenagers will not talk to their parents about their interests, and you may be right ... at first. A cardinal aspect of coaching is that small steps matter. Things take time, and every step forward is a move toward your goal.

If your efforts don't seem to be going anywhere, fall back on an easy way to connect. Ask your older children what they would like to do on the weekend. Let your child choose if you have a family night tradition, such as movie or game night. Asking your younger child, "What would you like to play?" puts them in the driver's seat.

Interests change over time, so be adaptable.

A Path Forward

I invite you to reflect: "What are my child's interests?" "How often have I asked for my child's input when planning activities?" Then, take action using the LEARN approach.

What could be better than having your efforts communicate that you value your children as individuals and are willing to let them lead you into their worlds?

Denise Colpitts, MSEd, is a PCI Certified Parent Coach® who has received Parent Coach Certification®. She has over thirty years of experience working at the elementary, middle school, and college levels. In her work with parents, Denise has developed and implemented multiple strategies that work for families with toddlers to teens. She combines her training from the Parent Coach Institute with her experience as an educational leader, mother, and grandmother to help families meet the challenges of today's world by reimagining parenting. For more ideas and a list of ways to connect with your children, please scan the QR code or visit www.inpoweredparent.com.

23

THE POWER OF FAMILY MEETINGS

Sheryl Ang

———

"Can you tell your parents everything?"

My children were participating in a live poll and were asked to move to different parts of the room based on their answers. My heart sank as I saw my two oldest giggle and walk toward the "No!" group. They were only six and five years old. Despite practicing peaceful parenting almost all their lives, this defining moment felt like a reality check. What did I do to make them think I was unapproachable? What was I missing here?

Upon reflection, I realized I needed to make changes. Disconnection creeps in innocuously in modern family life. Our lives are busy, and dual-income families mean parents spend less time with their children. Children are often overscheduled with numerous after-school activities. Easy access to digital devices prevents us from being present and connected. You may feel you're doing well by providing for all your children's needs, but as they grow, your conversations become purely logistical—"Hurry up, you're late! Have you had your dinner? Go shower and prepare for bed." The delight you once had in your child is now overshadowed by emotional disconnection and distance.

Stephen Covey said, "Ninety percent of relationship problems can be eliminated if we communicate better." His words hit home: What values am I imparting to my children when our conversations lack depth?

Disconnection leads to a lack of shared reality, fuels misunderstandings, increases emotional distance, and can lead to outright conflict and aggression. Without open lines of communication, children might turn to peers or external influences that may not act in their best interests or provide appropriate support. Research has shown that inadequate family communication can lead to mental health issues.[11]

A working mother once reacted in frustration to her teenage child, "Do you think our house is a hotel?" This question, born of pain, was met with rolling eyes of dismissal. The disconnection took many years to repair before the teenager felt safe enough to confide in her mother again.

That teenager was me.

My stakes are high. Do I want to see the reflection of my teenage self in my children? Am I ready to risk my adult child walking away because he feels misunderstood and unheard?

Determined to change course, I realized that adopting family rituals encourages connection and conversation. When we incorporate family rituals as regular practices, they serve as checkpoints for review and reset. I schedule them on my Google Calendar to manage them easily. These rituals allow us to pause and reconnect, giving children a sense of love, stability, and familiarity. They might include spending special focused time with each child, having monthly pizza nights, or hosting game days. For us, one game-changing ritual is our monthly family meetings.

Why Family Meetings Work

Family meetings provide a space where everyone has an equal right to speak and reflect. Regular family meetings yield benefits beyond strong family bonds and positive relationship skills. They offer children opportunities for growth, including personal empowerment, confidence building, positive identity development, enhanced collaborative skills, problem-solving and conflict resolution abilities, decision-making, and more.

We kept the initial meetings short (15 to 30 minutes). As they grew, we expanded into deeper discussions.

We ask questions like:

- What are you grateful for?
- What upsets you?
- What's not working for you?

We assess actions that may have led us down a slippery slope:

- I've noticed you've been asking, "What do I do now?" a lot.
- How might you avoid taking it personally and absorbing someone else's emotions when they are having a bad day?

Responses vary from thoughtful insights to simple "I don't knows." As we model self-reflection, our children learn to find their own answers.

There is no one way to hold a family meeting. Some families spend significant time discussing values, vision, and mission statements. In today's complex family structures—whether you are a single parent, co-parenting in a blended family, or raising children with extended relatives—introducing family meetings can transform your family dynamics. Your family meeting may look different from mine, and that's perfectly fine.

Here are some considerations when setting up your family meetings:

1. **Be consistent.**

   Choose a frequency like fortnightly, quarterly, or monthly, depending on your family's needs and season of life. Consistency creates opportunities for progress.

2. **Keep the agenda simple.**

   Don't try to cover too much. We have a lifetime to do this. Keeping it short makes it manageable and sustainable.

3. **Make it enjoyable.**

   Family meetings shouldn't be a source of dread or just another task. Build positive and enjoyable memories to strengthen family bonds. Effective family meetings flourish with a collaborative and inclusive mindset. An authoritative and one-sided approach quickly loses its impact. No one wants to feel silenced or overlooked, even in a forgiving family.

At its core, the success of a family meeting lies not in its structure but in conversations that promote emotional safety, collaboration, and family alignment. I have found that family meetings that result in healthy relationships and personal growth have the following in common:

- **Listen actively** without interruption or judgment. Respond in a way that understands the positive intention behind the words.

- **Observe with empathy**. Use objective statements like "I noticed ..." to initiate difficult conversations without accusation.

- **Value each family member's contribution** regardless of age or perspective.

- **Explore solutions** collaboratively while respecting personal choice.

Together, this is the LOVE success framework.

Like any new habit, the biggest challenge faced by many families is time. Scheduling these meetings like a work meeting has worked for many. Another option is to tie it to an existing activity, such as dinner time. It's easy to focus on logistical matters rather than contemplative questions. Keeping the agenda short forces you to discuss what matters rather than what's on the calendar next month.

Young children engage better with drawing materials. One family with multiple children successfully held family meetings during the toddler's naptime! Meeting while walking, inside a hot tub, with yummy treats, or with a ceremonial process of lighting and blowing out candles can bring elements of fun and excitement. If calling it a "meeting" brings unpleasant memories or feels too formal, try giving it an unconventional name, such as family fun time or family gathering.

Family meetings are just one of many connection rituals that bring lasting benefits. The most important thing is to take the first step. Start small with just 15 minutes today, and watch your family strengthen in ways you never imagined.

Sheryl Ang understands the overwhelming challenges parents face in balancing life, educating their children, and fostering meaningful connections. She is an educator, coach, and advocate for child-centered learning. With certifications in Peaceful Parenting, Wunderled Education, Mindfulness, and Woman-Centered Coaching, Sheryl's interests, including neuroscience and social-emotional learning, have allowed her to take a multidisciplinary perspective. She helps mothers find aligned pathways that create the greatest ease in their lives. Before becoming an educator, Sheryl built a career in business and finance and is a Chartered Financial Analyst and a Chartered Accountant. She now spends time nurturing communities and homeschools her three boys.

For close to a decade, Sheryl's work has touched thousands of families through summits, children's entrepreneurship fairs, workshops, podcast appearances, and individual consultations. She guides parents in making self-directed learning and mindful parenting a natural way of life, without adding more to their already full plates.

Access additional resources for family meetings via the QR code.

24

STOP PARENTING AND START CONNECTING

Atousa Maleki Nikirk

D id you know there's something you can do in just five to fifteen minutes a day that will make your child willing to consider anything you ask?

"Adults are so boring," says every kid ever.

"Remember how it felt to be a kid and have FUN, Mom?" my son asks as I rattle off the evening to-do list.

We read many parenting books, but they're all from an adult perspective. We often forget our children's viewpoint. Maybe it's time to change that.

So how do you get kids to do the work needed to get to the fun part? If you ask kids, they'll tell you all they want to do is play with their friends. Why? Because it's fun! It's as simple as that. They connect with their friends and decide what to do together.

As parents, we often get trapped in command mode and forget how to just have FUN! We're so busy running errands, checking off our to-do lists, worrying about bills, and stressing over the kids' homework—did it all get done? Did they practice piano? Make it to soccer practice? We forget about the #1 attention-grabber for our kids: having fun. Does this mean we should throw away the lists and give in to playing games all day? I wish. But as parents, we must remember that to help our kids understand what we feel is important, we must translate the word FUN to its adult equivalent: connection.

Who I Am

I have a Ph.D. in Biological Sciences with a minor in Behavioral Science. I've read many parenting books to understand parent-child relationships, and it took me several years of actual parenting without great success in persuading my kids to see things my way until I realized that the key lies in the wise words of the internationally acclaimed cartoon character Bandit, Bluey's dad: "I am not Dad; I am Magic Claw!"

Channel Your Inner Child

To be a great parent, it is essential to channel our inner child, set aside the stresses of the day, and truly connect with our kids at their level to have fun. Of course, this is age-dependent.

For toddlers, it may mean getting down on the floor at eye level and playing silly games; for adolescents, it may involve running around, playing their favorite game, and laughing with them; and for teenagers, it might mean committing to putting phones away and having a cup of coffee together while listening to their favorite songs and being silly while singing along.

These fun activities are much more than just fun. They're the building blocks of a trusting relationship that helps you bond and should always be followed up with listening time, allowing your kids to know you are there to talk about anything.

When you show up for them, their self-confidence improves, their desire to do what is right increases, their willingness to complete necessary tasks (like homework) readily improves, and a hidden gem begins to glisten: their deep desire to build a stronger bond with you grows. This establishes the magic circle of self-driven accomplishments, where the reward is simply building a stronger family bond.

How to Start

If you've never tried this approach before and want a fresh start with your child, the best way to begin is with genuine honesty. Start by saying something like, "Hey, they don't give you a manual when you're a parent, so you just try your best, and sometimes we mess up too. I'm sorry if I wasn't great at it in the beginning. But I love you so much that I keep reading and trying to connect with you. Will you let me keep trying to get it right?"

Kids are generally forgiving and eager to connect, so they will give us many chances to improve. Plus, they are usually delighted to see how concerned and invested we are in them. As parents, we will find that if we take a little time to do things their fun way, the return on investment is so great that it's worth the extra time every time.

In summary, follow the **SOFUN** method:

- Stop
- Open your heart
- Find humor /inner child
- Unplug /listen
- New bond

Studies show that spending even 15 minutes a day focused on connection can help children feel better connected to their parents.

Stop Parenting

"Stop Parenting" means breaking the habit of telling your kids what to do and what to think, and instead, treating them emotionally like your best friend. However, when I say connect and communicate as if you are talking to your best friend, I do not mean that you should literally become your child's friend rather than their parent. This is very different from parents who compromise their judgment to fit in as the "cool friend." I mean to imagine you are having a sincere conversation with your best friend.

By the time my children were 10 and 11, I realized this approach transformed everything for us. Suddenly, when there was genuine connection, they not only complied with our requests but became invested in fulfilling their responsibilities. Once invested, they developed a personal desire to complete their morning routines, finish their homework, and, best of all, maintain their end of the "connection." Knowing they had a constant cheerleader gently guiding them, rather than simply ordering them around, empowered them to achieve anything.

Mishaps and Failures

Were there mishaps? Of course. Were there failures? Yes. Were there still occasional meltdowns, particularly when we stayed up too late for something fun or when dinner was delayed? Yes. But overall, this strengthened our relationship for life and became the magic glue that melted our hearts together again. It transformed necessities into inner desires for the kids to achieve, rather than external demands from us as parents.

Once regular, consistent connection is established, it stimulates a sense of inner motivation, confidence, and strength that makes them understand the importance of planning and visualizing their future. The world becomes their oyster. Then, you can discover what they dream of and envision for their ideal future. Imagine the new confident, positively driven generation of young people with positive self-talk and exemplary achievements we could create if we all did this.

Atousa Maleki, Ph.D., is a board-certified clinical cytogeneticist with 30 years of experience. She received her Ph.D. in Biological Sciences, with a minor in Behavioral Science, from the University of Texas Health Science Center in Houston, Texas. She completed her fellowship at the University of Colorado and UT Southwestern Medical Center. For the last 15 years, she has directed XS Genetics, LLC. However, her favorite job is being a mom to her two kids, ages 12 and 13, whom she adores. She couldn't do any of it without her amazing, loving, and brilliant husband, Chris, and her wonderfully supportive and open-minded parents. Currently, she has started a new venture combining coaching and motivational organization for parents and small business owners called Moti-Vision™, where she offers regular motivation sessions with a custom-designed vision planner, the Moti-Vision™ Planner (MVP). She can be reached for coaching at amn-llc.com, where her organizational products can also be found. She welcomes new clients of all ages to help them get organized and reach their short- and long-term goals! For more information about Positive Connection Coaching and organization tools for reaching your goals and helping your kids reach their dreams, visit our website and connect with her at atousa@amn-llc.com.

25

TEACHING SELF-ADVOCACY SKILLS DURING THE TODDLER YEARS

Heather Schalk and Amy Fieldman

We can't tell you how often we hear from parents who are at their wit's end, trying to manage tantrums and challenging behaviors, saying things like, "Why won't my child listen to me no matter what I try?"

Removing your child from a situation or saying, "No! Stop that," might seem like the only solution, but it misses the most important part of learning to regulate emotions and does not teach appropriate prosocial skills.

Advocacy skills are among the most important skills to teach children in early toddlerhood. Most parents do not know that teaching advocacy skills is integral to developing age-appropriate social-emotional skills, such as requesting, sharing, and turn-taking. Without these skills, children may struggle upon entering formal educational settings. A recent study shows that 72% of kindergarten teachers report children struggle in multiple areas of social-emotional development. Specifically, 53% face challenges with working collaboratively in small groups, and 50% struggle with making friends and peer interactions.[12]

Is This Your Child?

If you're concerned that your child struggles and exhibits the following:

- Not listening and talking back
- Physical behaviors of hitting, throwing, kicking, pushing
- Screaming to communicate
- Unable to share and take turns
- Tantrums and big emotions that disrupt the entire day

Then, you may want to pay close attention.

The Birth of Our Approach

We dug deep into our combined 35 years as special educators, drawing upon our expertise, and decided to try some revised methods of building self-advocacy that focused on communication skills with my (Heather here) twin toddlers. The twins were throwing, hitting, and tantruming throughout the day. Yes, it was tough! It was tougher for them because they couldn't figure out how to better meet their needs.

If you feel your child struggles with getting their needs met and, in response, is acting out, know there is hope and a skill your child can learn. According to a study, children who have access to better language skills by age four demonstrate an increase in coping skills, such as waiting for attention or a turn with a toy, and, in turn, exhibit less aggressive physical behavior.[13]

After implementing our simple-to-use strategies, the twins became happy, communicative, and better adjusted in less than a day. That's when we knew this method needed to be shared. As a parent, you may see hitting or screaming as just tantrums or meltdowns, but often, they are really signals that our toddler is missing an important skill—**advocacy**. These big reactions are a child's way of communicating a need they don't yet know how to express in a healthy, prosocial way. Here's the rundown of the simple, proven approach to help your toddler manage their feelings by advocating for their needs:

Five Steps to Fewer Meltdowns

Step 1: Identify the Trigger (what brings on the tantrum)

Even if you're unsure about the exact emotion your toddler feels or what triggers them to hit or throw toys, you can still teach general replacement behaviors. Example: The child wants to be noticed or interacted with and to have a turn first. Waiting is hard, so they hit or scream.

Step 2: Understand the Emotion (Recognize the emotion your child is experiencing)

Once we know what is upsetting them and can identify which emotion they are feeling, we can help them find a replacement behavior through what they say and do physically—for example, disappointment—not getting expected outcomes or responses (attention from you).

Step 3: Choose Empowered Communication (simple, clear phrases) and/ or Appropriate Physical Actions

Have a replacement behavior for what our toddler is doing. This can be verbal (communication) or physical (body movement), replacing the behavior that doesn't serve them or you (e.g., hitting). Example: Instead of screaming or hitting, teach "my turn next" or teach a gesture for "turn." They can also cross their arms if feeling frustrated or stomp their feet.

Note: When choosing a communication mode, make sure it's a skill they are already practicing, such as saying "turn" or giving a hand gesture for "turn."

Step 4: Practice and Praise

We need to use proactive strategies like praise and practice this frequently with our toddlers when they are calm. Example: "Awesome job saying you want a turn next." Practice by modeling during play or supervising siblings or peers: "Turn, please!"

Practice crossing your arms when angry and showing angry facial expressions.

Step 5: Adjust as Needed

Make adjustments along the way to ensure your child is successful.

Example: You might find your toddler struggling with saying "my turn next" and just saying "turn" or using the sign for a turn instead. It's essential to meet your toddler where they are now. You also might find that the physical behavior of stomping feet doesn't work, but squeezing a squishy stress ball does! Finding physical strategies for your toddler that work for them is crucial.

Set realistic expectations for results. Once your toddler learns a replacement skill for their behavior (e.g., throwing toys), you might be happy they learned the skill but still find other behaviors popping up! You're not doing anything wrong; you need to keep re-implementing the five steps to reduce meltdowns in other areas where your toddler is struggling with communication.

Our five-step solution for teaching advocacy skills is a successful evidence-based process. It works for us and for the clients in our program. Some examples include: when a toddler learned to wait patiently for adult attention by communicating his needs first instead of throwing toys at the parent, a twin who found ways to request a turn with toys with their sibling instead of screaming, and a child who navigated transitions calmly without hitting their caregiver.

Make Modifications, if Needed

Even children who are nonverbal or delayed in communication can learn the social skills of asking for help, a turn, a toy, and food by using gestures or picture cards. Take pictures or print out images of your child's favorite items and show them that the picture card can be used to request the item they want. When your child grabs a toy, demonstrate how to use the picture card or a gesture to request a turn. These simple techniques will give your child the tools to communicate with others and significantly reduce tantrums.

You are an Invested Parent/Caregiver

Communication and advocacy are key cornerstones that your toddler must learn to have their needs met now and in the future. Parenting is a journey that isn't perfect, but together, we can support, connect, and grow through every challenge. When you use the skills provided in this chapter, you'll see an increase in your child's positive and pro-social skills.

Heather Schalk is a twin mama and the founder of *The Toddler Toolkit Podcast* and *The 3 Steps to a Calm, Kind, and Caring Toddler Cohort and Course*. She has a master's degree in education and taught pre-K through ninth grade for ten years. Her passion is helping parents develop long-term customizable strategies that work, giving young children the skills needed to advocate for themselves and joy.

Amy Fieldman is a parent and grandparent with a master's degree in special education. She has 25 years of educational experience as a parent coach, teacher, and administrator, supporting developmentally delayed and at-risk children in public and private educational settings.

26

THE FOUNDATION OF YOUR RELATIONSHIP IS CONNECTION

Mrs. Jay Anderson

As a psychologist, counselor, and play therapist with around 30 years of experience, my specialty is problem-solving with struggling families.

My journey into child protection allowed me to use my people skills and help those in the community. I connected with families and children, helping them improve their relationships, recognize their feelings, and keep children safe. I encountered many children who simply needed their parents to care for and connect with them.

I developed my ability to connect with children and listen to them.

I also developed skills in helping parents connect with their children. I remember one very young woman whose little boy was in foster care. I helped that young woman be seen and heard and given an opportunity to show that her life had changed. She was older now, had undertaken some changes, and had a partner to support her. This interaction enabled her to keep her baby. She succeeded, and I witnessed the happiness of her little boy upon being reunited with her and returned to her care. This family situation ignited my passion for helping others and making a difference in their lives.

In my other roles in child protection, I was trained to connect with children and use my skills to engage and communicate with them. This led me to a role in interviewing children, where I developed deep skills in hearing their stories, pain, trauma, and life experiences. For example, some of the core skills that I was trained in involved not asking children direct questions. The key to communicating with children was simply to ask, "Tell me about that," or to say, "And what happened next?" I enjoyed helping children communicate with adults to be heard and truly experience safety.

I learned how to understand children profoundly and how crucial their attachments were. I also learned skills for helping parents understand how to truly connect with their children. Understanding that children communicate differently from adults is at the core of understanding how to connect with children. Being in a relationship with children is so much easier when adults can understand that children communicate through play. Parents can slow down their interactions, notice feelings, and truly listen.

I also assist children in counseling and processing significant trauma and grief experiences. I recall one child who undertook play therapy with me. She was in foster care and had been removed from her mother as a baby. In her play therapy sessions, she would play with little toys and give them a voice, saying, "Where's my mummy? I lost my mummy," and enacting play with a baby animal and its mother. Over time, in her play, she worked through and processed her distress and her grief, and knowing how to connect, reflect, and listen was crucial to this process. In my work with parents, I can train them in some of these core skills that assist them in building greater connections with their children and improving their relationships.

I have found that the key to happier families is spending time together—connecting, communicating, and caring.

In my roles, I developed skills to understand children and help parents deeply connect with their children to improve their relationships. I remember two parents who described their distress that their toddler was so challenging—how he was naughty and demanding of their time. When I heard their story, I could see the challenge, and I knew the solution could be discovered. We talked about how their child was not in their direct care for most of his day. These parents were working so hard, each of them in a job; their little boy was in long daycare, from early until late. They would pick him up and go home for the "dinner-bath-bed" routine. But he would be so naughty, so upset and disruptive, not sleeping, temper tantrums—they were distraught and didn't know what to do.

Together, we discussed and learned about child attachment, emotions, and needs. I helped them understand their child's need for connection and how they could all be more connected as a family.

As they spent more time together, they saw their child's distress reduce and noticed that he was a happier boy. They realized that when he was spending time with one or both of them, he was getting his emotional needs met. The family then told me that they had decided that he needed a parent at home with him instead of in extended daycare, and the mother decided to leave her job and spend more time with their boy. They made this decision when they realized how to connect with their child and spend more time with him.

I have discovered that when people take time to listen and respond with respect and care, each child and parent can develop a deeper attachment. In our fast-paced world, I can help parents connect with their children, resulting in happier children and happier parents. It can be as simple as spending more time together.

I encourage you to explore your relationships, connect, and communicate—to discover the foundation of family relationships. I wish for you and your children to experience with all of your senses and see what change is possible.

Mrs. Jay Anderson is a psychologist, counselor, and play therapist. She practices in southwest Western Australia at the Southwest Wellbeing Centre. Jay has worked in the human services field for about 30 years, with her primary focus on counseling and therapy. Jay's passion is "making a difference," and she works with children, adults, and families. She enjoys helping parents with their challenges, assisting families to connect and improve their relationships, and helping many people enjoy life more. You will find Jay at www.swwellbeing.com.au.

27

IT'S TIME TO FEEL GREAT ABOUT YOUR PARENTING

Leah Brown and Michael DiVirgilio

For many of us, the idea of having children fills us with dreams of being great parents and envisioning amazing lives for our children. We imagine moments of smiling, laughing, playing, and growing together, forming strong bonds, and feeling fulfilled.

Holding your newborn, you feel those dreams are all but certain. After all, you are smart, caring, hardworking, and fun. You seek out parenting advice and follow the latest methods. You are an amazing person. Your spouse is, too.

Yet somehow, parenting becomes a struggle, with mixed and unsatisfying results. You know it could be better, but knowing hasn't made it so. Well, you're not alone.

Only 16% of parents consider themselves excellent parents.[14]

But why? Because you are looking for answers in the wrong place. Yes, parenting strategies are beneficial, but excellence (and fulfillment) comes from looking in the mirror.

We have found that doing so in specific ways that reveal what's driving you—and how previously hidden aspects of yourself play out in your parenting—makes all the difference.

With our framework, you will be able to immediately choose new, effective, rewarding ways to parent, while outdated and ineffective ways you've become used to will melt away. You will be and feel excellent in your parenting.

Facing Uncomfortable Truths

One of our favorite approaches is what we call "Facing Uncomfortable Truths." This practice involves identifying parenting conversations where you're less than honest and then working to come clean with your children by communicating from a place of truth.

Yes, we all work hard to be honest with our children. But we also regularly pass off things that aren't true. We want you to find big and small ways you are not telling the truth to yourself and your children.

Taking this courageous step—even with mundane circumstances—will create a new reality in your parenting. In our own lives, this regularly helps us resolve specific problems and elevate our relationship with our children.

Leah discovered that her frustration with her children for not listening to one another stemmed from unrelated experiences. Seeing the impact this had on her children, she resolved her past experiences and addressed the situation head-on with them. This direct communication made Leah a more effective parent and a positive model for her children, but it also helped eliminate any shame her children might have felt over something unrelated to them.

Sometimes, we give our children directions or set rules to make ourselves feel better or more comfortable. Other times, we pass on "truths about life" that we were told as children, pretending to know something we don't—all so our kids like us, respect us, and do what we want.

Michael noticed he was habitually telling his twelve-year-old daughter to dress warmer to avoid a cold. Instead of doubting his daughter's experience and creating a negative future to justify his demand, he faced the uncomfortable truth that his fear and his grandmother's voice had taken control. Michael and his daughter had a good laugh about it all.

In our work with parents, we help them with deteriorating relationships with their child; where there are fewer conversations, the child no longer listens, and the disconnect causes pain (often for both parties). Almost immediately, we see opportunities for parents to face uncomfortable truths.

There's the client who says they "trust their child" but also describes covertly checking on their child, peeking at their items, and doubting what's said. Another client gives their child a phone, accompanied by restrictions that go unenforced for fear of upsetting the child.

In each situation, we help these parents see the contradiction—and the truth that it hides. We then support them in exploring what internally drives their behavior.

By facing the uncomfortable truth and communicating the insight to their children, the resulting conversations transform the behaviors and the relationships forever.

It's a permanent upgrade on a path toward feeling excellent.

Pursuing Honest Communication Is a Game Changer

As adults, we appreciate people who speak plainly and truthfully. We value friends and colleagues who are honest, direct, clear, vulnerable, and empowered. These rare individuals embrace their imperfections and dare to communicate difficult or embarrassing truths in a brave, inspiring way.

These individuals are imperfect, too. They might have judgmental or selfish thoughts, avoid confrontation, be inconsistent, and focus on appearances. However, they recognize where things aren't working and prioritize taking responsibility, knowing that messing up leads to cleaning up, which leads to a better life.

We prize adults who do this. Wouldn't our children value the same from us?

Parents, you too can be transparent with your children. You can admit when you want to look good in front of other parents. You can acknowledge that you restrict your children from doing something you regularly do (like eating in your room, texting while driving, or pretending to like something). Investing in your own self-awareness and honesty pays dividends forever.

One classic example we have come across involves parents pushing their children to be honest and do the right thing regarding a sensitive family matter. Clients Felicia and Jim ultimately saw their own pattern of dishonesty! While an extremely uncomfortable experience, acknowledging their shortcomings elevated their relationships with their children. It also created a safe, collaborative space for their children to confront their own struggles.

The value of telling the truth is universally understood, but by building a practice of regularly finding new truths to face, you will gain access to new ways of being as a parent.

You may think that your circumstance is more complex or unique. The truth is that this works within all family dynamics and all types of relationships.

It will feel great, and you will be on the way to becoming the parent you dream of being.

Imagine the impact on your children. You'll be real with them, and in turn, you'll have engaging conversations that transform their experience of you, at school, and in other relationships.

Grounded by the strength of their relationship with you, they will emerge as confident, compassionate individuals ready to influence society positively.

By looking in the mirror and openly facing uncomfortable truths, your parenting will create a better world for you and your children. You will feel—and be—an excellent parent.

Leah Brown is a lifelong educator, thought leader, and change agent. With degrees in psychology and public policy and a master's in special education, Leah's perspective on parenting is comprehensive. She has worked as a counselor and teacher in settings ranging from underserved New York City to the "Gold Coast" of Connecticut and from private to public to homeschooling communities.

Michael DiVirgilio is a skilled leader, coach, and author. A former mayor of Hermosa Beach, California, a trained engineer, business strategist, and author of *Beyond Burnout*, he has coached hundreds of individuals in leadership and personal transformation. He and his daughter live in Saratoga, New York. Leah and Michael are out to make the world a better place. Download their free guide, *5 Ways to Feel Excellent About Parenting*, at parentwithdistinction.com.

28

FROM FEAR TO TRUST: A NEW WAY TO CONNECT WITH YOUR TEEN

Arlette Chinappi

Do interactions with your teen—even simple questions such as "How was your day?"—turn into arguments? Ever wonder whether it's worse for them to lash out or just give one-word answers? Does fear set in? Where's the child who looked up to you for advice? The unexpected behaviors, the risks they start to take, the importance of their friends, and, of course, the constant presence of their phones! You yell, feel guilty, yell some more, and before you know it, your fear takes over, only for them to yell back. Thus, the cycle of parent-teen life continues.

You're Not Alone

Parenting during the teen years can feel like navigating a storm. It may feel like nothing works, but their behavior is normal, and your connection isn't lost; it's just waiting to be rediscovered. How do you go from the storm of communication battles to a calmer trust system where they feel they can tell you anything? Join me as I share how to start transforming your fear into curiosity to help you reconnect with your teen. I did it, and so can you.

A Little About Me and Brains

As a mom of three (18, 16, and 13), I'm right here with you. Do I always get it right? No! But parenting is a journey; taking it one step at a time is okay. I love breaking things down into simple steps—especially when it comes to understanding the brain.

Step 1: Recognize how our thoughts shape our interactions.

Our brains generate thousands of thoughts daily—most are negative and repetitive! Many of these negative thoughts stem from fear of failure, rejection, or not being good enough—and these fears can significantly impact how we interact with our teens.

Fears can hijack both the parent and teen brain. However, unlike adult brains, the teen brain is still in a "remodeling" phase, coined by Dr. Dan Siegel in *Brainstorm*. His book explores the teenage brain and outlines four key pillars, which I simplify here and you'll likely recognize. The teen brain is constantly rewiring itself to prepare for adulthood, which means they are driven by intense feelings, a focus on friendships, a desire for risk and adventure, and the ability for deep thinking.

Remember: Their brains are still developing. They're not giving you a hard time—they're having a hard time!

Connection Begins When Fear is Replaced by Curiosity

As parents, we often find ourselves on an emotional rollercoaster, right? We have a choice: We can allow fear to blind us and grip us tightly until the ride is over, or we can embrace curiosity and revel in the thrill of the ups and downs. With our eyes wide open and our arms raised high, we can find joy in every moment! Key to navigating this ride?

Step 2: Shift from fear to curiosity.

Be curious and remain curious. What do I mean? Shift your perspective. Consider if your thoughts stem from fear and why your teen's behavior triggers you so much. Is it really about you? Probably not.

Curiosity is about exploring and learning, but too many questions can feel like pressure to teens. Constant lectures or probing often make them pull away.

Stay curious. Instead of, "How dare they speak to me this way?" reframe to, "They're struggling; what do they need from me?" Resist the urge to jump in, judge, lecture, or fix things—just listen, and truly listen.

On to Empathy Leading the Way

Curiosity opens the door, but empathy keeps it open. How we respond to our teens' struggles builds trust or pushes them away. When we choose empathy over control, we create a safe space where they feel heard and understood.

Step 3: Lead with empathy.

What is empathy? I appreciate Dr. Laura Markham's explanation; she emphasizes that in parenting, empathy is about "accepting our children's emotions." When we express empathy, we are not trying to solve problems, cheer them up, or distract them. We're not asking more questions; we are simply conveying to our children that we understand they are struggling. We see and feel their anger, sadness, and frustration. It is essential for them to feel our presence and know they are understood.

The concept of empathy is challenging in the heat of the moment, especially with teens. So, what's the secret? It lies in learning to shift your thoughts and stepping off that negative train. How can we do this? Catch your thought: "Why can't they just follow the rules? I'm so tired of this defiance." Challenge it: "Are they trying to be defiant?" Change it: "They're testing boundaries because they're trying to figure out who they are. How can I guide them without controlling them?" Be curious and stay curious. When you self-regulate, you will discover your compassion grows and empathy flows.

From Fear to Trust

Shifting your perspective changes how you interact with your teen, strengthening your relationship and deepening connection. "I've failed as a parent if they're behaving like this." Sound familiar? Try this instead: "Their behavior doesn't define my worth as a parent. This is a moment to teach, not to judge." Trust yourself, the process, and most importantly, them. This is the beginning of building a trust system with your family.

Use these three reminders to keep building trust:

- Your teen is not the problem; connecting with your teen is the challenge. Don't let your fear get in the way.

- The teen years are not simply a time to endure and hope to survive. If you choose to make it so, this period can be a time of growth and connection; stay curious.

- The teenage brain is still "under construction," which means it's critical to be present, supportive, and to lead with empathy.

Your teens need you more than ever—to feel heard and trusted. They need a safe haven, not a judge, even when they push you away. Do you want them to come and tell you anything? I do, and you do, too. Open the door for them and let them trust you to be there when they need you the most. If they fear your reaction, judgment, or lack of understanding, they will turn to other sources that are less capable of helping them, which could lead to worse issues. They are filled with curiosity. Join them in this curiosity. Allow them the space to roam and explore.

Trust Them

You can choose to be a guiding light or a hindrance to their growth, as fear can keep them from spreading their wings. Which path will you choose?

I understand it's challenging, but I choose to let them spread their wings—how about you?

Arlette Chinappi is a lifelong learner who loves to ask questions and is curious about how things work. While she enjoys seeking out new challenges, she strongly believes in the power of finding joy in small moments. As an engineer, she's passionate about solving problems and breaking down complex issues into simple steps. Most importantly, she loves being a mom to three incredible children and a wife to a wonderful man with whom she has created a family rooted in trust, open communication, and connection. As she embarked on her own parenting journey, she was introduced to the realm of coaching and discovered how valuable it was to walk alongside other parents facing similar challenges. She found joy in learning more and is now a dedicated parent coach guiding families to build what she built in her own family: a trust system that bridges the gap between parents and their teens. Arlette is on a mission to empower families with strategies for lasting change. Download her free guide, "The 5-Step Blueprint to Communicating with Your Teen," at www.trustthem.ca/5stepblueprint. Or book a free discovery call to explore deeper at www.trustthem.ca/bookme.

29

HOW TO HANDLE TEENAGE EYE ROLLS, MOODINESS, REFUSAL, AND CLOSED DOORS—AND RECONNECT WITH YOUR TEEN AGAIN

Dr. Kirstin Barchia

L et's be honest: teenage eye rolls, moodiness, refusal, and closed doors are annoying. No, scratch that; it's more than just annoying. Being huffed at, sworn at, and having all your buttons pushed at once is exhausting. When punishments, warnings, and consequences aren't working, and ignoring, placating, and walking on eggshells don't change anything, it can feel like waiting until they are 25 is all you can do.

The truth is the key to calming moodiness is learning to "talk teenager." I don't mean learning the latest slang—that will definitely earn you an eye roll. I mean understanding that teens communicate and seek connection not always through words but through huffs, shrugs, and one-syllable responses. These behaviors are not necessarily disrespect that begs for discipline. They are also not just "teenage" behaviors that need to be accepted.

Contrary to how it may appear, your teen wants you to break through to them. One thing that surprised me early in my career as a clinical psychologist working with teens was how often they expressed heartache over losing closeness and connection with their parents. In my 25 years working with teens and their parents as a therapist and researcher, I have learned that teens want and need a good relationship with their parents.

Huffs, eye rolls, one-syllable responses, yelling, stomping, and door-slamming are all ways your teen communicates with you. While it seems as though they are shutting you out, they are actually communicating a lot, just not with words. Responding to these behaviors in the wrong way can cause disconnection, heartache, and disruption in households.

I have seen really amazing parents doing things they thought were helpful for their teens but were actually unhelpful. For example, what if their head-down posture and shrug at the dinner table means, "I'm sad"? And you interpret it as being rude and say, "Stop being so rude! How hard is it to just answer a question at the table?" While it may feel justified in the moment of frustration, this often results in teens sharing less about their emotions or yelling over the dinner table. However, a small acknowledgment that matches the teen's mood, saying something like, "Hey, you seem a bit down; how was your day?" may be the beginning of opening the conversation and reconnecting. The behaviors shift when we're curious about their behavior and respond by acknowledging their emotions with compassion.

When parents get this right, teenagers and parents reconnect. Teens engage in meaningful conversations with their parents about important issues and seek their support. With less conflict at home, these teens are more agreeable, help without fuss, listen to their parent's advice, and even set their own healthy device limits and go to bed on time.

You may be reading this and thinking, "I do ask them about their day and their feelings, but that's when they give me moodiness, frustrating shrugs, and one-syllable responses." I hear you. Teen behavior is complicated, and so are the dynamics of interacting with them.

Following a script alone won't bring the changes you want. Several key elements are needed to shift the communication dynamic and help teens open up, listen, reflect, and change their behavior:

1. The Mood in the Room

When emotions run too high, it's hard for any brain to think. Your teen will struggle to answer well-meaning questions like, "Is something upsetting you?" and may become even more frustrated. The timing of your approach matters. Instead, simply acknowledge their feelings and delay the discussion about their behavior or mood. Be patient and allow time for them to calm down. Later, you can approach a conversation about what's behind their behavior.

2. Your Anxiety

No one wants to talk to someone who may panic about what they have to say. If you approach a conversation with your teen with too much concern, they won't share for fear of upsetting you further. In my experience, this is the most common reason teens refuse to open up to their parents—they don't want to worry them.

Parent anxiety is often exacerbated by two types of thoughts. First is when the imagination fills in story gaps. For example, if your teen tells you their friends left them out, you might imagine them eating lunch alone when your teen meant that their friends didn't ask for their opinion. Or you get a call from school that your teen was kicked by another student, and you picture them lying on the ground being kicked when, in reality, they were kicked under the table in class while joking around. You can manage your anxiety by sticking to the facts you know rather than allowing your imagination to fill in the gaps.

The second common cause of anxiety is "what if" thoughts about the future. You might worry: if it's this bad already, how will they be when they are older? What if they never stop gaming and don't find a job? What if they talk to their future partner the way they talk to their sister? Bring your focus back to the present. Focus on tackling today's problems. Future "what ifs" are not reality. Your teen needs you to believe they will be okay.

3. Your Past

Another common barrier to connection is using your teen years to try to relate. To connect with empathy, you may be tempted to "put yourself in their position" by thinking of times when you were their age. The danger of connecting this way is that you may fail to see your teen's unique problem when you introduce your own experiences.

No teen wants to hear "in my day ..." stories, but it is a common trap—one I have stumbled into with my own kids. Leave your past in the past and focus on their present, and you will have a better chance of connecting with them.

4. Giving Solutions

Suppose you have managed to "crack the code," and your teen finally tells you what's really upsetting them. In that case, it can be tempting to jump in and provide the "solution" so everyone can feel better. But there are two reasons why this is unhelpful. First, anyone who has ever been told "you should just ..." when trying to share their day with their partner knows that giving advice too soon leads to shutdown or conflict. Like us, teens need a space where they can share their feelings and experiences. A lot shifts when someone just listens.

Second, you are likely wrong. Teens often respond with "you don't understand" because if we haven't fully listened to all their stories, we cannot understand.

Listen calmly. Time your conversations and stay in the present. And listen some more. Then, when they ask, give them your advice. It is worth the patience to finally have a teen who calms down and listens to what you have to say.

Dr. Kirstin Barchia, PhD, MClinPsych, BPsych (Hons) is a clinical psychologist working with teenagers and their families. For the past 25 years, she has witnessed many great parents unknowingly make mistakes that have worsened their difficulties with their teens, all because no one gave them the support and guidance they needed. When she looked for resources for parents, she found vague tip sheets that advised them to "connect" with their kids without providing practical strategies. That's why she developed the Calm Connection Program and other online resources for parents of teenagers.

She has conducted studies with teenagers on bullying and aggression, lying, delinquent behavior, and resilience. Her goal as a researcher is to support parents with strategies based on scientific and psychological research.

She cares deeply about supporting teenagers and their parents and wants to offer you a free resource to improve calm and connection in your family at www.kirstinbarchia.com.au/connection.

30

MY HIDDEN HEARTACHE HAS A NAME: RESTORING HOPE TO RECONNECT WITH MY CHILDREN

Sally Bennett

R esearch reveals the devastating scope of parental alienation worldwide, with studies showing that over 35% of parents report being alienated from their children.[15]

I felt my heart aching with hidden grief during the years of disconnection from my children, experiencing a profound emptiness as they unconsciously chose to refuse contact. This evolved into a deep sense of powerlessness at being rejected, impacting my self-worth and often causing me to second-guess myself as our mother-child bond weakened.

Today is different. I rejoice as a parent.

After combing through research articles, I studied the signs of coerced attachment behaviors, splitting behaviors, and the silence of parents hesitant to speak about their estrangement. With this information, I found a path to navigate the judgment and misunderstanding from society. I pursued a new perspective, realizing that my overwhelming darkness had a name: parental alienation.

Here, I wish to share my journey in becoming a conscious parent, empowered by reframing my heartache to advocate for myself and support my children in their positive emotional development. My hope is to give voice to this often-hidden pain and foster strength for mothers on a similar path, helping them recognize that each new day holds the promise of light for understanding, healing, and change.

The Journey from Darkness to Dawn

My life froze the day my daughter and son left without notice, slipping out of the house and into a waiting car. A disagreement over family values had surfaced, slowly percolating throughout the separation and my second marriage.

Looking back, I can now see that there was little discussion about how my two eldest children were coping with navigating two differing family beliefs. At that time, I did not realize they were entrained with negative narratives through a misguided, anti-social, addictive lens.[16]

In the following days, I waited in hope as my children's loyalty conflict escalated, staying away for one night, then two, then a week, and eventually stretching to years. I grieved for three months, thinking I was alone, yet my trauma had become our family's pain.

My turning point came when I saw my youngest son's concern. I had valid reasons for my pain, but as a mother, my whole family needed me to be present. The shift to mindful parenting helped foster a sense of self-worth, clarify disillusioned feelings, and open the opportunity to re-enter my children's lives.

The first reconnection of two came when my son was a teenager, and I was called to help manage his growing anxiety. Here, I discovered a path to rekindle our bond—a message, a phone call, a visit, a small outing that extended to an overnight stay, and eventually, visits became regular. In this space, shadows faded, the air felt sharper, colors were brighter, and the world felt balanced again.

I clearly remember my two youngest children playing happily in our garden, reunited with their siblings. In that moment, laughter and connection soaked into my soul. I had found our family stability again, akin to discovering my bike balance for the first time as a young girl.

Like learning to ride a bike, I experienced that fleeting yet unforgettable perfect moment when body and heart align. My wobbles faded into steadiness, and I felt as if I had unlocked the hidden skill of flying. My childlike joy overcame the fear of failure, replaced by an inner lightness.

This is where knowing our relationship is an uncharted journey prepares me to embrace my inner calm. In those fleeting moments when the exhilarating rush of freedom and control merge, allowing me to find outer balance, connection can quickly topple—like brakes screeching against the exposed gaps in our relationship.

A Navigation System to Communicate Calm

One particular afternoon, my eldest son fell over, tears flowing as I tended to his physical injury while his aching heart spoke. It was our first real conversation in over five years. I needed to stay steady with wounded thoughts that had fractured our connection before.

"You were not there for me!" he cried. I felt my heart sink; he was right. Just like on a bike, we sometimes wobble, the wheels move out of alignment, and we fall.

I needed the strength to remove the blame and anger that had consumed my life as the excluded mother. I didn't want to repeat past mistakes; my child wasn't seeking answers but craving reassurance and comfort.

So, I took slow breaths, exhaling past triggers, and leaned forward, releasing tension. I responded with a gentle touch, saying, "Yes, I wasn't there for you, but I wanted to be. I've always loved you and always will, no matter what anyone says."

The 4-Step Calm Process

This was the process that helped me when I was stuck in past moments. It became my self-care practice during wakeful nights and a reconnecting tool with my children.

1. Naming

Recognizing the awareness of the issue cognitively supports biological regulation by stimulating neurotransmitters.

2. Calming

Taking slow breaths self-regulates emotions by releasing serotonin.

3. Directing

Using a bending-over movement physically relaxes tension by flushing out cortisol.

4. Reconnect

A hug or a hand on your heart creates a sense of well-being, supporting social bonding by activating oxytocin.

The calming process was only the beginning of our repair work. We had to focus on rebuilding too.

Family Connections to Minimize Challenges

As a conscious parent, I have learned to adjust gears to steer my family, where joyful activities have become as important as sunshine and drinking water.

1. Green Tea Gratitude

We all enjoy the gratitude game, stating three things we appreciate about the day or person to the left or right, or a rapid response of positives on a person's birthday. This creates amusing dinner times that deepen our family bond and offset undermining messages.

2. Family Fridge Funables

Our children make decisions easily by referring to our family values poster, where individual beliefs and contributions to our family bucket play-personality list are voiced. Here, they feel seen and heard, which is vital to developing a sense of self.

3. Chalkboard Chit Chat

In the kitchen-dining area, I have a self-love chalkboard where I stay uplifted by sharing positive quotes. I know from research that even though my children are now young adults, their prefrontal cortex continues to develop until age thirty. So, I stay optimistic and be gently proactive.

Pedaling for Connection on the Path Forward

Drawing from my personal experience, understanding that this ride is a journey of connection and rejection, not perfection, helps me pedal through the dark days. According to studies on parental alienation, it may last over two years and, in severe cases, up to six years, disrupting family life for 22 years.[17]

So, stay on the path of hope, enjoy the ride with those beside you, and shine your motherly light for all your children, even from a distance. I have experienced firsthand that how you show up for your children shapes your path, so find your rhythm in love by tapping into your inner child joy balance.

Sally Bennett is a mother of four in a successful second marriage who enjoys simplifying research studies to support families. She created a simple *4-Step Calm Process* based on the natural healing cycle of the human body, designed to help families remain regulated through meltdowns. She has also formed a Happy *HACKSS Guide* compiled from numerous articles to support mothers in navigating parental alienation behaviors. She draws from over 20 years of knowledge in teaching, with her Master's degree in Educational Counseling, Graduate Diploma in Information, Qualified Reiki Practitioner, Children's Yoga Therapy Teacher, Educational Consultant, and over 25 years of experience as a dedicated parent.

Connect with her on Facebook, "The Conscious Calm Parent," to learn Happy Hacks, mindful communication scripts to connect with children, and how to co-regulate and shine your self-worth.

31

THE SEX TALK: A MANDATORY CONVERSATION

Rebecca Reber

———

If you're like most parents, the idea of discussing sex and relationships with your child is enough to make you break out in a cold sweat, begin to panic, and look for the closest exit sign. The thought of a root canal is more appealing than sitting down to talk about sex with kids.

But if we aren't having this conversation with our children, who is? We can't assume that they are learning about it in a classroom.

According to *The Power to Decide* webpage (2023), "At the moment, 28 states (and DC) require some kind of sex education. However, 29 states require schools to stress abstinence. Because sex education in schools is legislated at the state (or individual school district) level, not federally, the quality of what is taught varies widely across the country."[18]

So, if your children are not learning about sex ed in school or at home—guess what? They get their information from peers, the internet, or a boyfriend or girlfriend.

Parents must address these tough topics to ensure their children are knowledgeable during their teen years and capable of making informed decisions regarding their sexual health.

Why You May Want to Listen to Me

For over two decades, I have run a teen parent program in Southern California, working with hundreds of young parents who need to finish high school while pregnant or parenting. This program operates on a large high school campus and has two main focuses.

First, our parenting teens receive support while they complete high school, thanks to infant and toddler care and education provided during their school day. We want our teen parents to graduate high school and pursue college or a certification program.

Second, we aim to instill strong parenting skills to help them care for their children long after graduation.

Ninety percent of our teen parents report that they received little to no sex ed at home before becoming pregnant. Only after enrolling in our program did they learn anything about reproductive health, STIs, and birth control. Because of our program's sex education, only a few teens have experienced repeat pregnancies out of the hundreds I have taught. Education truly is the key to decreasing teen pregnancies and STIs during the high school years.

What I Hear Out of Teenagers' Mouths

Without comprehensive sex education, either in school or at home, our pre-teens and teens are blindly navigating their adolescence and relationships. I have repeatedly heard these phrases:

- "I don't even know how I became pregnant."
- "I just looked up sex on the internet and found a lot of videos (porn)."
- "I didn't even know that I was having sex."
- "What's a uterus?"
- "This baby is going to exit my body how?????!!!!"
- "I asked my friends about sex, and that's where I learned everything I know."
- "My boyfriend told me I wouldn't get pregnant if we had sex."
- "Sex is how I prove my love to my boyfriend."

The sex talk is uncomfortable to have—I get it. But if we aren't having these conversations with our children, you get comments like the ones above. I don't know about you, but I want to have some control over what my children learn about their bodies, their sexual health, and relationships. I want to provide them with medically accurate information that reflects the values and ideals of our family.

Families that don't tackle these tough conversations often have teenagers who face pregnancy, drug and alcohol experimentation, pornography exposure, sexual assault, and sexually transmitted infections.

It is uncomfortable to discuss sex and sexual health with kids. Initially, it will be just as uncomfortable for your children. However, the more you engage in these conversations, the easier it will become, and you may be surprised at how many teachable moments arise.

Prepare Yourself for the Conversation

Here are some tips to help you prepare for the conversations:

1. Educate yourself on medically accurate information regarding reproductive anatomy, puberty, and STIs. The more you know, the more confident you will feel.

2. Commit to having truthful, non-judgmental conversations with your child. Build a foundation that lets your child know that you are an open and loving place to ask questions.

3. Realize that this is not a one-time conversation. Depending on your child's age and developmental level, this topic will come up many times as they grow, mature, and encounter new information in their world.

4. Decide what values and expectations your family would like your child to follow when making relationship decisions. Consider religious and cultural beliefs as well as educational expectations.

5. Be ready to truly listen to your child. If you want your child to come to you with questions about sex and relationships, they must know that you will listen to understand and react with love and empathy.

How to Begin

So, how do you begin the conversation? I have always leaned into the organic moments that arise in everyday life with my children. These can be a television show, the news, a question they bring to me, or a story they tell about a friend.

Here are some tips for finding discussion openings:

1. **Start young**—this doesn't mean telling your 5-year-old every detail you've learned while doing your research. Begin by accurately naming their body parts and discussing consent regarding their body and touch.

2. **Answer questions about sex and their bodies in a developmentally appropriate and truthful way.** Provide just enough information to satisfy their curiosity.

3. **Be prepared to have the puberty talk around fifth grade.** Or find a class in your area that you can attend together. I signed my daughter and me up for a mother-daughter class to start the conversation. Check in with them after the talk/class to address questions.

4. **As your child grows, listen to the stories they share about their peers and their relationships.** You can turn some of these into teachable moments or ask your child how these situations make them feel. Ask what information they know or have heard at school from peers.

5. Finally, once the foundation of trust is established, if your child is in a relationship, you may need to **ask direct questions**

about whether they are engaging in sex and if they need birth control or STI protection.

It is no secret that discussing sexual health is an uncomfortable and challenging aspect of parenting. However, our children genuinely want guidance, education, and a trusting adult with whom to discuss this part of their development. I have heard hundreds of teenagers express that they wish their parents had talked to them about sex. I believe every parent can navigate this with a little preparation, an open heart, and a hefty dose of bravery.

"I wish I had had positive role models who openly discussed relationships with me. I believe that with support from adults, teens would be more confident to make wise decisions—whether it is to leave a toxic relationship, to take birth control, or to abstain from sex altogether. Teens just want to feel comfortable enough to talk about sex— they don't want anyone making them feel weird or like they are wrong for asking questions." —Former Teen Parent

Rebecca Reber has led a teen parent program in Southern California for over two decades. She earned her Bachelor of Science in Child Development from Cal Poly San Luis Obispo in 1998. In 2015, Rebecca received the Heart of Extraordinary Service Award, and in 2017, she was named the Riverside County Office of Education Early Childhood Education Teacher of the Year. She is the founder of the Freshman Preventative Program for her high school, which ensures that the entire freshman class receives classes in healthy relationships, sex education, and online safety. Rebecca is a mom to a young adult son (21) and a teenage daughter (15). Use the QR code below to connect to Rebecca's webpage and receive your free gift on tackling the tough conversations.

32

SEX ED CAN BE YOUR SUPERPOWER: FOSTERING HEALTHY SEXUALITY IN YOUNG CHILDREN TO BUILD TRUST AND CONNECTION

Laura Hancock, PhD

———

There are countless reasons to intentionally teach young children about sexuality from infancy through first grade. It helps them feel good about themselves, express their thoughts and feelings, learn about privacy and boundaries, and be safer from sexual abuse. One of the most powerful reasons to start sex ed early is that it lays the foundation for a stronger, more trusting relationship with your child. This deeper connection increases the likelihood that *you* will be their go-to person when they are older and the stakes are higher.

Consider Shannon, for example. She is the mother of ten-year-old Hadley. Shannon reached out to me about a situation she didn't see coming; she discovered Hadley messaging about boys in her class who wanted to have sex. After looking through other recent chat messages, Shannon found there was a lot of discussion at school about sexual behaviors, including oral sex. Understandably, Shannon was upset. "I'm feeling so angry, and I'm freaking out," she wrote.

As a parent, I can relate to the vulnerability and overwhelming feelings that arise when we learn our child is being exposed to inappropriate or potentially harmful sexual content. However, I have good news: Shannon had been having ongoing, age-appropriate conversations with Hadley about sex and sexuality for several years. This prior experience was crucial because it allowed Shannon to stay calm, ask questions, and truly listen to Hadley, keeping the door open for future conversations. If Shannon hadn't already developed a strong rapport with Hadley over time, I believe their conversation would have gone very differently. In this case, Shannon turned an uncomfortable situation into an opportunity for connection.

As children grow older, we can't control everything they encounter, but we can choose how we respond and how we lay the groundwork for open, ongoing communication. One of the most valuable things we can do for our kids is to build that trust and openness before the tricky conversations arise. This is a critical reason why sex ed during early childhood is so important.

When we teach our young children about sexuality, we're imparting two major categories of knowledge:

1. **Cognitive Information:** The *what* — facts, definitions, expectations, and values we want to convey.

2. **Experiential and Emotional Information:** The *how* — how we talk about sexuality, how we respond, and how we model emotional safety around it.

Here, I'm going to focus on the second category: the emotional aspect, where the relationship magic truly happens. How do you feel and respond when your child explores their body, touches other people, resists a hug, refuses to use the toilet, or asks questions like, "Why are your boobs so droopy?" How can you show your child that they can come to you for honest and reliable information about sex and sexuality without feeling scared or embarrassed? If you want your child to feel safe asking questions and learning about their body, you must model that safety through your behavior.

The beauty of teaching sexuality early is that children do not yet view these topics as awkward or embarrassing. At a young age, they are naturally curious and approach sexuality with openness and wonder. This developmental stage presents a unique opportunity to engage in shorter, simpler interactions before the topics become more complex or emotionally charged. The challenge is that most of us feel awkward or uncomfortable when talking about sexuality, at least some of the time. That's why I want to equip you with four steps to help you feel more empowered and peaceful as you teach your young child about sexuality:

1. Know what's typical for your child's age

It's essential to understand what typical sexual behaviors look like at each stage of development. The vast majority of the time, the behaviors your young child displays are appropriate for their age. If you are the parent of a toddler, for instance, you likely know that toddlers are master explorers, curious about everything around them. This includes situations where they might publicly ask, "Is that a man or a woman?" or "Why is my penis hard?" Recognizing that your child's behavior isn't out of the ordinary helps you regulate your feelings, respond calmly, and avoid shaming them. At the same time, it's important to learn about red-flag behaviors that may indicate a potential concern so you can intervene if necessary.

2. Reflect on your own beliefs and feelings

Take time to reflect on your own experiences, values, and potential triggers. What do you hope to teach your child about sexuality? What messages did you receive growing up, and how do they shape your approach today? A main goal of this self-reflection is to clarify which triggers may cause you to feel uncomfortable or dysregulated. Having this clarity helps you identify topics that may require more time or resources to process. Reflection can look different for everyone, but I recommend doing at least some of it in a structured way. Take time to write or talk about how you learned about sexuality, how you want your child to learn about it, what hopes you have for them, and what values you want to impart. Pay attention to which topics make you feel uncomfortable. The more you process in advance, the more present you can be for your child when questions arise.

3. Practice, practice, practice

Talking about sex can feel awkward, and it's normal to feel nervous. However, the more we practice, the easier it becomes. Talk with friends about situations they've encountered with their own children and share your experiences. Practice saying phrases like, "We only touch our own genitals." Ask other parents to read a book about early sexuality education alongside you and discuss it while the kids play or after they're in bed for the night. Read a children's book about sexual health relevant to your child's developmental stage when they *aren't* present. Practice reading it aloud and reflect on your feelings about it.

4. Equip yourself with facts and strategies

Sexuality is a broad subject that encompasses topics such as body autonomy, gender identity, consent, and safety. The more informed you are, the more confident you will feel discussing these issues with your child. Review the basics of anatomy, reproduction, sexual health, and age-appropriate ways to teach your child about boundaries and respect. Knowing when and how to address each topic will help you respond in a way that is accurate, compassionate, and feels good to you.

Final Thoughts: Keep the Door Open

These four steps may seem overwhelming at first, but the beauty of early childhood sex education is that it unfolds gradually over several years. Building trust and connection through many small, open conversations about sexuality creates a foundation of safety and security that will benefit your child for years to come. So, take it one step at a time and ask yourself, "Am I keeping the door to future conversations open, or am I closing it?" Then, do what you can to keep the door open. If you need guidance, my book is full of information and inspiration. And if you need support, I'm here to help.

Laura Hancock equips parents and caregivers with the tools they need to teach developmentally appropriate sex education in the early years. She empowers parents to guide their children with confidence and empathy, helping to build the groundwork for healthy sexuality for a lifetime. Laura is the co-author of *Sex Ed for the Stroller Set: How to Have Honest Conversations with Young Children*, published by the American Psychological Association. She lives with her family in Amsterdam, the Netherlands, and can be found online at drlaurahancock.com, where visitors can download resources for teaching a variety of sex education topics to young children.

SECTION FOUR:
NAVIGATING POWER STRUGGLES
WITH WISDOM AND GRACE

33

TRANSFORM CONTROL FREAK PARENTING INTO CONTROL-FREE PARENTING

Vibha Arora

——

"Is everything under control?"

This became my dad's standard greeting during our phone calls after I became a mom. For years, I responded with variations of "Yeah," "Sure," or "I guess so." I never truly grasped the question's meaning, nor did I take the time to ponder my responses. What exactly was meant to be under control? How was I supposed to maintain that control? As a single mom juggling a three-year-old and an infant, everything often felt completely out of control. And even if I did manage to seize some semblance of control, wouldn't wanting too much of it just make me a control freak? That certainly wasn't the goal.

A key moment in my personal growth journey came when I took the time to explore the concept and implications of control. Control is creating or manipulating a situation to achieve a desired outcome. The Cambridge English Dictionary defines control as "to order, limit, or rule something, or someone's actions or behavior." As parents, control translates to having power or decision-making ability over what our kids think, feel, and believe.

However, most parents would likely agree that "controlled" is not the first word to describe our interactions with our kids, our daily lives, or even our overall parenting journey.

As a parent coach, I frequently hear parents express annoyance, frustration, and outright anger at their perceived lack of control over their children. This frustration isn't their fault; we are conditioned to believe we should be able to control our kids. The reality is that we cannot control any other human being—and yes, our kids, though smaller, are still humans. So, what does this mean? How can we navigate the chaos of daily life as parents if we relinquish the notion of control?

The valuable tool I offer my clients and one I remind myself to practice daily is what I call the Circle of Control. The inside of this Circle is relatively small, consisting of three elements: your thoughts, feelings, and actions. Everything else you experience lies outside this Circle. Understanding and utilizing this powerful tool can genuinely change your life—no joke—if you allow it.

Let's give it a try right now. Take a moment to grab a piece of paper. Draw a small circle, and inside it, write "My Thoughts, My Feelings, My Actions." Next, think of all the things, situations, conversations, and interactions—especially with your children and others—

that have caused you frustration, annoyance, and unease. Write these down outside the Circle, without filtering your thoughts, until you feel it's a good stopping point. Once you're done, take a look at what you've written. Keep this visual handy, and feel free to add to it. That's your very own Circle of Control. Now it's time to focus on what you can control and practice letting go of the rest. While this isn't easy, with persistence, it will become easier over time.

Consider how much of our time, effort, emotion, and energy (TEEE) we spend as parents trying to control things beyond our Circle of Control. It creates an endless loop; we can never win this exhausting game. It's like trying to fill a bucket with a giant hole in the bottom—it just won't work. You'll only deplete your precious resources. Banging your head against a steel door won't open it; it will only give you a headache. Instead, try shifting your perspective. Look for the open door that invites you to practice surrendering perceived control, allowing you to step onto the path of peaceful living.

Did you ever truly control your toddler's eating, sleeping, or toilet habits? No, you did not. Occasionally, all the stars would align, and the desired outcome would happen magically. However, when we try to exert control—whether with toddlers or teenagers—we often move away from connection and toward struggle. While we don't have control, we do have influence as parents.

You may be telling yourself, "But they're my kids, so I should have control over them!" Oh, dear parents, please stop "should-ing" on yourself! This belief is often shaped by culture, religion, our families of origin, and society at large. But have you ever considered whether this mindset is healthy for you or your kids? Is it even what you truly want? Remember, a child who cannot make choices becomes an adult who relies on others to make decisions for them.

There is a quiet yet powerful strength in the art of surrender and letting go. We fear relinquishing control, but that control is just an illusion. What we're truly letting go of is an imagined reality, allowing us to embrace the authentic, present reality of life. While it may seem counterintuitive, there are magical and beautiful—what I like to call "magiful"—experiences awaiting us on the other side of releasing control.

When I asked my client Nicole about her experience with the Circle of Control, she shared, "It released me from stress and anxiety and allowed for deeper connections with my daughter when I stopped trying to control her and everything else around me." Another client, Nik, explained that after applying the Circle of Control concept, "My kids learned that I trusted them and began to express themselves more naturally while exhibiting greater confidence." And Cindy, a mother to two "kidults," said of this tool, "It allowed me to be more truthful with my feelings. It made me so much more authentic and aligned in my relationship with my kids." These are wonderful outcomes to look forward to on the journey toward releasing control.

One final note: there's a flip side to the control coin. What feelings do you think reside there? Fear? Anger? Unhappiness? In reality, it's anxiety. Consider this: when you feel out of control, doesn't your anxiety increase? Contrary to what social media and other sources often suggest, we shouldn't strive to eliminate anxiety. Instead, we should welcome it and heed the message it offers. Anxiety is signaling that we are out of control! Our task is to soothe our anxiety by acknowledging, "You're right because this is outside of my Circle of Control. Thank you for the alert; I've got this."

Remember, connection—not control—is the true currency of resilient relationships.

Practicing this shift in perspective will not lead to perfection—it will never be perfect—but it will lead to progress. The goal isn't perfect parenting; let's focus on taking one step at a time away from controlling behaviors and toward a more liberated approach to parenting.

So, no, Dad, it's not all under control—and that's a wonderful truth to embrace: parenting can be both messy and magical at the same time.

Vibha Arora is a Transformation Coach and Parenting Coach specializing in helping her clients look beneath the surface to find solutions that are more than just a quick fix. She works with clients and parents via Zoom video from wherever they are. She also facilitates parent education classes and playshops online and in person. Vibha has her master's degree in Marriage and Family Therapy, is a certified parent/teacher Positive Discipline Facilitator, and is a Conscious Parenting Guide. For over a decade, she has been providing a safe, judgment-free space for parents to process thoughts, feelings, beliefs, challenges, and celebrations while learning out-of-the-box parenting tools.

By combining the concepts of Positive Discipline and Conscious Parenting, Vibha helps parents practice Control-Free Parenting, which sets families up for long-term connection and compassionate communication.

Her latest endeavor is her recently launched podcast, *Kaleidoscope— Shifting Perspectives With a Twist*, which you can tune into wherever you listen to podcasts.

Take the Control-Free Parenting Quiz and follow Vibha on social media using #iparentplus or email her at wiseheart@vibha-arora.com.

34

STOP MANAGING, START GROWING: HOW A MINDSET SHIFT CAN BUILD STRONGER CONNECTIONS

Melanie Zwyghuizen

A ccording to a 2023 American Academy of Pediatrics survey, one in three parents report feeling burned out—largely from the constant struggle to manage their children's behavior. Honestly, I'd bet the real number is even higher.[19] I hear from parents all the time who feel the same way. Parenting can feel exhausting, especially when it seems like every day brings another behavior battle.

I've been there too. As a young mom, I spent so much energy trying to manage every little thing—correcting behaviors and constantly reminding myself. At that time, as a high school teacher successfully teaching around 150 teenagers every day in groups of 30+, I couldn't understand how my three tiny beings could throw me off my game. I loved them more than I could have ever imagined, but something had to change!

I began to realize that what was needed had nothing to do with my kids and everything to do with me—I just needed to apply the same principles in my home that I did in my classroom. I was showing up for my students in a way that I wasn't for my own kids. When I recognized and made that shift, things felt different. It wasn't overnight, but it made a real difference in how I connected with my kids and how much less stressed I felt.

You're not alone if you've ever found yourself at odds over even small things—like getting your child to clean their room or put on their pajamas. You might even find yourself thinking, *Why can't you just listen and do what I say?*

But what if you, too, shifted the way you thought about parenting?

The Behavior Manager Mindset: A Battle to Win

Imagine this: You walk into your child's room to find clothes scattered everywhere, homework untouched, and music blaring. You've asked them *at least* three times to clean up, but nothing's happening. As a behavior manager, your immediate reaction is likely frustration, followed by a need to take control and perhaps issue threats: "I told you to clean up! Get this done now, or else. And what about your homework?"

The focus is on fixing the behavior right now—so you take control, and your child is expected to comply. Some parents may resist at this point and say, "But I'm the parent! They *should* do what I say!" Let me reassure you—I'm not suggesting you give up your authority. But let me ask you this: Have you ever really "won" one of these battles? Sure, the room might get cleaned, or the homework might get done this time, but at what cost? More often than not, this approach leaves both of you feeling disconnected and stuck in a seemingly never-ending cycle of battles where *everything* just feels hard. Does that really feel like a win?

The Growth Guide Mindset: We're in This Together

Picture this situation: Your child's room is messy, and homework remains untouched. Instead of reacting with frustration, you pause. You take a deep breath and ask yourself, What's *really going on here?* Maybe your child is tired, overwhelmed, or struggling with a particular task.

As a growth guide, you understand that behaviors are what we see on the outside, which can give us insight into what is happening on the inside. You know that growth only occurs in an environment of understanding, not confrontation. So, instead of issuing commands, you ask, "Hey, how are you feeling about your homework? Is something making it hard to start?" This shift opens up communication rather than shutting it down. Now, you're less focused on behaviors (like cleaning the room or doing homework) and more on the growth process: "What skills do they need to develop? How can I best support them?"

Sir Ken Robinson wisely said, "The gardener does not make the plant grow. The job of a gardener is to create optimal conditions for growth." Similarly, as parents, we can't make our children grow or develop, but we can create the right environment for growth to happen. This means stepping back from trying to manage every behavior—an exhausting and fruitless effort—and instead supporting growth. When we focus on nurturing growth instead of enforcing compliance, we empower our kids to become capable, confident individuals. Even in tough moments, this approach fosters teamwork, reduces conflict, and encourages cooperation while building a lasting connection based on trust and mutual respect.

Now, *that's* a battle worth winning!

How Shifting to a Growth Guide Mindset Made a Real Difference

Tom and Carissa came to me feeling exhausted and frustrated. Their 17-year-old daughter had already been through an outpatient behavior program. However, they didn't see the hoped-for success, and their home still felt like a constant battleground. They loved her deeply but struggled with connecting with her and were frankly tired of her disrespect. Like many exhausted and desperate parents, Tom asked me to "fix her."

We focused on shifting their mindset from fixing her to understanding and supporting her through actionable steps that led to more connection. It was no longer about managing her actions but about creating a safe space where she felt seen and heard. Within weeks, their home began to feel more peaceful, and the challenging behaviors started to improve.

Simple but Not Easy Ways to Start Your Shift

Making this shift is simple. It's just not easy. We often have long-entrenched patterns and thoughts about the "right way" of parenting that can cause us to resist and struggle with changes. It's okay to go slow. Your effort will be worth it for you and your kids.

1. Pause and reflect.

Before reacting, take a moment to pause and check in with yourself. Ask, "What's really going on here?" This helps prevent an automatic, reactive response that usually focuses on managing behavior.

2. Focus on the problem, not the person.

When issues arise, remind yourself that your child is not a problem—they are experiencing a problem. This helps you adopt a *me & my child vs. the problem* approach rather than a *me vs. my child* approach.

3. Ask open-ended questions.

Instead of issuing commands and threats, engage your child with questions that invite conversation, such as: "What's making this difficult for you?" or "How can we work together to solve this?"

4. Practice empathy and active listening.

Show your child that their feelings matter. Respond with empathy—acknowledge their struggles and frustrations. You're more likely to gain cooperation when they feel seen and understood.

5. Shift your focus to growth.

Avoid focusing on immediate compliance and instead think long-term: *What skills do they need to build? How can I help them grow through this experience?*

The Path to More Connection

Parenting is not a one-size-fits-all process, and every day brings new challenges. By choosing to parent as growth guides, we create an environment where deeper communication, stronger connections, and lasting respect can thrive.

Ultimately, it's not about winning behavior battles—it's about creating the conditions for growth, connection, and mutual respect to flourish as you face life's challenges together.

In addition to raising her own three children, **Melanie Zwyghuizen** has spent over 30 years working alongside families. She believes that with the right mindset, tools, and knowledge, parents can create a peaceful, joyful home while raising confident, emotionally healthy kids. Melanie's approach focuses on building a strong foundation for thriving families—centered on a respectful parent-child relationship, healthy boundaries, and a collaborative, solution-focused mindset. Through personalized coaching, workshops, and small-group classes, Melanie has helped numerous families, from littles to emerging adults, achieve lasting results: improved child behavior, stronger connections, better communication, and less stress. Parents often share that they feel more confident in guiding their families, leading to greater harmony at home.

To get started today, download your free guide, *"Setting & Holding Limits,"* at gen1parenting.com or contact Melanie to schedule a free consultation and learn how she can help you transform your parenting.

35

BE LIKE THE V IN THRIVE

Sandra Wartski, Psy.D.

Within the same week, two mothers came to my office with different concerns about managing issues for their maturing children. Both were loving, thoughtful parents wanting the best for their children, but they faced challenges.

Theresa was distraught about her teenage daughter, tearfully describing the sudden surge of conflicts over recent months. She noted that her daughter had plenty of freedom as a younger child, as meltdowns could be minimized with minor adjustments. However, now her daughter was resisting all rules. The teenage activities her daughter wanted to pursue were risky, leaving Theresa feeling angry and scared. She needed a new strategy.

Melinda wanted to discuss her middle school son, who had been struggling with significant anxiety and learning challenges since early elementary school. Although Melinda had been actively helping and protecting her son, she now worried that she had sheltered him too much. Her son was showing increased anxiety and relying excessively on her. Melinda felt frustrated and conflicted. She knew her approach needed to change.

Pivotal Parenting Principle

All parents want their children to thrive, but not all parents consider the evolving guidelines they must provide throughout the parenting process.

I like using the visual of a capital V, which perfectly represents the changing shape of the guardrails we must provide as parents. We give children increasing latitude, decision-making power, and responsibilities as they age while maintaining solid boundaries at each stage. The space within the provided guidelines ideally expands proportionately to a child's capabilities. We strive for Goldilocks-just-right margins: not too wide, not too narrow.

Some children frequently test those boundaries, while others hardly approach them. Ongoing monitoring of such boundaries helps kids move from merely surviving to thriving.

By visualizing parenting as the V, we are reminded to provide space for slow, steady growth. The V-visual serves as an overarching intervention principle from which other subgoals can be developed.

Shifting Needs

When our children are very young, we hold them close. This stage requires intimate supervision, with fewer decisions to be made but closer guardrails in the sleep-eat-diaper-change phase of life. The love story with our child is just beginning; we are at the bottom of the V.

As development continues, we still hold them close to our hearts but allow for more autonomy. We provide a safe, secure harbor while gradually allowing the child to explore the world. We are slowly expanding the V-shaped guardrails.

Just as we buy new clothes for our kids as they outgrow their old ones, we must also stay alert for and adapt to their psychological growth spurts.

Application in Many Domains

The V-visual can be applied broadly in parenting. As children grow, the boundaries we set for them naturally change. For example, a second grader may only be allowed to bike on the sidewalk near the house, while a seventh grader may have more freedom to ride to a friend's house. The way we communicate also evolves—what we say to a 6-year-old about sexuality will be much simpler than what we discuss with a 16-year-old. Our connection with our children shifts, too. When they are young, we know nearly everything about their daily lives, but as they reach their teenage years, they seek more independence, and we may know less. This is normative and expected. Being aware of these needed changes and adjusting helps us support our children effectively as they grow.

The V-visual can also help in difficult parenting moments. When a dysregulated child is angrily shouting embarrassing things in public, it can be hard to stay calm and balanced. It takes effort to avoid reacting too loosely ("Fine! Do whatever you want!") or too harshly ("That's it!

No phone for three months!"). The key is finding our center—responding with firm but compassionate guidance rather than reacting out of frustration.

Too Wide

The case of Theresa's teen daughter reflects an inverted-V situation. Theresa was initially more permissive, leading her daughter to have little experience with guardrails, but then felt the need to impose strict restrictions during the challenging teenage years.

Many parents of young children may have looser boundaries, choosing to buy the toy at the checkout (rather than manage an impending tantrum) or do the chore themselves (rather than get their child to follow through on the agreed-upon task). This may seem easier initially, but often there comes a time when those too-wide margins no longer work.

During our work together, Theresa developed a better understanding of the situation and learned to trust the process of establishing age-appropriate guardrails. She became adept at calmly managing instances when her daughter challenged her and provided incremental steps toward increasing privileges.

Too Narrow

The case of Melinda's son seemed to involve narrow guardrails for too long. She had been providing tremendous support for her son's unique needs but struggled with letting go. Melinda's V needed more of a sloping outward path for her son to flourish.

Family support for children with specialized skills is indispensable, but many struggle with knowing how to allow more independence. The best growth generally occurs somewhere between being too comfortable and too challenged.

During our work together, Melinda gradually altered her approach. She began to recognize that her son's anxiety about a challenge didn't mean he required immediate rescuing. She observed how stepping back allowed him to develop more self-sufficiency. This shift in approach gave both Melinda and her son more confidence.

Variance Exists

Variability in providing solid and supple guardrails for a new generation can be influenced by the type of parenting we experienced in our own childhood. If we had limited, variable, or no exposure to supportive boundaries, developing a strong, evolving V-shaped guardrail for our children becomes more challenging. Parenting is more difficult if we did not have strong role models.

While we strive for progress, there are times when a child's position in the V-trajectory needs to temporarily backslide. When children struggle with serious mental health issues or substantial life transitions, parents may need to adjust the level of guidance or supervision. This is not a failure on either the parent's or the child's part; it is an intentional regrouping to meet the child's current needs. Sometimes we need to lean in.

V is For Victory

Parenting is an important job, yet it often feels elusive due to its continuously shifting responsibilities. There is virtually no training, qualification test, or pay; yet we all want to do our best in raising our children. Ultimately, we aim to work ourselves out of this complex full-time job.

Noticing those small but meaningful victory moments helps us recognize progress. Triumphs are evident the first time a child ties their shoe, puts dishes in the dishwasher, or chooses to step away from unscrupulous peers. We can also feel proud the first time we didn't nag about an overdue project, upheld a significant promise, or listened rather than commanded when our child approached us with a problem. These moments matter.

Holding onto the metaphorical V-visual doesn't replace the countless tricky parenting moments we must contend with each day, but it reminds us to maintain a mindset of stable, flexible margins as we parent onward and upward.

Sandra Wartski, PsyD, is a licensed psychologist with over thirty years of experience at Silber Psychological Services, a North Carolina-based group practice dedicated to helping families navigate life's challenges. Dr. Wartski finds immense fulfillment in building relationships with her clients, fostering positive growth, and creating opportunities for meaningful change. She notes that her background in psychology provided valuable insights into raising her own two children—now young adults—though professional knowledge did not mean that the parenting journey was always easy or simple. Beyond her work as an active clinician over the past several decades, Dr. Wartski enjoys sharing her expertise outside of the office. She has provided presentations on various mental health topics for professionals and the public, and she is available for speaking engagements. Dr. Wartski also values writing as a means of sharing the benefits of psychological science; she is especially passionate about the power of visualization in personal growth, such as envisioning a V-shaped guardrail, and contributes regularly to her *Mindful Metaphors* blog at *Psychology Today*: www.psychologytoday.com/us/blog/mindful-metaphors.

36

THE GRACE OF REPAIR: STRENGTHENING BONDS THROUGH IMPERFECTION

Natasha Ching

"STOP!" I screamed, grabbing my almost three-year-old from his learning tower and placing him in his bedroom. "Mummy needs a moment," I managed to say before closing the door. At the sink, my hands shook as my child's cries echoed. I had broken. As I cleaned up the cacao powder sprawled across the kitchen, I knew it wasn't the real problem. My reaction was disproportionate and had nothing to do with my child. Ten minutes earlier, I'd received unexpected, stressful news and was struggling to process it. Guilt sank in—this was entirely about me and my mental state.

Overwhelmed, I'd ruptured our connection. My son was likely feeling scared, isolated, and confused. I returned to his bedroom, picked him up, and gave him a hug. "I'm sorry, buddy. I shouldn't have screamed. It wasn't your fault—Mummy was feeling stressed." My husband stepped in, giving me space to go for a walk and regulate myself. Later at bedtime, when things were calm, I apologized again, reaffirming that my reaction wasn't his fault. He leaned into me and whispered, "I love you, Mummy. Don't do it again." This was the repair.

Moments like these are challenging, but they also provide an opportunity to reconnect. This is the essence of rupture and repair, a concept well-supported by attachment theory.

Research by Dr. John Bowlby, Dr. Donald Winnicott, and Dr. Daniel Siegel shows that children develop secure attachments when parents intentionally reconnect after ruptures. This means validating emotions, apologizing, and showing compassion—to our children and ourselves.

Life is a never-ending journey of growth. We all have ungracious moments, and guilt is natural—even healthy. Shame, however, is not. We must find compassion when we fall short for the well-being of ourselves and our children.

While ruptures are inevitable, this doesn't mean we should simply accept them as the status quo. In medical school, we learned that prevention is more effective than symptom management. Similarly, reducing ruptures and optimizing connection improves children's and parents' mental health outcomes.

Even as a pediatrician with years of experience working in the field, I still lose control, as the story demonstrates. If we, as adults, struggle with stress and emotional regulation, why would it be any different for our children? They experience stress and overstimulation but process it with immature, developing brains. What children need as they learn to regulate is compassion. This is especially true for neurodivergent children. However, unless we are able to show compassion to ourselves, we cannot extend it to others.

Secure attachment is critical for optimal child development, and our mental state plays a pivotal role in fostering it. Over the years, I've observed that many behavioral challenges parents seek help for in their children could be significantly alleviated by first addressing and supporting the mental health of the parents themselves. Just as we cannot share from an empty glass, we cannot be for our children what they need us to be if we are empty.

With this understanding in mind, here are four practical steps to help reduce ruptures caused by our mental state and foster stronger connections.

Step 1: Reflect and Identify Triggers

After a rupture, reflect and try to identify your triggers and beliefs. The ABC Model of Cognitive Behavioral Therapy is a useful tool for reflecting on triggers.

1. **A (Activating Event)**: The moment that triggered your reaction. In my case, my toddler ignored my instruction to leave the cacao powder alone. Ask yourself:
    1. What specifically triggered my response?
    2. Was it really the situation, or was I carrying stress from elsewhere?
2. **B (Belief)**: The narrative you attach to the event. I believed, "My child should listen to me because I told him I was feeling

stressed." This wasn't a realistic expectation for my toddler to be responsible for helping me re-regulate—the belief reflected my own dysregulated state. Ask yourself:

1. What belief was driving my reaction?

2. Is this belief fair or helpful?

3. **C (Consequence)**: The reaction that follows. For me, this was feeling angry at him for ignoring my request, yelling, and putting my toddler alone in his bedroom while I stepped away, physically shaking in my dysregulated state. Ask yourself:

   1. Was my reaction proportional to the situation?

   2. How did it affect me and my child?

Identifying these patterns can be challenging and may require professional support, but it's a valuable step toward reducing emotional ruptures.

Step 2: Develop Strategies to Regulate

My toddler's behavior was developmentally appropriate. Regulating wasn't his responsibility—it was mine. When you recognize your own warning signs, pause and implement strategies to de-escalate and regain control. Potential strategies to regulate include:

1. **Tapping out**: If another adult is available, let them step in so you can take a break.

2. **Adult time-out**: Find a safe space to briefly step away, even if it's just to take a few deep breaths.

3. **Getting outside**: A short walk or some time in nature can help everyone reset.

4. **Breathing exercises**: Pause, close your eyes, and take 5–10 slow, deep breaths.

Step 3: Repair the Relationship

Once you've regulated yourself, repairing the relationship after a rupture helps prevent the repetition of generational patterns of unresolved conflict. This process works best when the situation is calm, often later in the day. Begin by naming an emotion your child might have felt: "Did it make you feel sad when Mummy got angry?" Then listen. Offer a sincere apology, taking full responsibility for your reaction without justifying it. Acknowledge your mistake and affirm your intention to do better next time.

Step 4: Be Self-Compassionate

Throughout this entire process, remember that parenting is a skill, much like learning to walk. Imagine a child taking their first steps. They stand, wobble, and fall—over and over again. At first, they may not even manage to take a step before tumbling. Sometimes, they get hurt or cry, but they keep trying. With practice, they grow stronger. Their muscles develop, their balance improves, and soon, they're walking more than they're falling. But even then, stumbles still happen. Uneven ground, distractions, or new terrain can trip them up, just as life's challenges can destabilize us as parents. When a child falls, we don't criticize them for not being perfect. Instead, we offer encouragement, pick them up, and let them try again. Parenting is no different.

We will stumble and fall—sometimes in ways that hurt. But like that learning child, every effort we make strengthens our capacity to navigate challenges. Every attempt at repair and every moment of reflection helps us grow. Just as a child grows stronger with each attempt, we as parents grow through our efforts to reflect and repair. Guilt can guide us, showing us where we want to improve, but shame holds us back. The most important thing is to keep moving forward, focusing on progress, not perfection. When we show ourselves the same grace we'd offer a learning child, we model resilience, patience, and self-compassion—not just for ourselves, but for our children too.

Just as my son forgave me and asked me to do better, we must offer ourselves the same grace. Parenting is not about perfection; it's about showing up, reconnecting, and growing together. By embracing our imperfections and modeling resilience with love, we empower ourselves and our children to thrive. This is the true grace of repair.

Dr. Natasha Ching (Doctor Tash) is a Melbourne-based pediatrician and proud mother of two. She graduated from Monash University with honors in Medicine (2011) and Biomedical Sciences (2017). Doctor Tash completed the majority of her pediatric training through the Royal Children's and Monash Children's Hospitals in Melbourne, where she also served as the Chief Resident Medical Officer before obtaining her fellowship. In 2018, she became a Fellow of the Royal Australasian College of Physicians and has since held consultant roles at Monash Children's Hospital. Doctor Tash is passionate about child development, responsive parenting, and empowering families. She aims to blend professional knowledge with personal insights from her parenting journey. She champions the belief that "connected kids thrive" and that "by embracing our own growth, we empower our children to reach their fullest potential." Doctor Tash seeks to provide practical tools and compassionate guidance to help families grow and thrive together. For more insights and tools, join her on her journey to help families grow together. www.doctortash.com/connect.

37

WHEN LIFE SAYS NO, STOP FIXING

Emma Gleadhill

L ast night, our daughter told me about being passed over in group work at school yet again, in what ought to be her favorite subject. Her joy. I asked her how she felt about it. She looked me in the eye and held the pause. Her eyes reddened beneath the weapons-grade eyeliner. Her breath became ragged, then settled into a deep sigh: "Drained. I just feel drained."

The intensity of exclusion, the dreaded disappointment of the need to belong. The pain of yearning filled the space between us.

I wanted nothing more than to hold her in my arms. To fight in her corner against unfairness. To protect her. To tell the teacher. To make the other kids include her, be nicer. Anything to make it better.

The unbearable helplessness of being a parent. We've all been there. It activates us. We wade in with "fix-and-solve" solutions when our teens need our presence most.

Emotional mismatches like this happen all the time in family life. I see this pattern both as an established parent coach and through my many years as a school leader. As a parent, I have done it myself, often.

The problem is it feels good to displace pain with activity. It worked when they were babies. They cried; we fed, changed, or cuddled them. Now they are teens; not so much.

The effect of going into fixing mode is similar to being in a duet when one person stops being in tune with the other—it jars. Inadvertently, we teach our child that we're not good at listening and that we shortcut or preempt their struggles. This is the opposite of our loving intentions. It is caused by our entanglement with their pain.

There's a reason why the villain (Lord Business) in the *Lego* movie had a robot called "Micro-manager." When we are activated and reactive, we become Lord Business—and they become our problem to fix, rather than the capable, resourceful kids they also are.

When this forms a pattern in the dynamic with our teens, it erodes trust. They will tend to take their private, vulnerable inner world elsewhere.

Many of us learned from a very early age that hurting and being needy is horrible and hard for others to bear. We were praised when we stopped crying. We learned to be less freely expressive—because that's what being a "big girl" or "big boy" is supposed to mean.

We learned to fend off sadness with anger, blame, and displacement activities. We "grew up"—but perhaps without tending to the vulnerable parts of us—which means our capacity for healing and growth is capped. This is, after all, the purpose of physical and psychological pain: to indicate a rupture and the need to take protective action.

As parents, we can collude in this by avoiding our children's suffering, mistakenly seeing our role as getting them back to happy as soon as possible rather than being steadfast and supporting them through emotional hardship.

I'm often asked in talks and workshops why young people stop talking to parents and teachers. The answer is simple: if they don't feel seen, heard, and understood when they speak to us about their struggles, they will stop telling us what we find so hard to hear.

Without trust, the parent-teen relationship becomes functional rather than fulfilling. Teenagers become secretive or closed off to protect their autonomy and ward off what can feel like intrusion or overreaction.

As a mother myself, I know it's easier to stay with vulnerability as a professional. It is a courageous and rigorous practice that enables us to face fear and hurt, and to find more purpose as a result. When we self-regulate better around our own vulnerability and develop our capacity to tolerate discomfort, we can provide space for their courage to emerge—for them to step up into self-awareness, learning, and growth.

Six Things Worth Knowing:

1. Develop awareness of your relationship with vulnerability.

Do you tend to express anger more than sadness? How easy was it to be vulnerable when you were growing up? Did you receive praise for self-sufficiency? Were reactions to your vulnerability overwhelming? Where do you find it easy or hard to be present with other people's vulnerability? At work? At home?

2. Healthy relationships—secure attachments—are characterized by the capacity to be vulnerable.

Having a track record of getting our vulnerable needs met with our caregivers is key. It forms a powerful model for authenticity, connection, and resilience in future relationships. They will know in their core that it's worth taking the chance to ask for help when life gets hard and they feel bad. With an inner working model of being heard and understood, they become more resourceful and feel better equipped in the face of challenge or suffering. They will develop more self-compassion and strength to face their struggles.

3. Slow down, move into curiosity, and observe.

The cues, tones, and gaps between what is said and what is actually going on in our teens are easy to miss or misread. It's often in the minutiae of movement, facial expressions, pauses, breaths, and the energy in their voice. It pays to tune in and pay attention. Look closely, listen, and learn. Say less, listen more. Let the silence do the work.

4. Notice when you are just waiting to insert yourself and your solutions.

Label it: "Ego ears." Dialogue with it: "Stand down, Micro-manager." Instead, trust in the strength and wholeness of your teen. As a coach, I know I earn my fee in the power of the pauses, where attention comes to the emotional core of our pain points—not the resistance narrative. It is important to come together and see the hurt with compassion and clarity.

5. Stay with those moments when your child or teen is in touch with their pain.

Trust them to feel their feelings. Allowing a more spacious awareness, rather than shutting down their pain, will provide the courage and the tools for their path to healing, transformation, and mastery.

6. Bear witness.

What values do you see in them as they wrestle with the pain in their heart? What is the privilege of supporting them in their humanity? What are they learning? What do they want? What can they do? What first steps can they take? Tell them about the strengths you see in them. It's less about us and more about them. Trust in them.

As parents, our children's hurts confront us powerfully with our own helplessness, life's unfairness, and the residue of our own growing pains. We learn to bear the reality that life can be unkind, unfair, and hard through experience. It is only this that will help our children develop the emotional musculature and resilience needed to face the inevitability of unwanted change—and open up their capacity for connection, strength, and joy.

Emma Gleadhill brings a wealth of experience as a leading educator, with 28 years of experience as a teacher, school leader, and governor. She served as Deputy Head with responsibility for safeguarding and well-being at one of the UK's leading independent schools. Emma specializes in psychological well-being, emotional intelligence, and healthy relationships. She completed the preclinical training in psychotherapy at the Tavistock Clinic in London. She then found her second calling: to apply her knowledge of child development to support teachers and parents. She now works with over 50 schools across the UK and with parent groups in corporate settings.

38

THE GOOD FIGHT: HELPING OUR KIDS WITH AGGRESSION WITHOUT SHAME OR PUNISHMENT

Caroline Griswold

———

Slowly, he lifted one finger: my cue to stop talking.

I paused. Something important was dawning on him.

In that coaching session, the dad of two was working on his daughters' physical aggression—when they kicked or hit each other, especially when they turned their aggression on him.

When he spoke again, he shared that when he was young, he was never able to fight back—to do what his girls were doing. Not when he and his siblings got into it. Not when he was hurting. Not even when his parents hurt him.

Feelings with Nowhere to Go

One key thing I've learned from supporting hundreds of parents in my coaching practice is that most of us have a well of pent-up hurt that had nowhere to go when we were young.

Our parents struggled to respond skillfully when we lashed out—especially if we got physical, and especially if they were on the receiving end. We have a hard time when this happens with our kids for the same reasons. We fear they'll never find a better way to express their anger, or others won't see the sweet, loving kids we know they are.

How to Help an Aggressive Child

If you have a child who behaves aggressively, I'm sure you've tried many strategies to shift the behavior: taking something away, sending them off to "calm down" or think about what they did, or promising a reward if they can go a week without hitting others.

None of it works—or works for long.

But we also can't ignore our kids' aggressive behavior. So, how can we respond in a helpful way without spinning our wheels or resorting to punishment?

The first thing we can do is understand that *fear* often lurks beneath aggression.

A child who lashes out is a scared child.

A scared child needs a parent to come close and help. All off-track behavior is a cry for our attention, and behavior rooted in fear is the biggest howl.

If we punish, ignore, or harm our children when they become aggressive, it does not heal their fear. It increases their hurt or sends it underground, where it festers.

When their behavior turns aggressive, our kids need three things: us to stop them from hurting others (including us), allow them to fight, and remember their goodness.

Stop Them from Hurting Others

Our kids are born wanting to connect with others and wanting things to go well with others. They especially want things to go well with their closest others (us!).

As confusing as it is, this is precisely why they "choose" to lash out at us. We're the people most likely to help them feel safe and less afraid again. There's also a chance that we might remember that they're a good kid and offer our help.

When our kids become aggressive, we must intervene. When they recover from this particular bad dream, realizing they harmed someone they care for will only add to whatever hurt triggered their aggression. Therefore, it's a kindness to stop them as quickly as we can.

We also need to intervene as *warmly* as possible. Try carefully moving your body between them and their target. If you're the target, blocking hits gently or catching kicks before they land can be effective. This can be tricky, so just do your best!

Allow Them to Fight

As counterintuitive as it may feel, I suggest that you find a way to allow your child to fight—without harming anyone.

When our kids are hurting, allowing them to physically expel that hurt from their bodies is a gift. Unburdened by fear, a child can remember how to be loving.

So let them fight if you can. Try to hold a warm space for them to kick, scream, and thrash. If possible, allow them to continue until they're finished or until the tears or laughter come—a common and positive outcome when we create a loving space for anger, frustration, and aggression. When our kids are able to sweat, tremble, cry, and laugh, they can effectively release tension and hurt.

Remember Their Goodness

Perhaps the most significant thing we can do to help our kids with aggressive behaviors is to remember their goodness—not their "good behavior," but their deep, intrinsic goodness—what every child is born with.

Good kids get angry. Good kids sometimes fight. Good kids can kick, punch, and bite.

Your child is good, even when they engage in these behaviors.

Remember their goodness as you move close to help them, and they will notice. You will also be able to be more present as they work through the feelings driving the aggression.

How to Begin

Here are a couple of suggestions for how to try this approach in a way that is beneficial for everyone (including you).

1. Go slowly and take breaks.

This approach takes courage and persistence. It can feel strange, even wrong, when we first try it. So go slowly. Start by simply sitting with the idea for a few days and noticing how that feels.

After that, try allowing your child's aggression for just a few minutes at a time. If you start feeling overwhelmed, step back as gracefully as possible. Your child will give you another chance!

2. Get support for your feelings, too.

Know that it's also natural for strong feelings to arise for you in this process. Like the good dad I coached, you likely never had the chance to express your feelings like this as a child.

Anger, confusion, and grief are just a few emotions that can emerge when we start to allow these feelings from a child. This is hard work and may be very different from how you were parented.

If you find it difficult to hold both your own feelings and your child's feelings, be sure to seek support. You might turn to a trusted friend or therapist. Hand in Hand Parenting can also help you find a Listening Partner—a very supportive, free resource.

The Best Medicine

"Just imagine," I said to that loving dad in our coaching session, "if even one time, you could have fought.

Imagine if you could have kicked and screamed like your daughter does and if your parents could have allowed it. And not only that—

if they could have allowed it while still remembering that you were good."

The tender look on his face said it all. We needed that from our parents, and our kids need the same thing from us.

We can model the warmth, understanding, and kindness we want them to develop. When we do, we provide them with the best medicine for this kind of hurt: our love, patience, and trust in their goodness.

The best news is that things often shift regarding our child's aggression with this approach, just as they did for the dad in my practice. As our response to the aggression shifts, so does our child's instinct to lash out. Safety and connection begin to replace fear and aggression. Our children learn that they can trust us to help them with whatever feelings arise, however difficult they may be.

Caroline Griswold is a parenting coach, mother to a preteen son, and the founder of Fertile Ground Parenting. She is a certified Hand in Hand Parenting instructor and is also trained in the Educaring® Approach (RIE®). Since 2018, she has been helping parents grow into their parenting with grace, insight, and humor. Download her free guide to helping kids with aggression at learn. fertilegroundparenting.com/aggression.

39

SIBLING CONFLICT – MORE THAN JUST A NUISANCE?

Susan North

We've all been there: your family is going about its business as a fight breaks out between siblings. Emotions explode. There is shouting, perhaps tears. If you don't step in, someone could get hurt. Conflict can strike at the worst moments; you might be late for the dentist or shopping for a week's worth of groceries. It even disrupts a perfectly lovely outing, such as a day at the beach or the zoo.

Like generations of parents before us, we wish to resolve disputes quickly and arbitrate. We listen briefly and then decide on a solution. We act as judges making a ruling or umpires making a call. Our goal is speed and efficiency. This approach may shut things down for an hour or even a week, but it often turns out to be a postponement rather than a solution. Notice how the same conflict (or some variation) often breaks out soon afterward?

Students in my parenting classes tell me they find the constancy and repetitiveness of sibling conflict most overwhelming. They say that even though they try to be evenhanded, their children are often upset about the decisions they make. "That's not fair!" is a familiar refrain.

I have two big ideas about conflict to share. One is basic and simple, and the other is more complex, with many moving parts. Both are useful.

The first big idea is that conflict is not misbehavior. When you put two people together, they will not agree about everything. Their wants and needs will naturally collide. This is conflict, and it's perfectly normal. (True, conflict can lead to misbehavior—like hitting, pushing, and the like—which is why we try to intervene early.) Understanding that conflict is not misbehavior helps you start approaching disputes as opportunities to explore and strengthen your children's relationship with each other.

The second big idea is this: mediation works better than arbitration. Mediation leads to more durable, doable solutions. As a mediator, you don't advise, judge, or decide.

Mediation is ages old, yet it still isn't well understood or widely practiced. It has only been practiced as a profession for about a hundred years in North America. I didn't invent the steps to mediation, but I framed them in a format that's easy to remember when you're in the trenches, mediating a passionate conflict between two people you love dearly. I call it "The Opposite of COMBAT" because COMBAT spelled backward is TABMOC, which outlines the six steps:

T is for Talking

Invite each child to discuss the situation. They can take as long as they need, with no interruptions. Say something like, "Let's hear what's happening for you. Then it will be your sibling's turn." Coach them to frame their complaint as an I-message: "I felt [emotion] when you [verb]." Be helpful with emotion words such as discouraged, frustrated, angry, insulted, disappointed, etc.

A is for Acknowledging

Now that both children have vented, invite them to repeat what they heard the other say. This kind of perspective-taking can be challenging for kids. Allow no arguing back or critical comments at this point (assure them that this will come later). Encourage them to use each other's emotion words by saying things like, "You felt scared when I shouted." Acknowledgment is key to helping two disputants calm down and listen better because they get to be heard. This is what Interpersonal Neurobiologist Dr. Dan Siegel calls "feeling felt."

B is for Brainstorming

Ask the kids to suggest solutions to the problem. No idea is too wild or far-fetched, and criticism is not allowed at this point, as it shuts down creativity, and brainstorming should feel creative. You can write down their suggestions or make simple drawings to illustrate their ideas. During brainstorming, you may detect a shift in tone from "you and me against each other" to "you and me against the problem." Collaboration has begun.

M is for Mulling-Over

This is the time to negotiate all the ideas on the table. Your kids will learn how to critique someone else's ideas respectfully. Children are very nimble thinkers, so don't be surprised if they combine different ideas to create a workable solution!

O is for Organizing

You begin to wrap things up by clarifying what the kids can agree on. You may have to slow the momentum by asking probing questions—who, when, where, how?—to firm up the plan. Have they both made promises or concessions? The goal is a practical and lasting win-win resolution.

C is for Contracting

This is the big finale. Your two kids have designed a resolution, and now they each commit to holding up their end of the bargain, whether it's a signed contract, drawing, or spoken promise. Thank them and celebrate their collaboration. As educator Ruth Beaglehole said, "Siblinghood is a workshop for intimacy."

It's both freeing and exhilarating to take a neutral stance toward your children's conflicts. Mediation requires more effort than arbitrating but is less emotionally wrenching. Moreover, it's a wonderful opportunity to get to know your children better. Does mediation work every time? No, but every attempt deepens your understanding and strengthens your children's sibling bond. This is a priceless investment in a relationship that will likely outlast you.

Should you mediate every dispute? No. Is mediation as swift and efficient as arbitration? Absolutely not. However, it may save time and aggravation in the long run while generating many small miracles: improved emotion regulation, empathy building, emotional literacy, perspective-taking, and negotiating skills.

You don't have to be a master mediator to bring these small miracles to your family. By following the steps outlined above and practicing in good faith whenever possible, you will see wonderful changes occur. Every mediation is a ceremony of respect, and every conflict is an opportunity for growth.

For a deeper look at mediating sibling disputes, see **Susan North's** book, *The Opposite of COMBAT: A Parent's Guide for Teaching Siblings How to Collaborate & Solve Their Own Conflicts.* This book bridges the disciplines of child development, parent education, and mediation. In it, North explores time-honored conflict resolution techniques and provides lively, real-world scenarios involving children ages two to eighteen. Susan North has worked with children and their families since completing UC Berkeley's Early Childhood Education program in 1971. Her early professional experience included teaching and administration for Head Start, running parent/toddler programs, and directing full-day preschools. She later served as a Master Teacher with the Los Angeles Unified School District's Parent Education Division. Subsequently, she opened her mediation practice in 2007. She has divided her time providing conflict resolution, parent education, parent coaching, and volunteering with Southern California Family Mediation in the Child Dependency Courts. She serves on the board of RIE (Resources for Infant Educarers).

40

BUILDING STRONG SIBLING RELATIONSHIPS

Ng Wei Lin

———

As a child, I often felt pitted against my sister. She was the adorable, beautiful one, while I was the reserved, bookish nerd. "This is the beauty and the brains," some relatives would say. Although they meant no harm, adults frequently commented on our looks. Once, when I was ten, a family friend asked his toddler to run to my little sister for a hug, saying, "Run to the cuter *jie jie*! (sister)."

When I became a mom, I promised to prevent unhealthy rivalry between my two sons. Some sibling rivalry is inevitable, but if unchecked, it can lead to animosity and resentment into adulthood.

Here's my journey of minimizing rivalry between my children and creating a strong bond of brotherhood.

Be Intentional

From the start, I read widely about sibling relationships to understand how unhealthy rivalry can take root. It's understandable that an older child, who has had their parents all to themselves for three years, must now share their time, attention, and energy (which diminishes significantly with a new baby!).

Then come the comments levied at the older child as they grow:

"She's having trouble with her homework. Why can't you help her?"

"You're older; you should know better."

"I know she pushed you first, but you're bigger and stronger; you could have hurt her."

Does any of this sound familiar?

I didn't want to impose any expectations that such careless comments (often made during moments of overwhelm) could trigger. I felt resentment when I was younger, so I was intentional in breaking this cycle.

When his brother was born, we didn't ask B (four years older) to:

- Hug or kiss the baby
- "Take care of and protect your brother"
- Be quiet because the baby was sleeping
- Share

Instead, we:

- **Maintained his routine**, especially quality time activities like reading daily, asking about his day, and building Lego together while breastfeeding the baby.

- **Responded to him first**, even if the baby was crying or fussing (unless it was an emergency).

- **Called each child by name**, instead of only referring to them as "*Gor Gor*" (big brother) and "*Di Di*" (little brother) as is common in Asian families, to help them develop their identities beyond their birth order.

- **Scheduled one-on-one time** with each parent, so they would know how uniquely they are loved. We still do this today, to celebrate them individually, doing activities they each enjoy. My husband took B to climb Mt. Kinabalu, the highest peak in Southeast Asia, as his "coming of age" trip. He is now planning a dive trip with J, who turns 12 this year, as J loves the ocean.

Prepare, Don't Compare

When we're annoyed, it's tempting to compare our kids: "Why can't you sort out your mess like him?" Instead, focus on the issue at hand: "Please clean your room."

Nurture Their *Unique* Superpower

B loves music, and J is talented at building. We coach and prepare them to identify their unique strengths and capabilities, emphasizing their growth as individuals. We openly praise them for their progress in their respective projects or fields and encourage them to do the same for each other.

Follow a Needs-Based Approach

There is no such thing as fair and equal. Yes, you heard that right. What is fair? Do you spend equal time helping each child with homework when one struggles with procrastination while the other rushes through it?

I openly discuss this with both sons to normalize a needs-based approach. I buy new shoes only for the child who has outgrown his. I tell his brother, "When you've outgrown yours, let me know, and we'll go shopping together." At a café, I get a brownie for the brownie lover and a curry puff for the spice lover. Now, when Lego is on sale, B suggests buying it for his Lego-loving brother for Christmas. Likewise, J excitedly points out guitar shops because he knows his brother's passion. I don't always succeed or remember, but when I do, I say, "It's so thoughtful that you know his favorite thing!" or "It's really considerate of you to wait without complaining while he looks at guitars, as I know you find it boring. I do too!"

Acknowledge Feelings

Allow them to feel disgruntled and upset with each other. Disagreements, feelings of jealousy, or a sense of injustice are normal and human. Sometimes all they need is to be heard. I listen to them privately vent about the other but refrain from making any comments or judgments. They don't need me to be the judge, as this often pits them against each other. Many times, all they need is a safe space and a sympathetic ear. I always tell them it's okay to argue, as they are practicing their social-emotional and conflict resolution skills! To their credit, they always make up afterward and have never physically hurt each other, as we are firm on this.

Take Small Steps

Despite good intentions, we have had bad days and made careless comments that could undermine their sibling relationship. But take heart; small, intentional steps will accumulate. Values take root slowly, but the harvest is worth the wait.

Start small:

- At dinner, we share what each person did that was kind. This helps diffuse any ill feelings from a recent spat.

- Notice and commend small wins. When one helps the other pick up something, or, in our case, when they fill each other's water bottles, notice and praise.

- Create bonding traditions. We always read together before bedtime. Now my teen and tween enjoy being in the same bedroom to read and chat before sleep.

- Ensure personal space and me-time for each child. I had to explain to J, who adores his older brother, that it's important for B to spend time with his friends without him. Is it always easy? No. But I suggested that B "fill his brother's cup" before he headed out—perhaps with a simple 30-minute computer game together or 20 minutes of volleyball. After that, J is perfectly fine spending the day alone.

- I emphasize "relationships before things." This perspective helps them when they squabble over who took whose charger or lost the other's headphones.

Remember, it's not a perfect journey, and we shouldn't expect one. Imagine how much pressure that would put on our kids! If your children are struggling to get along, have grace for yourself. Choose one small step you can start doing consistently and build it into a habit. Once you have that down, try another small step that fits your family dynamics and circumstances. Showing your children that you care about their relationship will resonate as it becomes an important family value they will uphold.

Wei Lin Ng lives with her husband and two sons in Malaysia. Passionate about a play-based childhood, she believes that giving her children unstructured time allows them the freedom to explore and be creative (read: creative mess). She also fosters an environment where her children can build strong sibling relationships and bond, where they are celebrated for their unique gifts. As a finance professional addicted to coffee, Wei Lin tries to balance her career with providing her kids a wholesome and authentic childhood, creating a home where they can be independent thinkers—even if that means they now possess the skills to outsmart her at every turn.

Navigating the Asian education system, which often emphasizes academic rigor, while carving out space for play and unstructured time can feel overwhelming, and she's often just trying to get everyone to bed on time! Afterward, she relaxes with her books and hidden stash of chocolates.

Follow Wei Lin on Instagram @colours.of.play, where she shares insights, practical tips, and real moments from her parenting journey to remind you that you're not alone in this.

SECTION FIVE:
UNDERSTANDING AND SUPPORTING NEURODIVERGENT CHILDREN

41

NEWRODIVERSITY: MINDS DECODED, POTENTIAL UNLOCKED

Dolores Gage

"Mama, why can't I make friends like everyone else?" enquired my nine-year-old son. I tried to find words to comfort him, but inside, I felt helpless to change his daily reality as the target of verbal and physical abuse from an increasingly aggressive group of classmates.

Most days, he returned home and erupted over the smallest things. My husband and I recognized these outbursts as stress responses to the humiliation, exclusion, and misunderstanding he endured at school. Despite regular contact with teachers, they were unable to stop the bullying.

The situation escalated. As Austrian psychiatrist Rudolf Dreikurs observed, bullying stems from the need to "deflate others in order to inflate oneself." My son, struggling with reading, math, and attention, became the go-to target for classmates seeking to boost their self-worth at his expense—an all-too-common scenario for children with neurodivergent learning differences.

At home, we tried everything to counteract the negativity he faced daily. But his trust in us was overshadowed by the constant messages he absorbed at school that labeled him "lazy," "stupid," and "weirdo".

His self-esteem plummeted. One night, he confided, "If next year is like this, I'll kill myself." His words filled me with fear and despair. My own brother, creative and sensitive like my son, had taken that same tragic path just shy of his 30th birthday. I couldn't let history repeat itself, but what could I possibly do?

The Human Cost of Outdated Thinking

Through my educational training, including an M.A. in International Education and an IB Certificate of Teaching & Learning, I realized that most teachers lack the tools to recognize and support neurodivergent thinkers like my son.

As parents, we were trapped in a cycle of worry, fear, and confusion from the intimidating labels that "defined" our son (dyslexia, dyscalculia, and ADHD), and the explanations from educational and medical professionals felt incomplete.

Traditional perspectives on neurodiversity focus on what a person can't do or what "doesn't work." Experts refer to "intellectual disability" or use technical, deficit-laden terms like "disorder" and "impairment." For decades, neurology even attributed neurodivergent learning difficulties to brain damage! Only in the 1990s did advances in neuro-science start reframing them as "neurological diversity."

Equally, phrases like "it's in the genes," "caused by trauma," or "brain structure anomalies" were insufficient. The experts couldn't explain the significant overlap between neurodivergent conditions or why these "disabilities" coexisted with incredible creativity, prob-lem-solving skills, resourcefulness, and perseverance. I felt lost, and my child felt "broken."

The rise of well-known neurodivergent figures celebrating their strengths provided little solace. Their success stories added pressure as my son continued to struggle without explanation or solution.

The consequences of misunderstanding neurodiversity are pro-found. My brother's story haunts me, but statistics are equally harrow-ing: neurodivergent children face higher risks of school failure, men-tal health challenges, and even suicide—the leading cause of death for people under 35. Misunderstanding also paves the way for addiction, underachievement, and criminal behavior. Alarmingly, up to 80% of incarcerated individuals have learning differences.

Misunderstanding neurodiversity has a devastating human cost. The YouTube video "Las Vidas de Mario" poignantly contrasts how under-standing, and the lack thereof, impacts the life of a neurodivergent indi-vidual. I urge every parent, educator, and caregiver to watch it.[20]

Neurodivergent Minds Decoded; Potential Unlocked

In my quest for answers, I discovered Ron Davis' book, *The Gift of Dyslexia*. It was like a light switching on. Davis' insights into neurodi-vergent thinking explained the mechanics behind my son's struggles and strengths in a way that finally made sense. Better still, his transformative approach offered actionable solutions.

Ron Davis' journey is nothing short of extraordinary. Born autistic and severely dyslexic, he was labeled "uneducatably retarded," yet he grew up to become a mechanical engineer with an IQ of 169. Davis didn't learn to speak until he was 17 or read until he was 38, but through intense self-observation, he overcame his challenges. In just three days, he discovered how to correct the involuntary perceptual distortions behind his dyslexia and subsequently read *Treasure Island* in a single sitting, understanding everything! His breakthrough in 1981 laid the foundation for the Davis® method, which has helped countless individuals worldwide.

Davis identified three common traits behind neurodivergent challenges:

1. **Non-verbal/picture thinking**: a natural ability that is explorative and fast (often subliminal), enabling neurodivergent individuals to excel at imaginative, creative, and empathetic thinking, solving problems by seeing the whole picture rather than following step-by-step processes.

2. **Heightened sensory sensitivity**: their nervous systems respond intensely to physical, social, and emotional stimuli.

3. **A talent for disorientation**: This temporary disconnection from reality is caused by emotions such as curiosity, confusion, boredom, pleasure, fear, or instinctive self-protection (e.g., from trauma, sensory overwhelm, etc.). It fuels creativity and problem-solving but also causes *perceptual distortions* in sight, hearing, balance, coordination, and sense of time.

These traits, while individually advantageous, can lead to states of disorientation that hinder learning and development because we learn from experience. However, since we only experience what we perceive, the accuracy of our perceptions is a fundamental filter affecting our identity, ability to learn and relate to others, and function in life.

Dyslexia Explained

For neurodivergent thinkers, disorientation becomes their go-to strategy for exploring and understanding the world. This works well with 3-D objects but not with 2-D symbols. Letters trigger confusion, disorientation, and involuntary perceptual distortion. Consequently, the child can no longer discern the correct version of the letter and assimilates/interprets it incorrectly. This leads to mistakes, frustration, anxiety, and compulsive solutions that impede learning.

ADHD Explained

With ADHD, emotions such as confusion and boredom trigger disorientation. When the interest level in the physical world is lower than what they can create in their thought world, children disorientate for entertainment. Often referred to as "switching off" or "having one's head in the clouds," this results in *inattentional blindness,* meaning they only take in things they find significant. This explains why individuals with ADHD struggle to focus on some things but *hyperfocus* on others.

Living with repeated and uncontrolled states of disorientation is like watching two movies simultaneously without fully understanding either. Gaps in understanding in our thought world may be inconsequential, but in the real world, they can be debilitating. Essential life concepts like change, cause-effect, time, and order explain the mechanics of life, and their absence causes individuals to exist in a state of disorder.

Davis® addresses these challenges by teaching individuals how to control their perceptions, manage disorientation, and correct/complete any gaps in their understanding. Through creative, strength-based strategies, neurodivergent thinkers can unlock their potential and build self-esteem. When taught to five to seven-year-olds, learning difficulties drop by over 80%.

Davis® changed my son's life. His explosive outbursts disappeared, and his confidence blossomed. We moved him to a culturally diverse school with methods better suited to his experiential learning style. With Davis® insights and tools, he's now thriving academically, recently earning a spot on the High Honors List with grades of 90% or higher.

I never foresaw becoming a Davis® Facilitator, but now I can't imagine doing anything else. Helping neurodivergent individuals of all ages transform their learning and lives is profoundly rewarding.

Davis® unlocked my son's potential, restored his self-esteem, and positively changed our family dynamic. If you or a loved one struggle with neurodivergent challenges, consider exploring this approach. It may change your life.

Dolores Gage is a Davis® Facilitator, Presenter, and Supervisor-in-Training based in Madrid, Spain. With over a decade in education and a background in strategic branding, she specializes in supporting neurodivergent individuals with ADHD, dyslexia, dyscalculia, executive function challenges, and autism. Her academic credentials include a degree from Cambridge University, an Executive M.B.A. from IE Business School, and an M.Ed. in International Education and Bilingualism from UCJC. Fluent in English, Spanish, and French, she works with clients both in person and online.

After experiencing the life-changing impact of the Davis® method, she dedicates her work to empowering others. She is passionate about how Davis® provides insights where traditional approaches fall short: explaining the causes of various learning differences, their frequent overlap, and how they can be both prevented (*Davis® Learning Strategies*) and resolved (1-to-1 Davis® Programmes). She also runs *Davis® Parent Power: Dyslexia* to support parents.

Discover how Dolores unpacks dyslexia, ADHD, and autism with Davis insights—watch *Neurodivergent Minds Decoded: Potential Unlocked* below.

42

NOTHING IS WRONG WITH YOU OR YOUR SENSITIVE CHILD

Miranda Eiseman

Y ou probably came to this chapter because your child is sensitive, and this has been challenging. You may even feel like something is wrong with you, your child, or that you're destined to suffer forever. I'm here to reassure you that your highly sensitive child is not only normal but also possesses amazing superpowers that the world needs.

Research by Elaine Aron, PhD, identified high sensitivity as an inherited trait found in about 15 to 20 percent of children.[21] This is a normal trait with real evolutionary advantages. We need people who pause and reflect before acting, think through consequences, and notice subtleties. In my own family, several individuals over four generations possess these traits, including my children. However, the characteristics of these individuals are often undervalued and misunderstood. Your approach to caretaking will help them thrive.

My hope is to calm your fears and provide actionable steps that will help you and your sensitive child lead a joyous and meaningful life. Before we proceed, know that these steps are designed to help you build connections, which enable both children and adults to navigate challenging situations and separations with ease.

A Few Simple Practices

1. Indulge in inside jokes and pretend play, which can quickly build connections during difficult transitions.

For example, getting to the bathroom to brush teeth before bedtime can feel like a chore. You might pretend to be cats, crawl down the hall in the dark to practice your night vision, and then brush your sharp teeth to strengthen your bite.

2. Build connection through routines, which are comforting.

Sensitive children don't like surprises or being caught off guard. Even seeing new faces at the bus stop can be alarming. I've found that secret handshakes and a consistent order of backpacks, kisses, and hugs keep everyone in motion.

3. Open the door with uninterrupted, no-agenda play.

Do you get silence or a simple "OK" when you ask your child about their day? This special play helps you understand their world and benefits children from babies to teens. For 10 to 20 minutes a day, your only job is to observe and follow their lead. Set aside distractions and your to-do list. No teaching or interrupting—just enjoy. You'll be surprised by how much you learn, as children express and process their world through play.

4. Contain and don't fan the flame.

During big emotions or meltdowns, which you can expect from time to time, adjusting your approach can help. Sometimes, the tone of your voice can escalate the situation. The greater the hurt your child is experiencing, the more explosive and feral they may become, exhibiting animalistic behaviors, including hissing or growling. Using a soft voice or whisper, maintaining little to no eye contact, getting low, and breathing slowly can help. If possible, move to a smaller, safer space. Stay there as long as you feel strong enough to ride it out. You may need to take breaks.

5. Prepare for events that can bring about big emotions.

Going to the doctor's office? In my experience, showing up without warning does not go well. We mark it on the calendar, discuss the events, play check-up, and my children will give me the vaccines while I cry and get better. We talk about the steps we can control and wonder together about what might be surprising. Preparation also reduces the need for discipline.

6. State your boundaries.

Sensitive children have a strong desire to do what's right, and knowing your boundaries and house rules goes a long way. Be sure to share these out loud and often.

7. Respect their reality.

It's okay to validate their feelings, even if you don't understand them. This helps with big reactions to situations that may seem trivial to us. Phrases like "you know your body best" provide validation and give them more autonomy to do what's best.

8. Less is more for big lessons.

Keep big lessons private and low-key. Highly sensitive children can be distressed even by a change in your tone. As Elaine Aron, PhD, shared in her research, highly sensitive children feel shame readily, and this feeling is very distressing for them. This is part of how they learn.

9. Watch the discipline.

We want to be mindful in our discipline approach and avoid inducing more shame. Public displays of correction will only cause more shame and resistance. Harsh punishments wreak havoc. Avoid techniques that increase isolation or withdraw love. Outside of the moment, talking calmly in the car or while on a walk usually works best.

10. Talk to the fear of failure.

Whether it's trying something new, performing, or competing, the fear of failure can be loud for sensitive children. Discussing this can be uncomfortable for caretakers. We often want to reassure them or convince them otherwise. They already have these thoughts and discussing them together builds their ability to cope. Avoiding or dismissing these feelings will only leave them feeling isolated.

11. Respond appropriately to comments.

Your approach to your highly sensitive child can attract attention and unwanted comments. You may encounter prejudice against sensitivity in your family and community. My children have been called "the most dramatic child in preschool," "overly sensitive," "hysterical, can't be calmed down, and I can't help her." You may have experienced something even more severe, or your child may have been asked to leave a school or program. Be proactive with teachers, family, and other caretakers about the language and approach you use. Share techniques that are effective at home. Encourage teachers to have a calm corner in their classroom with low stimulation. Many sensitive children have self-soothing techniques that can be accommodated in the classroom.

A Word of Caution

Approaching your child in this way can bring up a lot for you as a caretaker. Perhaps you have faced hostility, judgment, and misunderstanding. You may feel a sense of loss because your child is different.

You may have dreamed of your child being a soccer star, but they won't step onto the field. They may be an artist or poet, but that "isn't acceptable." You just want them to be like the other kids and enjoy the birthday party. Maybe you want to go on adventures, but your child needs more rest and less stimulation. I encourage you to take time to process these losses and show yourself compassion.

Change will take longer than you hoped. It's not uncommon for situations to escalate before you see improvement, as your child may not be used to having their emotions met with calm compassion. It's never too late to start, and you and your child are worth this investment.

Dr. Miranda Eiseman noticed early on that her child's sensitive traits were often viewed as a problem. Also, the "recommended" parenting techniques were not effective and left her feeling distant and alone. Knowing she wanted to do things differently, she embarked on a journey to understand the richness of her children's gifts and how to be their fierce advocate in a world of misunderstanding. She recognizes the demands of caring for highly sensitive children and now works to support families in improving understanding and building deeper connections so caregivers and children thrive. Dr. Eiseman is also a board-certified OB/GYN and enjoys supporting others in the transition to parenthood. She lives in Bellevue, Washington, with her family, cat, and chickens. She loves the outdoors and looks forward to all that each season has to offer. Her happy place is on a trail in the mountains. Her mission is to increase awareness and support for families so all children can embrace their unique gifts and live deeply meaningful lives. Download her free guide "Responding to Comments About Sensitivity" at www.guidinggenerations.com.

43

TEN SECONDS TO TRANSFORM A MELTDOWN

Wendy Leung

D id you know that parents of autistic children experience stress levels comparable to combat soldiers? I didn't realize this until I found myself in the trenches of early motherhood, raising three children under three—one of whom is autistic.

I was completely overwhelmed. This 24/7 mothering lifestyle turned my life upside down, as I was doing everything for everyone except myself. I would clench my teeth every time I had to wash the dishes, thinking, *Why does everyone else get to go out and have fun while I was left behind to do chores and deal with tantrums?* I'd tell myself I could handle it; it's no big deal. However, I was also the same person who yelled at my children, and whenever my partner and I talked, it would often end in a fierce argument. I was so tired.

Before I tell you how I found my way out, let me jump ahead to the "happy ending."

How Having an Autistic Child Transformed Me

Having an autistic child changed me in different ways. I learned to be more flexible, patient, and open-minded—qualities I never realized I needed to develop.

1. Flexibility

I used to thrive on schedules and plans set in stone. But life with my autistic child taught me the beauty of adaptability. Now, I choose classes and programs that allow for changes or don't sign up for classes at all. Suppose we have something planned, and it doesn't work out. In that case, I always have a Plan B or C. Flexibility has become a cornerstone of our family's happiness.

2. Taking judgment with a grain of salt

Before, I worried about what others thought of my parenting and my child. But over time, I learned that other people's opinions don't define me or my child. I began to trust my instincts and focus on what's best for our family rather than conforming to societal expectations.

3. Listening with All My Senses

My child doesn't always communicate with words. Sometimes, he shows us what he needs through gestures, facial expressions, or behavior. I learned to listen with my eyes, ears, and heart—to pick up on the subtle cues that reveal his thoughts and feelings. This deepened our connection and taught me to be more present in every interaction.

But it took a while to get here ...

The Key to This Transformation

I remember a time when I cleaned up spilled milk on the living room carpet. Toys were everywhere—I had just tidied them up five minutes ago—and a pile of laundry was sitting on the couch, waiting to be folded. As I passed the kitchen, I noticed a full sink of dirty dishes, and then I saw my two-year-old son sitting on the floor with an empty can of baby formula. He had managed to take the can from the pantry, opened the lid, and tipped all the milk powder onto the floor. He played in it and even took some with his hand to eat. I was shocked—how did he get the can so high up in the pantry? The budget was tight, and now I had to throw all that expensive baby formula in the bin. Why hadn't I even realized he was hungry? I felt like I was the worst mom as voices started to ring in my ears: "Why is the house such a mess?" "You will never be a good mom." I began to lose myself, stuck in the role of what I thought an "ideal mom" should be or what everyone else thought I should be. That's when I realized I needed to find a way out.

Picking up my camera one day, I found myself pausing. Taking a photo offered me a chance to stop and observe; it forced me to focus on the beautiful things around me, no matter how dire the situation was. Taking photos taught me that I can choose what to focus on. It interrupted the overwhelm.

Did you know that when we're overwhelmed, our brain triggers a fight/flight/freeze/fawn response? To short-circuit this impulse, we can use a tool.

The Ten-Second Pause

This is where the power of a ten-second pause comes in, which I call a ten-second meditation. Taking a brief moment to stop and breathe can calm this response and help us engage the more logical, thoughtful part of our brain.

Anytime you feel overwhelmed or on the verge of losing control, whenever you get swept up in the chaos of meltdowns, feel the urge to stop them immediately: Pause. Breathe. And ground yourself.

Your calm presence is your child's anchor. When you regulate yourself, you show them how to do it for themselves. (Easier said than done, right?)

Just like taking photos helped me pause, I want to help you install your own "Pause." Parenting an autistic child isn't about controlling behaviors—it's about creating safety, and that safety starts with you.

I remember one day when an autistic child suddenly grabbed a broom and started swinging it in anger. The whole place froze. The children and educators stood in shock, unsure of what to do. While everyone else hesitated, I felt a deep sadness—not just for the fear in the room but for the child, who must have been overwhelmed or triggered by something. I slowly approached him, trying to understand what was wrong. Another educator yelled, "Don't go near him; you'll get hurt!" I nodded to acknowledge her concern but continued moving calmly toward the child. I spoke softly. "It's okay. Just put the broom down." I gently gestured down with my hand. The child looked at me. I repeated, "It's okay, just put the broom down," keeping my tone low and even and my body relaxed. When I saw his tension ease slightly, I moved closer and gently took hold of the broom. "Let's put this down now," I said, and he let go. When a child doesn't see you as another threat, it's easier to communicate with them through words or actions. Your calm presence—born of pausing—can be the bridge back to safety. Once the storm passes, practice the ten-second pause together with the child when emotions are calm. Practicing this regularly can help rewire your child's brain to exit the fight/flight/freeze/fawn mode more easily next time there is a trigger.

Other Ways to Create a Pause

While photography worked for me, you might find your own unique way to pause. Here are some ideas:

- **Step outside for fresh air.**

  Sometimes, a simple change of environment can ground you.

- **Touch something grounding.**

  A piece of jewelry, a smooth stone, or even the fabric of your clothes can help bring you back to the present.

- **Use music as a reset.**

  Play a calming song or hum a familiar tune to interrupt the stress response and refocus your mind.

- **Focus on your senses.**

  Notice three things you can see, hear, and feel to bring your attention back to the moment.

By practicing this regularly, you rewire your brain to exit survival mode. Next time the storm rises, try it: pause, breathe, and be present. In ten seconds, you can transform the moment—and your parenting. Create your own happy ending.

Wendy Leung is an autism advocate who navigates the world of autism both as an early childhood teacher and a parent. She understands the unique challenges parents face every day. With over a decade of experience as an early childhood teacher and a background in behavior management, she specializes in helping children on the autism spectrum, as well as those who are shy or have English as a second language, find their voice. Her journey is deeply personal, and she strives to empower other parents by sharing practical strategies and compassionate insights. As the creator of the Autism Advocacy Academy, her mission is to bring calmness and confidence to parents' journeys.

Over the years, Leung has collaborated with multidisciplinary teams, parents, and caregivers to develop and implement personalized strategies that cater to each student's unique needs. This has driven her endeavor for continuous learning and advocacy for the autism community.

She strives to engage and inspire through her work, imparting knowledge and passion that translate into tangible support for autism and the Chinese migrant communities.

44

UNLOCK YOUR HOME'S POTENTIAL TO NURTURE EMOTIONAL REGULATION

Dana Denning

What if I told you that the key to unlocking your child's emotional well-being isn't another parenting strategy but something far simpler—your home?

The day I realized our home was adding to my child's stress rather than easing it was a turning point. My son was experiencing frequent meltdowns, and no behavioral strategies seemed to work. I felt powerless, exhausted, and deeply worried about his emotional well-being.

One evening, as I walked through our cluttered, noisy living room with its harsh overhead lighting, it hit me: our living environment was exacerbating everything.

This realization wasn't about clutter or decor—it was about understanding how a child's nervous system interacts with the space around them. I began making small adjustments, experimenting with lighting, creating a sanctuary for sleep, and curating a calming retreat for him. The change was slow but undeniable. Our home became more than just a place to live—it transformed into a nurturing nest that supported my son's emotional regulation and, in turn, our entire family's well-being.

Drawing from decades of experience as a designer and as a mother navigating life with a differently wired child, I've had the privilege of helping countless families create environments that truly support their unique needs. I'm excited to share the insights and strategies that transformed living spaces that soothe rather than overwhelm.

The Invisible Weight: Understanding the Total Load

Parenting a neurodivergent child means navigating their needs and the external pressures they face every day. One concept that reshaped my approach is "total load." This term refers to the cumulative stressors on a child's nervous system—everything from emotional challenges to environmental triggers.

Imagine a scale. Each stressor adds weight to one side until the scale tips into meltdown territory. Emotional regulation becomes nearly impossible if the home environment adds more stress rather than alleviates it.

Consider how cluttered spaces increase visual noise, making it harder for kids to focus. Loud, unpredictable sounds can keep their nervous systems on high alert, and harsh lighting may feel like a constant sensory assault.

But here's the good news: we can shift the balance by identifying and addressing these triggers. Your home can become a place that supports and strengthens your child's ability to self-regulate.

The Power of Space in Emotional Regulation

By designing a space that nurtured emotional regulation, we were able to support our child's mental health, reduce overwhelm, and foster a deeper sense of peace in our home.

As you embark on this journey, know that the space you create can truly be a sanctuary for your child's emotional growth. With small, intentional changes, you can unlock your home's potential to nurture emotional regulation and provide the stability your child needs to thrive.

Actionable Steps: Transforming Your Home

You can create a holistic haven that isn't complicated, expensive, or time-consuming. Here are the keys to unlocking your home's potential:

1. Address lighting to soothe the senses.

Lighting can have a powerful effect on the nervous system. Harsh, fluorescent lights can overstimulate, while soft, warm lighting helps promote relaxation.

- Quick Wins:

    o   Replace bright overhead bulbs with dimmable, warm-tone LED lights.

    o   Open curtains to maximize natural light during the day.

    o   Use soft, low-light lamps in the evenings to cue the brain for rest.

2. Prioritize rest with a sleep sanctuary.

Sleep is foundational for emotional regulation, and the right environment can make a huge difference.

- Quick Wins:

    o   Invest in blackout curtains to block light and reduce external distractions.

    o   Use a white noise machine to create a consistent auditory backdrop.

    o   Keep the bedroom free of clutter and designate it as a calm, sleep-focused zone.

3. Create a quiet retreat for regulation.

Every child needs a space where they can reset and recharge.

- Quick Wins:

    o   Transform a corner of a room into a sensory-friendly retreat. Include items like a beanbag chair, weighted blanket, noise-canceling headphones, or a sensory bin.

o   Keep the area calm by minimizing visual distractions and using soothing colors.

o   Personalize the space with your child's input to make it feel safe and inviting.

By addressing these key areas, you create a home environment that supports not only your child's emotional well-being but also your family's overall harmony.

What This Looks Like in Real Life

Eight-year-old Liam was a bright, energetic boy whose parents felt at a loss. Their home was chaotic, with toys spilling into every corner, the TV always on, and fluorescent lighting casting a harsh glare. Liam, who was already navigating sensory sensitivities, struggled to focus, and frequently melted down during transitions.

When they began making changes, they started small—turning off the TV during meals and replacing the fluorescent bulbs with softer, warm lighting. Next, they tackled the clutter, using bins and baskets to create a more streamlined, organized environment. They transformed an unused living room corner into a sensory retreat, adding a bean-bag chair, a small shelf of calming activities, and noise-canceling head-phones.

Within weeks, Liam's behavior shifted. He started using his sensory corner during moments of overwhelm, giving himself the time he needed to regulate. The family also noticed a calmer atmosphere during meals, where everyone could connect without the distraction of background noise. Liam's parents were amazed at how small, intentional changes to their environment helped create a foundation of calm for their son—and for themselves.

Overcoming Challenges

Like any transformation, there will be bumps along the way. Maybe you don't know where to start, or your child resists changes. That's okay; I can help.

- **Limited budget?**

  Rearrange furniture, thrift storage solutions, or repurpose items you already own.

- **Resistance from kids?**

  Involve them in the process. Let them choose colors, textures, or items for their spaces.

- **Time constraints?**

  Break it into small tasks. Declutter one drawer or swap out one lightbulb a day.

Moving Forward

Your home is more than walls and furniture—it's the foundation for your family's well-being. By making intentional changes, you're reducing stress for your child and creating a space where your family can thrive together.

Remember, this journey isn't about perfection—it's about progress. Every choice you make to support your child's emotional regulation is a step toward creating a home that feels safe, nurturing, and calm.

Dana Denning is the founder of Nourished Nest, an online holistic interior design and coaching resource that helps families create homes designed to meet core needs—nervous system regulation, connection, rest, and the reduction of environmental triggers. As a mother of a differently wired child, Dana understands the transformative power of small, affordable changes in fostering family well-being. Through virtual courses and consultations, Dana shares actionable, budget-friendly strategies to reduce overwhelm and create homes that soothe rather than stress. From promoting restful sleep and minimizing overstimulation to crafting calming spaces that encourage connection, she provides practical tools to empower families to take control of their environments—and their peace of mind.

Are you ready to create a home that supports your family's emotional well-being? I've created The Personalized Calm Space Plan (Mini Home Review)—so you can get straight-to-the-point, doable changes that make your home work *for* you instead of against you. I'm also including the Bonus Calm Tracker, a simple and stress-free way to check in and see real progress. Go to https://www.nourishednest.com/minihomereview to start today.

45

ADDRESSING "SCHOOL SHAME" IN ADHD ADOLESCENTS

Gavin Front

———

B rené Brown, the well-known researcher on emotions, often cites a statistic from her early research on shame: 85% of her adult participants could recall a school experience so shaming that it forever altered their self-perception as learners. Based on my decade of working with neurodivergent adolescents, I would bet the figure is closer to 100% for those of us with ADHD.

Fifteen-year-old Tara walked into my office—arms crossed over her backpack straps, bangs covering her face—and cautiously took a seat across from me. "Your mom told me a little about what's going on," I said, "but tell me how I can help."

"I don't know," she replied. "I have a bunch of late work, and my mom is super mad at me about it. I'm pretty much failing my classes right now ... which is fine, I guess. But my neighbor said he worked with you, and he's cool, so I thought I'd give it a try."

Tara was genuinely failing classes and couldn't bring herself to do schoolwork. In class, she zoned out during lectures and doodled through assignments. At home, she was locked in a perpetual battle with her mother, who was frustrated that Tara "refused" to do homework. Tara was a quick thinker and a good reader—after an hours-long fight one night, her mom watched as she read an assigned chapter in just ten minutes. Mom believed Tara was ruining her future through some misdirected expression of teenage angst and defiance. Tara thought she must be stupid, and neither knew how to move toward a better reality. The core issue soon emerged: Tara would be diagnosed with ADHD (Attention-Deficit/Hyperactivity Disorder) about four months later.

ADHD is not truly a deficit, as the acronym suggests, but a specific pattern of cognitive and neural functioning. Students with ADHD often struggle to initiate and sustain attention (or, as I phrase it with students, "turning on" their brains). Longer-term rewards, consequences, or priorities—functions of the prefrontal cortex—do not stimulate focus and action; instead, an ADHD brain focuses and sometimes hyper-focuses when situation-specific cues like urgency, interest, or novelty activate their limbic (emotional) systems. This different way of thinking can lead to brilliant and creative problem-solving, but it can also cause school and learning issues if not thoughtfully managed.

The School Experience: Who I Am Is Not Enough

ADHD students struggle in school systems that are not designed for their cognitive patterns. In a typical seventh-grade math class, a teacher may present a lesson on adding fractions, give students a worksheet full of practice problems, and assign any unfinished work as homework. A student with ADHD likely has trouble focusing on the lesson; instead, his attention is drawn to the PE class playing soccer outside. ("Jason, eyes on me please!" says the teacher, for the umpteenth time.) Once the worksheet is distributed, he pays more attention to entertaining his tablemates with jokes and receiving social reinforcement. ("Jason, you need to stop distracting everyone and work on your fractions. If you don't do the practice, you won't do well on tomorrow's test.") At home, with most of the worksheet incomplete, he plays Minecraft instead of trudging through 15 more math problems he doesn't understand. He then doesn't turn in the worksheet because he doesn't want the teacher to know he left most of it blank. When the test arrives, he tries to recall the math concepts and gets one or two of the ten problems correct. The test is returned with plenty of red marks and a "come see me" written at the top.

Odds are that Jason shrugs off the experience—it's not the first time he's done poorly on a test, and he just thinks he's bad at math anyway. But with every one of these experiences, an insidious internal message reinforces itself: "My failures are my fault because that's just who I am." Consider my student Tara from earlier. What she heard, both at school and at home, was that the tasks she couldn't focus on "should" be easy and doable. Her takeaway was not the mismatch between school structures and her cognitive functioning patterns—it was that she must be stupid.

Inoculating Against School Shame

What I call "school shame" occurs when a student internalizes the belief that they are fundamentally flawed as learners. School shame, as it worms its way deeper into an adolescent's psyche through repeated experiences, eventually shapes their identity—"I'm stupid," or "I'm bad at math," or "I'm not a school person." The bad news is that there is no real way to prevent students from facing shaming situations at school—those intense moments when their faces flush, their stomachs sink, and they wish to run and hide. The good news is that we, as parents and professionals, can help our kids learn to prevent that shame from becoming part of their identity.

First, we need to communicate to our ADHD kids that while their brains may work differently than many classmates', they are not broken. Approach conversations from a strengths-based perspective; instead of focusing on what is inherently difficult for your child, identify their natural strengths. Then, explore ways to apply these strengths to challenging tasks. For instance, Tara could read and comprehend quickly. She and I developed the concept of "work sprints": she set a five-minute timer and did as much reading or writing as she could in that time. Through these short, focused bursts of effort, she was able to complete assignments, often much more quickly than her neurotypical peers. Now in college, Tara still checks in with me from time to time—and she still loves the sprint technique.

We also need to normalize the ADHD experience. Adolescence can feel isolating for anyone, and when you add ADHD to the mix, many kids feel like they are the only ones struggling. When they share school challenges with you, it can be tempting to immediately start problem-solving—but that only reinforces the impression that such struggles occur because they lack your skills. Instead, consider using phrases like "It makes sense that this is hard to do with ADHD." Once kids feel heard and believe their struggles are valid, they tend to be much more open to strategizing productive next steps. Even better, they learn an essential skill: when things feel hard, they can work to make them easier. And when kids leave home for college, work, travel, or whatever adventure lies ahead, they will have practiced shame-resilient problem-solving and will know how to grow from the inevitable future struggles rather than be crippled by them.

Gavin Front is a learning specialist and the creator of Shameless Learning®, a coaching program designed to foster confident, empowered, passionate learners who deeply know, even when they struggle, that they are enough. He has worked with hundreds of students, both neurotypical and neurodivergent, on improving learning skills and scholastic performance. Diagnosed with ADHD in his 30s, he intimately understands the struggles that neurodivergent students can face in the school system—especially when that neurodivergence has not been identified. Gavin is also the founder of Chronos Prep, a boutique tutoring company that supports students in academic subjects, standardized test preparation, college admissions, and executive functioning. He lives in Berkeley, California, and spends his free time gardening, making pottery, playing the guitar, loving his dogs, and spending time with his family and friends. He graduated with honors with a dual degree in neuroscience and English from Amherst College and is a member of Mensa and the Sigma Xi research society.

46

HOW TO TRANSFORM WORRY INTO MEANINGFUL ACTION

Dr. Glorianne Vazquez

Worry is a prevalent issue among parents of neurodivergent children. It keeps us awake, drains our energy, weakens our immune systems, and prevents us from living purposeful lives. Worry makes us lose sight of what we want and forget the endless possibilities before us.

I've struggled with worry for as long as I can remember. As a little girl, I would lie in bed, my mind spinning with endless "What ifs?" Fast forward to my becoming a mom of two neurodivergent children while trying to launch a private practice after my second out-of-state move in four years, and worry was still a staple in my life. It was no coincidence that many of my psychotherapy clients were women grappling with worry. As I worked with more parents experiencing uncontrollable worry, I wondered about worry's function.

Throughout my years working with clients, I've found that parents of neurodivergent children are more susceptible to worry as we are constantly problem-solving challenges. Worry takes over, and it's detrimental to our health. We have difficulty sleeping, focusing, and handling everyday tasks. Our ability to be grateful diminishes, and self-doubt increases. We begin to worry about our worries and our ability to cope with them. When we judge ourselves for worrying, we reinforce anxiety, which thrives on overestimating threats and underestimating our ability to cope. This vicious cycle, reinforced over time, makes us feel overwhelmed.

For example, one of my clients was feeling overwhelmed about how her child handled emotions. She was consumed by worry about their frequent meltdowns, believing they would never learn to regulate their emotions. Her worry spiraled into self-doubt: *What if I'm not the type of mom my child needs?* Her constant worry triggered a stress response in her body that clouded her perception of her child and herself. Over time, her child's real challenge, emotional dysregulation, turned into a catastrophic narrative: *My child is not going to be able to function as an adult because I was not a good enough mom.*

Navigating Worry

I've learned that worry is unhelpful, but it's a well-reinforced internal behavior, so we must be intentional about changing how we relate to it. Worry is often a form of emotional avoidance, an attempt to escape what makes us anxious. Anxiety, like all emotions, is valid and useful. It's a natural, adaptive response that alerts us to potential danger and prepares our bodies for fight or flight. This response is helpful when facing a real threat, but we often overuse it. Excessive worry triggers the same fight-or-flight response to non-threatening situations, creating a disconnect between our body's response and reality. Worry diminishes activity in the prefrontal cortex, which is responsible for emotional regulation and judgment, and overactivates the amygdala. Our capacity to regulate our worry is diminished, and worry takes over.

I've developed a simple formula with exercises to help transform worry thoughts.

Transforming Your Worries

This exercise helps you break free from the worry loop by distinguishing between worry thoughts and actual problems.

Step 1: Describe your worry.

Identify and describe your worry as if you were an objective reporter. Write down one specific worry thought and ask yourself:

- What is happening?
- Who is involved?
- When and where does it happen?

Step 2: Categorize your thought.

Determine if your thought is a worry thought or an actual problem by answering these three questions:

1. Is this thought completely true? If yes, then it's an actual problem. When calm, engage in problem-solving and brainstorm practical solutions.

2. Is it partially true? If yes, these thoughts are common for parents of neurodivergent children due to their unique needs and challenges. Break the thought into parts: the true part is the actual problem, while the false part is the worry thought. Problem-solve the actual problem.

3. Is it false? If yes, then it's a worry thought.

Step 3: Tune into emotions behind your worry.

Worry is an opportunity to explore the emotion driving it. Ask yourself: *What's the function of worry in my life right now?* When we worry, we unconsciously avoid the primary emotion we're feeling. By the time we notice we're worrying, this primary emotion may have shifted into secondary emotions, making it harder to recognize.

Break this cycle by asking yourself:

- *What am I feeling as I'm worrying?*
- *What is this emotion trying to tell me?*

Identify your primary emotion and its purpose. For example, anger can provide energy for setting boundaries, while sadness signals a need to address what you perceive is missing in your life. Recognizing your emotions helps you regulate them and use them as guides for meaningful action instead of dwelling on your worries.

If you have difficulty identifying your emotions, you can tune into your energy level (are you high or low?) and then choose a soothing or activating activity depending on your body's needs. You are working on regulating your nervous system by identifying your energy level and engaging in an activity.

Regularly engaging in this exercise can help rewire your brain. My clients have found using it as a journal prompt helpful, even when they're not worried. Through consistent practice, they become skilled at distinguishing between a worry and an actual problem without needing to write it down. They build emotional resilience by recognizing the purpose of the emotions behind their worry.

Managing Worry on the Go

Through my work, I've discovered on-the-go actionable tools to help clients change their relationship with worry. Labeling thoughts is a simple tool that even busy parents can integrate into their daily lives. When a worry arises, say, "I'm having the thought that ... " This creates distance, helping you see worry as an internal behavior, not a fact. You can also label recurring thought patterns as stories: "Here's that story again about me not doing enough for my child." Labeling thoughts and narratives teaches you that you are not your thoughts and that you don't have to believe everything you think.

When we've struggled with worry throughout our lives, we tend to worry about worrying, which leads to self-judgment. Parents with chronic worry may feel they aren't doing enough or that they aren't good enough. Self-compassion is an actionable tool to address this.

Practicing self-compassion transformed one of my clients' lives. She was consumed with worry and felt like she wasn't doing enough. She began picturing a friend with a child facing similar challenges and imagined offering understanding and validation, and then she repeated these words to herself. This shifted her perspective, easing her self-blame and helping her feel less alone.

A Final Note

By learning to differentiate between worry thoughts and actual problems, we become skilled at using anxiety as energy for problem-solving. This, in turn, boosts our confidence in tackling any issue as it unfolds. Recognizing the emotions behind our worry is essential for self-regulation. Worry will always be a part of our lives, yet we can practice changing our relationship with it. This shift has a significant impact on our families as we can model to our children how to navigate their own worries, and by doing this, we equip them with a lifelong tool that can transform their lives.

Dr. Glorianne Vázquez is a clinical psychologist with fifteen years of experience specializing in anxiety, worry, and parenting stress. She has worked extensively with parents of neurodivergent children in both community mental health and private practice. Motivated by her professional experience and her personal journey as a mother of two neurodivergent children, Dr. Vázquez founded *Regulated Parenting*. She equips parents with practical, research-backed tools through personalized coaching, group sessions, and emotion regulation skills training. Dr. Vázquez helps parents break free from worry and build emotional regulation skills, enabling them to gain the confidence to address their children's unique needs and view challenges as opportunities for growth. Her mission is for families to understand that they are worthy of living a life aligned with what truly matters to them. Beyond her work, Dr. Vázquez engages in activities that resonate with her core values of *connection, family, adventure, service, courage, and knowledge*. She gains energy from working with her clients, as well as from hiking, traveling, reading, and cooking. Recently, she discovered a love for aerial hiking, embracing it as a way to honor her core values of adventure and courage. Download her *Transforming Your Worry* guide at https://www.regulatedparenting.com/transform-worry.

47

GETTING UNSTUCK WHEN YOU AND YOUR CHILD ARE NEURODIVERGENT

Shelby Czarnick

———

That moment. That moment you realize you yelled ... again. You assess what to do. Do you leave, take a break, or try breathing and holding on? Can you even do that? You feel tears and say, "I need a moment," beginning to leave the room. Terrified, she screams, "Don't leave!" You're stuck ... again. You know you need to leave, and your child is asking you to stay. You fight the urge to leave and risk saying something you may regret. You choose to stay in silence. An image comes to mind of professionals telling you this tense situation is okay, maybe even normal. And your gut is telling you something is wrong. You need to help your child. You need to keep searching.

Moments like this led me to my specialty in ADHD, sensory issues, neurodivergent brains, and further trauma training. My goal has been to gather resources to provide answers for parents like me who feel stuck. It's awful to feel stuck. It also feels awful to possess a neurodivergent brain yourself and have professionals say they don't know how to further help you or make a situation like this better.

Here are four challenges designed to help you build the specialized parenting skills that will allow both of you to thrive.

Challenge One: Change How You Look at Struggles

Behind every struggle is a strength and a skill that needs to be found. Your job is to find it and teach it.

When you truly believe this statement, it will change the narrative of the defiant child needing punishment to one of wonder, curiosity, and connection. In order to see the situation as a connection opportunity, ask yourself and your child: "How exactly is this struggle happening?" The answer will allow you to find the necessary missing skill and sound less defensive and critical. Once you've identified the skill, you can partner with your child to learn it. This will also help ease frustration in those stuck moments.

Challenge Two: Focus on Connection

Build the connection! Feeling connected will allow you both to trust each other and feel safe enough to look at a situation with curiosity and wonder. When we feel unsafe, our brains freeze and block the ability to access information. This is especially true for neurodivergent brains. What looks like defiance can simply be the inability to access the information. "I don't know" truly means "I don't know."

A hard part about connection is understanding it takes time.

Here are some ways to begin building connection. During heated moments, utilize play, humor, or movement. Take a walk together, sit in a "wiggle chair" with them, hug, or massage them. List behaviors by saying, "I notice," then sit silently.

Sitting silently and not leaving is one of the hardest things to do. Not leaving shows you're staying, even if they unconsciously try to push you away. This begins teaching their bodies you are here for them.

Note: Touch is not to be used in heated moments for the first time. You must try things in calm moments and make them part of daily rituals and routines, like massaging your child's arms while reading her a book at night. Otherwise, it could trigger them more.

Challenge Three: Build a Good Support System

It's hard to weed out the unhelpful people in our lives, especially the ones we love. The best way to crowd them out is to find new team resources.

1. **Search for role models with beliefs who function the way you want to.** Then, find the most efficient way to learn from them. Listening to podcasts is my way.

2. **Assess your team.** List them and keep listing. Consider how they react and how you feel after. This will tell you if, right now, they help or hinder you. Be in the now!

3. **Ask questions** like, "Has anyone ever ... helped me with my kids, helped me brainstorm, etc.?" to find helpful individuals you may have forgotten.

Challenge Four: Practice Good Communication Skills with Your Team

1. Check in and see if potential team members are willing to change how they interact with you or your child. Say things like, "I feel _____ when you _____ (behavior). I need _____." Example: "I felt dismissed when you said Lilly's behavior was normal. I need you to let me vent and brainstorm other options to help."

2. If this member is willing to change, be prepared to remind them of the new response, as building new habits is hard.

3. If the team member is unwilling to change, understand that this is their boundary, and it is okay. If they're still in your life, consider what this person can do for you and reconsider how they might support you. Be prepared to call on another support during this transition to make it easier.

Challenge Five: Turn to Your Body

Consider treatments that calm the body down enough to use tools in the moment. Cognitive approaches do not always work, especially in kids and neurodivergent brains.

My sign to seek body treatments is when the body won't even try to use calming tools.

Masgutova Neurosensorimotor Reflex Integration (MNRI) was created by Dr. Svetlana Musgatova, who felt that the preferred cognitive approach was insufficient when working with children, especially those with a history of trauma. MNRI was developed for children who had been through trauma because their bodies were too restless and quick to get stuck in survival mode. Neurodivergent brains can also behave like this with or without trauma.

Other body treatments include the Wilbarger Brushing Protocol, massage, chiropractic, acupuncture, meditation, taekwondo, yoga, cross-body and balance movements, singing, and dancing.

Conclusion

We live in a world where, sadly, professionals often respond to neurodivergent parents and their children dismissively. Our current society's cultural norms also make it harder for neurodivergent brains. But we have the power as parents, neurodivergent or otherwise, to change how we respond to our children's needs. We can build stronger connections, curate support teams to assist us, and utilize body tools to calm our systems. Remember, behind every struggle is a strength and skill waiting to be found. Your job is to find it and teach it.

Shelby Czarnick, LICSW, ADHD-CCSP, is a respected clinical social worker, certified ADHD professional, child-care coach using the Pyramid Model, program developer, and visionary leader. As the founder of Essential Life Tools LLC, she has transformed mental health and leadership development with innovative, results-driven strategies. In therapy, Shelby helps clients shift weaknesses into strengths in under ten minutes. Her approach fosters deep trust, allowing clients to process and heal from unspoken traumas—often in their first session.

Beyond therapy, she builds high-performing teams and programs. Her ability to optimize environments for staff and clients—particularly neurodivergent individuals—has made a lasting impact across at least four behavioral health programs and an oncology navigation program.

As an expert and parent, Shelby understands firsthand the complexities of raising and supporting individuals with diverse neurological needs. This insight fuels her next endeavor: creating a retreat clinic and center specifically designed for neurodivergent individuals.

Book a free consultation today to begin living your best life at: essentiallifetools.org or info@essentiallifetools.org.

48

LISTEN, NOT TO RESPOND, BUT TO UNDERSTAND

Caroline d'Otreppe

"STOP! Don't hit me, or you will be crossing the line," I exclaimed.

My 28-year-old looked at me with his eagle eye and threatening glance—his left arm raised. He was deep in defense mode and ready to trigger "fight" mode. I stood firm, keeping my voice low and calm. My heart throbbed in my ears. He backed down and apologized, but how close were we to an explosive, out-of-control situation, and why?

As the primary caregiver, I have been the one to stand by my son's side through thick and thin. I have had to advocate for him since his birth and have had little guidance. He was the first with a diagnosis that was unknown and often misunderstood. My boy's condition was also invisible yet affected every moment of his life—his relationships, his perception of the world around him, his behavior, and his self-confidence.

As a new mother, I thought it was my responsibility to create a loving, peaceful household, maintain a routine, and provide structure and guidelines for how to behave. This was how I was raised, but it was not working for my firstborn. Family and friends stepped away from our family, unable to understand the situation and unable to accept "inappropriate" behavior.

Was It Possible to Build "Trust" with My Son?

My son had a very difficult time finding a therapist he could trust and who listened without reacting. I was his soundboard. I needed to break down the wall between us, or his anger could grow to a point that might be dangerous for both of us. My mind went to the school shootings around our country. No one should feel so marginalized that they become an outcast and are made fun of. It is impossible to find a life's purpose if one is in constant fear and does not have the opportunities to build relationships and pursue interests. Society loses when neurodivergent minds are misunderstood, and their talents go unused.

My son told me that he would never be able to trust me because I kept important information from him. His educational psychologist told me to be very careful when sharing his diagnosis because no one would know what is "appropriate" for him. What is a mother to do? I had to go with my intuition. I instinctively could not say "no" to his goals, as I felt he should have opportunities if he was ready to work for them.

Remarkably, he reached many of his goals despite having learning differences and being diagnosed with Asperger's syndrome in 1994. Not only did my son complete high school, but he went to college, joined the ROTC, became a pilot, and studied engraving overseas. Sadly, society did not follow suit and clipped his wings. All his hard work and determination brought him nothing, and this broke him. He craves recognition from outside the home for "work well done." Frustration and anger can percolate until he loses his temper and blames his parents.

As parents of this era, we had no choice but to follow our instincts. We raised our children in a traditional home where routines and manners were respected. We eventually learned that what was "fair" for one of our two children was not necessarily "fair" for the other. It would take decades before I realized that what we thought was right for our son was not. We guided him using our own experiences, common sense, and hopes, but we did not listen to him to understand better. Why did it take us so long to change our behavior?

When Everything Changed

It was like flipping a switch when I finally just listened to my adult son without needing to respond. He told me, "Just take the word "should" out of your vocabulary. I was not made to carry out my life like others. Please respect me for who I am and try to meet my needs."

We finally were on the same side of the fence.

What I Learned

Now that I listen without judgment or criticism, my son has taught me a great deal.

- Trying to reason with my son when he was in defense mode made him put up his guard and respond with anger.

- My son needs time to process a change in environment before engaging.

- He cannot respond to questions until he settles into a trusting situation.

- He cannot be rushed.

- Knowing what to expect is helpful to him.

- If given the chance to speak without being bombarded with conversation, he will contribute thoughtful, intelligent information and respond to questions in an appropriate manner.

- He cannot have a conversation when there is another conversation going on (whether it be on television, radio, music with words, or at a restaurant).

- He is bothered by light and needs adaptive lenses.

- He is very sensitive to changing weather and temperature.

- "Masking" and being constantly under stress as a child have led to physical ailments, including spinal compression, hunched shoulders, temporomandibular joint disorder, and digestive issues—all at no fault of his own.

Our son perceives the world and life differently from us, yet I admire no one more for his efforts, intelligence, and perseverance. His life is difficult and very frustrating.

Since flipping the switch, our son has lived independently and joins us three to four times per week for supper. We now know to turn off the TV or radio when sitting at the table, call ahead of time with the menu and to confirm dinner time, make some of his favorite foods available, wait for him to share what is on his mind before conversing, and show our appreciation for his help and all that he teaches us.

Our son now knows we accept and love him for who he is. He knows we are sorry about the decisions that we made for him without knowing any better. He trusts us to support him as he confronts life's challenges.

Advice for Parents

Parents new to "neurodiversity" recognize that human brains can develop very differently and that there is no one way to learn, process our environment, think, decide, and love. We can all learn from each other, but it takes listening, not responding, but understanding. There is not one way that a person "should" behave. It all depends on one's abilities to process, access, trust, decide, and act. Humans all need to develop "trusting" relationships to be able to take risks, learn, and grow.

Be that person who listens to understand!

Caroline Bissell d'Otreppe lives in Suffield, CT, with her Belgian husband and 42-year-old son. She returned to university studies in her forties to obtain her master's in special education and learn to advocate for adults with Asperger's syndrome. In 1999, Caroline joined the world of aviation (one of her son's passions) and ran the education department at the New England Air Museum for fifteen years. After retiring in 2015, Caroline started a non-profit called Partnering to Reach Aspirations to help high school graduates on the autism spectrum transition to independence and find work aligned with their strengths and interests.

If you would like to connect with Caroline by email at caroline.dotreppe@gmail.com, please write "Listen to Understand" as the subject of your email.

49

SEEING IS BELIEVING: HELP YOUR CHILD FOSTER ANY TARGET BEHAVIOR WITH EASE

Dr. Poling Bork

———

A s parents, we all want our kids to become the best versions of themselves and grow into happy, independent individuals. That's why we work hard to help them develop age-appropriate skills—from using the bathroom independently to following bedtime routines, building social skills, and speaking up in public. Our ultimate goal is to help them develop behaviors that set them up for success. But what if the secret to helping your child develop these behaviors could be as simple as having them learn by watching themselves?

Yes, that's right. According to Social Learning Theory (SLT), all behaviors—including those we want to encourage in our kids—are learned by observing and modeling others. For example, if I react fearfully during a lightning strike, my child will likely pick up on that reaction and imitate it, becoming fearful of lightning, too. What's even more powerful than learning from adults is when children learn by watching someone similar to themselves (like another child of similar age). In fact, research shows that the best role model for a child might be themselves.

This is where a technique called Video Self-Modeling (VSM) comes in. VSM allows kids to observe themselves performing a target behavior, learn from it, and then replicate it. I'll explain how I discovered this technique, how it worked even in challenging situations like overcoming phobias, and why it's such a game-changer for shaping behaviors.

My Personal Journey

My journey began when I learned that my children had selective mutism (SM), an anxiety disorder where they physically cannot speak in certain social situations. My eldest daughter experienced a near-drowning incident because she couldn't yell for help. My youngest, who was most affected by SM and also had ADHD, suffered numerous accidents early on, including broken bones. Since he couldn't speak up, he had no way to tell his teachers or babysitters when he was hurt. I felt completely lost and constantly worried.

What if my kids had another accident and I couldn't help them in time? How would they finish school, find jobs, or even have relationships if they couldn't speak? After years of searching for answers with little help, I decided to take matters into my own hands. I became a researcher on this topic and discovered SLT—it was an immediate revelation!

I was particularly intrigued by VSM and believed it could work. And it did! My research using VSM successfully helped all child participants with long-standing SM begin speaking in just eight sessions (less than three hours of active involvement for each child).[22] Most importantly, I was able to help my own children and many other families along the way.

More About Social Learning Theory

The Social Learning Theory, proposed by psychologist Albert Bandura in 1977, suggests that we learn new behaviors by observing and imitating others' actions. This means kids naturally look to the adults and peers around them to figure out how to behave.

Think about how often we model behaviors for our children. When we greet someone with a friendly "hello," say "please" and "thank you," or speak confidently in social situations, our children are watching. They learn from seeing us engage in these behaviors and naturally begin to imitate them. According to SLT, the best role model for a child is themselves—if a child can see themselves performing a desired behavior, they're much more likely to repeat it in real life. This is the foundation of Video Self-Modeling.

The Power of Video Self-Modeling

How does VSM actually work? It's surprisingly simple:

1. Record your child performing a target behavior.
2. Edit the footage to show only the successful moments.

3. Have the child watch themselves in the video.

This straightforward approach is remarkably effective. Watching themselves succeed on video encourages children to replicate that behavior in real life.

For instance, to help children with selective mutism speak in the classroom, we film the child speaking comfortably with a parent in an empty classroom. Then, we film the teacher (whom the child struggles to speak to) in the same spot, asking the same questions. We merge these videos so it appears the child is speaking directly to the teacher. After watching this video repeatedly, the child gains the confidence to speak with the teacher in real life.

Considering how VSM can effectively address a phobia like selective mutism, imagine how this technique can be applied to any behavior you want to encourage. Whether it's toilet training, falling asleep independently, finishing meals before dessert, or eating in public, VSM provides a unique and effective way to guide your child's development.

Why VSM Works So Well

VSM works because it builds what psychologists call "self-efficacy"—the belief in one's ability to succeed. When kids watch themselves successfully completing a task on video, they begin to believe they can do it in real life, too.

For example, if you want your child to become more independent with their bedtime routine, you can film them brushing their teeth, changing into pajamas, and getting into bed. When they watch themselves completing each step, they develop confidence that they can do it independently. Over time, that belief translates into real-life behavior. As the saying goes: "Seeing is believing."

How to Implement VSM at Home

Implementing VSM to foster any behavior is easier than you might think. Here's a simple step-by-step process:

1. **Pick the target behavior.**

    Decide on the specific behavior you want to encourage—brushing teeth, talking to others, or following a routine.

2. **Record the behavior.**

    Use your phone or camera to film your child doing the behavior with your help or guidance.

3. **Edit the video.**

    Edit the footage to show only successful moments. Remove your guidance or prompting and focus on moments where your child gets it right.

4. **Show the video.**

    Play the video for your child regularly to reinforce the behavior.

5. **Practice and repeat.**

    Encourage your child to practice the behavior in real life and continue using VSM to reinforce their success.

Final Thoughts: A Simple, Powerful Tool for Shaping Behavior

As parents, we often try various methods to help our kids develop the behaviors we want to see. Video Self-Modeling is a simple yet powerful tool that taps into a child's natural ability to learn by observing themselves.

By helping your child see their own success, you'll build their social skills, confidence, independence, and ability to handle new challenges. So, the next time you're struggling with a behavior, try giving VSM a go. After all, the best role model your child can have might just be themselves!

Poling Bork, PhD, is an author, consultant, and researcher based in Canada. She specializes in helping parents establish desired behaviors in their children using evidence-based techniques. Her book, *VOCAL*, has been translated into ten languages within three years. Dr. Bork and all three of her children experienced a "phobia-like" social anxiety condition called selective mutism (SM), along with other comorbid disorders, including ADHD and general and social anxieties. Over the past 20 years, she has conducted cutting-edge research and pioneered the use of technology to foster speech in those with SM. Dr. Bork's mission is to continue exploring evidence-based methods and to assist those affected by SM and social anxiety to the best of her abilities. Her passion led her to found Canada's nonprofit Selective Mutism Foundation in 2017 and to develop the world's first digital games and virtual reality systems as innovative tools for SM and social anxiety. Her reputation has resulted in speaking invitations worldwide. In 2024 alone, she was invited to speak at Oxford University on how digital games may help children with mental disorders and to share her expertise at Selective Mutism Conferences in Belgium, Norway, and the USA, among other local and global events.

SECTION SIX:
SUPPORTING MENTAL WELLNESS

50

DEAR PARENTS TAKING CHILDREN TO COUNSELING

Katherine Eastlake, LPC, RPT-S

L et me share something child therapists hate: the pressure to "fix" a child. Most child therapists have extensive training working with kids, not adults. At the beginning of our careers, we feel much more comfortable with toys, art, and four-year-old fever dream pretend play! Yet, working with adults is absolutely part of our job.

It gets sticky when a parent or caregiver presents the challenge as a broken part of the child: too loud, too messy, too rebellious, too violent, too quiet, too shy, and so on.

Our challenge is helping parents see that their child doesn't need fixing. We want to shift the lens to the whole family, environment, genetics, and events in the child's life.

Read this again: child therapists struggle with feeling pressure to "fix" a child. What happens in your body as you read that sentence? I notice my stomach clenching as I even type it.

The truth is, there's nothing to fix. Your child is amazing!

When your child is struggling or contributing to conflict within the family, they are holding a vital role in human dynamics. In these heartbreaking, agonizing times, the child is actually holding the potential to spur growth within the whole family.

My work with families began in 2007 when I worked in a day treatment program. We supported kids whose struggles were so big they were asked to leave their schools. Day in and day out, these kids came to our school program and worked on their emotional health. The families were asked to show up and engage in family therapy. One family in particular lingers in my heart. I remember sitting with the two adults and child in the therapy room, the air thick with tension. I remember the eyes of each of these individuals: dad's glossy and earnest, mom's full of tears, and the son's cast down towards the floor. All three wanted things to change but were at a loss as to how to move forward. With each difficult conflict, they drew further apart from each other. Much of our work was spent honoring their love for one another and working to come closer together, one inch at a time. For this to happen, the adults in the family needed to consider how they were parented. The preteen in this family had to address his really big feelings about being adopted. It was slow and vulnerable.

I have witnessed children's struggles ignite evolution for the adults in their families over and over. One common pattern I have supported is the child who is hurting so badly inside but presents an angry or even aggressive exterior to the world. Then, as the parent begins to understand this set of opposing forces, they start to melt. The angry, violent child helps me to understand their world; I help by translating to the parent, and the parent drops their wall of fear and protection, wrapping their child in a novel, accepting embrace.

Parents realize their child isn't broken—the disconnect lies in understanding and communication.

Another component present for those parents was vulnerability. They were courageous in approaching counseling for their child as an opportunity for family growth.

Here are a few things you can expect when you take your child to see a counselor:

- **Communication**

  Child therapists will discuss the child's behaviors, family patterns, and progress toward treatment goals with you.

- **Education**

  Child therapists will help you understand the type of counseling they use; play therapy is common and developmentally appropriate for children under the age of 10.

- **Guidance**

  Child therapists will invite you into the process and collaborate with you to create suggestions for parenting at home.

As you can imagine, all three require vulnerability from you, the parent. Let me assure you that, as a child therapist, I see you. I respect and honor the bravery it takes to step into my playroom and talk about the most painful moments from the week.

When you show up with openness, I can more effectively and lastingly support your family's growth.

Here's one way to think about this: imagine your family is a houseplant. Perhaps it is a lush, lengthy pothos vine with striking lime green and white variegation. Some of the leaves begin to fade; their shape holds, but their coloring dims until the whole leaf is a weak yellow. The change in color draws your attention, and you take action. First, you seek information. While at the local nursery, you bring this issue up with a master gardener, who asks if you have recently changed water, light, or feeding habits. With some hesitation, you admit that you have never fed your pothos.

The nursery employee gets you squared away with plant food and a feeding schedule. You then teach your whole family about feeding plants. Your kids and your grandchildren learn about feeding pothos when necessary. The yellow-leaf syndrome disappears from your home.

Your child is the color change; you are seeking education and support; the acknowledgment that you never fed the plants is the vulnerability it takes to create lasting change. Your education of your family is your power to disrupt generational patterns.

Note: Sometimes, children come to counseling due to events that occurred outside the family. I would never suggest that the parent solely caused the yellow leaves. Rather, they hold the power of awareness to help create a plan to address the yellow leaves.

Seeking counseling for your child is an act of courage and hope. It can feel daunting. I encourage you to find a child therapist with whom you feel comfortable and can engage in true collaboration. Your child has the power to spur action, and you have the power to interrupt family patterns that you learned elsewhere.

Your child is not broken; your family is not broken, and with courage to collaborate, we will create a path forward.

With warmth and support,
Katherine

Katherine Eastlake lives in Corvallis, Oregon, with her husband, aging dog, 400 houseplants, and one million books. Her mission is to offer effective counseling services to children and families and sophisticated education and supervision for clinicians, all rooted in relational neuroscience. She loves weightlifting, which literally helps her keep her feet on the ground.

Katherine is a Licensed Professional Counselor, a Registered Play Therapist-Supervisor, and a Certified Synergetic Play Therapist-Supervisor. She has experience in community mental health, youth detention, adolescent day treatment, wilderness therapy for at-risk youth, school-based counseling, and her favorite—the playroom.

For more insights on collaborating with parents in play therapy, visit Katherine's website.

51

THE POWER OF CONNECTION: NAVIGATING YOUR TEEN'S DEPRESSION

Kristina Nation

T he night she disappeared, my daughter was fourteen. During a movie night, I watched her and her friends enter the theater before driving off. When I returned to pick them up, the girls weren't there. I searched the theater and called my daughter and her friends repeatedly, but no one answered.

Panicked, I called the girls' parents, my ex-husband, and my sons. Together, we combed the neighborhood and surrounding streets. Finally, one of the friends' mothers called—the girls were at my apartment. When I arrived, my daughter wasn't there. Her friends revealed they'd gone to a party with boys from the theater. They said my daughter had gotten extremely drunk and refused to leave with them.

The parents contacted the police and went to the party house, which was empty except for discarded liquor bottles and the lingering smell of weed. My ex-husband and I found a drunk boy outside, who told us my daughter had left with another group of boys. Social media led us to them, and they agreed to bring her home. At 4:00 a.m., they dropped her off in a school parking lot, alone and drunk. Her dad and brothers brought her back home.

When she walked through the door, I could only hug her. Relief washed over me. The next morning, regret and shame hit her hard. Already battling depression, she impulsively took an entire bottle of anti-anxiety medication. She reluctantly told me, and I rushed her to the ER. Thankfully, she survived.

Seeing her in the hospital brought back memories of my own depression. I had attempted suicide as a teen, and now my daughter was following a similar path.

My Depression Journey

I grew up with a mother who had bipolar disorder, and I'd been fascinated by psychology from a young age. My own struggles began at twelve, with overwhelming fatigue that kept me in bed. I dropped out of school and moved out at fourteen, but depression left me unable to work or function. Despite trying numerous medications and therapies, I felt hopeless and overdosed. My mother found me and rushed me to the hospital. Though I survived, I had to rebuild my life step by step.

Becoming a mom at seventeen gave me purpose, but my struggles continued. In my late twenties, a new medication finally worked, allowing me to experience happiness for the first time. Medication isn't a cure-all, but for me, it was life changing.

My Daughter's Depression Journey

Knowing the genetic link to mental health issues, I wasn't surprised when my daughter began struggling at the same age I had. A dedicated gymnast for ten years, she quit at fourteen, losing her identity and social life. By sixteen, her depression and suicidal thoughts became severe. She called me to pick her up from school almost daily, unable to cope.

Despite my experience as a behavior specialist and parent coach, I had tools to help, but nothing seemed to work. Counseling, medications, and alternative schooling options failed. Her risky behavior escalated. I knew she was drinking, using drugs, and sometimes not coming home. Our relationship became strained, and I lived in constant fear.

Through intensive treatment and support, my daughter began to improve. She earned her GED, went to college, and is now thriving. Her journey taught me the power of resilience and support.

Finding Light in Darkness

Today, my daughter is an advocate for mental health, sharing her story to inspire others. Supporting a struggling teen is daunting, but it's one of the most important roles a parent can have. Here are strategies that helped us:

- **Take a multifaceted approach.**

  Recovery often requires a combination of therapy, medication, alternative schooling, and healthy coping mechanisms. Replace unhealthy habits, like substance use or self-harm, with positive strategies. Parents can't fix this alone. It takes a network of qualified help. You're there as the foundation of unconditional love and support.

- **Notice risky behaviors.**

  Watch for signs of depression, such as alcohol or drug use, self-harm, or sudden disinterest in school. A refusal to go to school can be a major indicator of depression. Open the dialogue early and often.

- **Build a strong connection.**

  A healthy parent-teen relationship is vital. Even in difficult times, nurture that bond so your teen feels safe opening up. Focus on the relationship, not the behavior. Spend quality time with your teen and ask them how you can best support them.

- **Seek specialized help.**

  Therapists, parent coaches, and school counselors can provide guidance tailored to your situation.

- **Self-regulate emotions.**

  Managing your own emotions helps you navigate high-stress situations and model emotional regulation for your teen. These skills enable you to teach your teen how to self-regulate and de-escalate stressful, tense, heated moments.

- **Advocate for safety.**

    If your teen is a danger to themselves, create a safety plan. Remove potential tools for self-harm, explore therapy, and consider 504 plans or IEPs at school.

- **Believe it can get better.**

    Depression is a lifelong journey, but it can become manageable. With the right support, life can be fulfilling and happy. Have hope and faith that your child will build resilience. Know you are not alone!

After the Darkness

Helping my daughter through her depression was one of the hardest things I've ever done, but it shaped me as a parent and professional. Today, I specialize in helping parents of teens navigate depression. I've created The Power of Everyday GRACE program to teach parents how to connect with, support, and advocate for their struggling teens.

There is hope. My mom got better, I got better, and my daughter got better. With support, resilience, and love, light can break through even the darkest moments.

Kristina Nation is a best-selling author, international speaker, and parent coach dedicated to helping families of teens struggling with depression. With a degree in Youth Development and years of experience as a youth and family therapist and a parent coach, Kristina provides parents with the tools to connect with, support, and advocate for their teens. Her mission is to empower families with practical strategies and guidance, foster stronger relationships, and create lasting transformations.

Kristina's mission is to empower parents with the knowledge, tools, and confidence to deeply connect with their teens, provide unwavering support, and advocate effectively for their mental and emotional well-being. She is a mother of four, a foster mother, and hosts international students. She loves to travel and to curl up with a good book.

52

SCREEN-DAMAGED BRAINS: WHAT EVERY PARENT OF YOUNG CHILDREN NEEDS TO KNOW

Dr. Carrie Mackensen

"**A** brain hooked on the internet, phones, or tablets looks like a brain hooked on heroin," says Dr. David R. Rosenberg, who has extensively studied the impact of screens on developing brains.

Recent MRI studies of preschool-aged children reveal alarming evidence about how screens and digital media affect structural brain development. The processing centers of children raised on screens differ from those of children who spend less time on devices. Moreover, screen time strengthens the brain's reward center, increasing the likelihood of addiction. Children are not only becoming addicted to devices now but are also more likely to develop addictions to other vices later in life due to increased interactive screen time. The evidence is clear: screens and digital media limit your children's brain development, manifesting in behaviors you don't want to see.

The Transformation of Childhood

Parenting is challenging enough, yet parents complicate matters by using screens as digital pacifiers. Well-intentioned parents often remain unaware of how these devices damage their children's personality development, cognitive function, impulse control, and emotional regulation. After the iPad's introduction in 2010, I noticed a dramatic shift in my private practice around 2013. Parents began reporting unusually explosive emotional outbursts in their children. While these outbursts were clearly abnormal, they were becoming increasingly common—even the new "norm." Having worked with children since 1997, I knew this wasn't typical behavior. Something had fundamentally changed.

With decades of experience, including a Ph.D. in Individual, Family, and Child Psychology, working at prestigious institutions and K-12 schools, private practice, and serving as Clinical Director of treatment programs, I was able to identify these abnormalities. Though anyone could see this cultural transformation, it was evident everywhere. Children sit zoned out in front of screens while their parents chat over dinner in restaurants. In grocery store checkout lines, two-year-olds in shopping carts stare, mesmerized by their mother's iPhone, its flashing lights and rapidly moving images capturing their undivided attention. We've traded presence for pixels. Parents give their children screens to buy uninterrupted time; however, they are unaware of the lasting impact on their child's brain development and subsequent behaviors, attention, personality, and emotional regulation.

Reclaiming Our Role as Parents

Parenting isn't meant to be convenient—it's an active commitment that requires our presence and dedication. While screens offer an easy escape from the challenges of raising children, our role as parents calls for something more. Our children deserve our best: not passive supervision that keeps our lives undisturbed, but active engagement that helps them reach their full potential. Yes, this path demands more from us, but watching our children grow into resilient, well-adjusted individuals who thrive is the greatest reward any parent could receive. It far exceeds any challenges faced along the way.

Of all parenting challenges, protecting our child's developing brain from the damaging impact of screens and reclaiming real-life connections is remarkably straightforward. While it may seem impossible, it's like picking low-hanging fruit on the parenting tree—easily within reach and yielding abundant positive changes. You don't need special training or complicated techniques. You simply need to start choosing presence over pixels by saying "no" to screens and "yes" to real-world engagement and connection.

The Science Behind Screen Impact

Brain imaging reveals how screens are literally reshaping the structure of our children's developing brains. MRI studies show troubling differences in brain regions essential for healthy development—areas needed for attention, emotional regulation, social connection, and learning to read. Children with more screen time show weaker language skills, slower thinking speeds, and less ability to regulate emotions. Think of a child's brain like a muscle—it grows stronger through exercise (real-life engagement) and weaker without it (when engaged on an interactive screen). Every moment spent on screens is a moment lost for the real-world interactions that build healthy brains and promote well-adjusted behavior.

The Presence Over Pixels Approach

While this research is concerning, there's hope. In my clinical practice, I've witnessed remarkable transformations in children aged 3-5 simply by implementing a digital detox and guiding parents in setting healthy boundaries around interactive screens. These changes inspired me to develop the Presence Over Pixels approach through years of clinical work. This practical method helps families shift from screen dependency to real connection while supporting healthy brain development. Rather than promoting complete screen elimination, it guides parents in making intentional choices that limit screen time, hand-select content, and prioritize presence, connection, and engagement over interactive screen time. While you should expect resistance initially—usually peaking around days three or four—most families see remarkable improvements within weeks.

The CARE Steps: Your Connection Roadmap

Step 1: Create space.

- Create presence-rich zones and times. While no parent can always be fully present, our children don't need screens to pacify them. Instead of handing your child a tablet or saying yes to video games, offer ideas and activities that engage their creativity, interests, and skills.

- Remove devices from bedrooms and mealtimes. Establish a house rule that children are never allowed to use screens behind closed doors in their bedrooms and that no family member should use screens during meals. Aside from television screens on the wall, portable devices should be stored out of sight to reduce temptation.

Step 2: Activate interest.

- Offer engaging alternatives to screen time. Keep puzzles, books, art supplies, blocks, and board games easily visible and accessible. Encourage outdoor play and physical activities.

- Participate to make activities appealing. Set aside short periods, even just 5-10 minutes, to engage fully with your child. Say something like, "Let's build something together!" and honor that commitment.

- Create a rotation of activities that includes independent and collaborative options, refreshing them regularly to maintain novelty and interest.

Step 3: Regulate emotions.

- Help children process emotions through presence.
- Name feelings and offer comfort.

- Stay calm and steadfast through initial outbursts.
- Use supportive language: "I see you're upset. I'm here. Let's take deep breaths together."

Step 4: Engage fully.

- Replace screen time with connected presence.
- Begin with short play sessions.
- Watch as attention spans grow naturally.
- Create special time: "This is our time together—you choose what we do!"

The Path Forward

The journey from pixels to presence isn't always easy, but the rewards are profound. As you practice the CARE steps, you'll see positive changes in your child's behavior, attention, and emotional connection. Most parents report that after the initial adjustment, their children appear happier, more creative, better at entertaining themselves, and more emotionally balanced—the whole family feels happier and more connected. Remember, as you maintain firm screen time boundaries, each moment of presence is an investment in your child's brain development and family bonds.

Your child's brain needs real-world experiences to thrive, and by choosing presence over pixels today, you're giving them the best possible foundation for success. The power to shape your child's future is in your hands, and it starts with one simple choice: presence over screens. Start today with one screen-free hour and build from there.

Dr. Carrie Mackensen (known affectionately as "Dr. Carrie" by her clients) brings 25 years of clinical expertise and real-world experience as both a psychologist and a mother of two boisterous boys. Her diverse background spans Cedars Sinai Hospital, K-12 schools, private practices in Beverly Hills and Manhattan Beach, and serving as Clinical Director for premier treatment programs. With a Ph.D. in Individual, Family, and Child Psychology, Dr. Carrie combines professional wisdom with the practical insights of a "battle-tested" mom, offering evidence-based strategies with warmth and humor. She understands that parents sometimes need an expert's perspective and at other times just need to hear, "I've been there too." Through her parent coaching business, Successful Parent: The Science-Backed Blueprint for Raising Emotionally Healthy, Resilient Kids, she helps families navigate modern parenting challenges through her practice, workshops, and online community.

For additional resources and support, visit www.successfulparent. com to download your free copy of "A Parent's Guide to Better Tech Boundaries" and join our community of parents committed to raising mentally healthy children in the digital age.

SECTION SEVEN:
FAMILY ADAPTATION AND TRANSITIONS

53

FINDING THE SCHOOL THAT FITS YOUR CHILD, NOT YOU

Siury Pulgar

A manda rented a two-bedroom apartment near a Trader Joe's in San Jose, California. She walked her son Nico to the playground and biked with him to his independent elementary school. In 2020, she and her husband joined the exodus of families leaving the Bay Area for towns with bigger homes and lower mortgages. Their search started with the best school districts in Texas. The numbers made sense: lower cost of living, free, quality public education. They started packing.

Two months and a down payment later, they moved into a spacious four-bedroom home within walking distance of the public school with the highest online rating. They felt elated.

However, when school started in the fall, Nico struggled, and Amanda did not feel connected to the parent community. The educational approach was new and unfamiliar. The homework load was unexpected, and while the teachers were understanding, they could not make significant changes. What to do now?

The family could not afford private school fees with the new mortgage, and moving to another district was not an option. The school was supposed to work. There was no plan B.

Amanda and Nico's story is not uncommon. According to a 2023 Gallup survey, Americans' view of public education is at a record low, so many families spend more time weighing attributes that differentiate their options. Some of these attributes are the quality of the curriculum, commute time, graduation rate, diversity in the school, parents' reviews, standardized test results, and a series of complex factors that put a heavy burden on parents. The process can be overwhelming, time-consuming, and stressful.[23]

Families from all socioeconomic backgrounds find themselves facing similar challenges. A 2024 study from Carnegie Mellon University looked at how we make school decisions and revealed that parents are not always aware of the factors that influence their selections. The researchers looked at decades of psychological research and conducted new interviews where participants had to choose from hypothetical school attributes. The authors found that, despite investing time and energy, we rely on the wrong information, which may lead to regrettable school choices.[24] There must be a better way—one that is more manageable and effective.

My Top Five Suggestions

Based on my conversations over the years with families, school leaders, and education experts, both as a parent coach and as a mom, I have gathered recommendations to help you find the best learning environment for your children.

1. Start with your child.

Finding a school begins with understanding who your student is, not who you "wish" they were. Ask these questions: When is my child the happiest, and where is she? What kind of people are around? What is he doing? When my child feels confident and empowered, what kind of interactions is she having? How does he engage with the new and unfamiliar? Does he take time to warm up or jump right in? Remember, children change over time, and the right environment celebrates their uniqueness as is while also helping them stretch out of their comfort zones.

2. Develop your non-negotiable list.

Let's break this down because family values tend to cloud everything else. As parents, we are tempted to start here, fearing our children will somehow be swayed away from what we consider essential. I get it. However, a great school attracts diverse teachers and staff whose primary job is to respect and welcome the rich differences their students and families bring. Therefore, what makes a school special is not that it perfectly aligns with your views but that it celebrates what you and others contribute.

3. Identify their approach to learning.

This is the hardest to fully grasp before formally joining the school. Recruitment officers already know what marketing buzzwords capture our attention, so we are flooded with terms like whole-child approach, blended, interdisciplinary, or project-based learning. Instead, I suggest you ask these questions: What does learning look like? How do subjects relate? What role does the student's personhood play? How is progress measured? What is the definition of success? How are students supported?

4. Be wary of online reviews and rankings.

School reviews provide perspectives from parents who may prioritize different aspects than you do and whose children learn and interact with the world in unique ways. While relying on online reviews may seem beneficial initially, it could steer you away from a school worth considering. Similarly, school rankings often rely on a list of variables that may not reflect what is important to you.

Additionally, in the United States, housing prices tend to rise when schools receive high rankings. Higher property values lead to increased funding for local public schools through taxes. Private schools also benefit, as rankings attract more affluent families to their neighborhoods. Therefore, it's clear that educational institutions have a commercial incentive to inflate their online ratings.

5. Go beyond the open house.

Connecting with teachers, administrators, parents, and students is a powerful strategy. You and your child will gain a genuine understanding of the school community. Is it welcoming and respectful? Do students seem to matter for who they are, not just for their achievements? Interact informally to obtain candid answers. For instance, when issues arise, what is the school's approach? Are they responsive? Are they easy to reach? Do you feel heard?

What if You Still Have Doubts?

Choosing a school is a significant commitment. If you are still unsure, consider asking yourself:

- Do I see my child growing beyond her own perceived limits?
- Do I like this place for the right reasons, or am I trying to fulfill my own dreams?
- When challenges arise, will this community offer us the right support?
- Is this an environment where my child will feel valued and can add value?

If you answered "Yes" to these questions, congratulations—you've found a great school. If you're still uncertain, keep looking. Be intentional and involve your child in the process. You are not alone; millions of parents are on the same journey. We are collectively cheering for you.

Siury Pulgar is a parent and education coach passionate about helping families navigate the complexities of parenting and school selection. With a master's degree in International Education Policy from Harvard Graduate School of Education, she combines academic expertise with real-world experience to support parents in building strong, lasting connections with their children. As a mother of two middle school-aged daughters, Siury understands firsthand the challenges of raising children in today's fast-paced world. Her work empowers parents to make informed educational decisions without succumbing to societal pressures or unnecessary stress. Through her coaching, she provides practical guidance on fostering meaningful relationships, choosing the right school, and creating a balanced family dynamic.

Having experienced parenting in a new country, Siury is dedicated to making the process of raising and educating children less overwhelming and more fulfilling. She currently runs her own consulting firm, helping parents find clarity and confidence in their choices.

Ready to strengthen your connection with your child and easily navigate school decisions? Visit https://www.siurypulgar.com/free-gift for a special bonus.

54

HOW TO HELP YOUR TEEN ADJUST TO A NEW ENVIRONMENT– SCHOOL, TOWN, CULTURE

Faramalala Ravaoarimanga

When your teen is adjusting to a new culture, school, or town, talk less and listen more.

I will never forget the time my family and I moved from Madagascar to the United States. My 14-year-old daughter, Judith, would sob every evening and say, "Mama, I want to go home. I don't want to stay here." Judith felt disoriented and frustrated as she faced an unfamiliar environment and a new culture. As she poured out her confusion, anxiety, and feelings of isolation in tears, my heart sank. I understood how she was trying to fit in while also wanting to escape the pain caused by cultural shock. These moments were opportunities for Judith to learn and grow. They were painful at the time, but they fostered frustration tolerance and resilience in her.

After a couple of years of adapting to a new culture, Judith embraced a third one and was able to navigate cultural challenges by balancing both individualistic and collectivistic values. She now has a master's degree in Information Systems and is currently pursuing her second master's degree. Supporting Judith during her challenging times and adversities has fostered a great deal of patience and empathy in me. I can share what to do when your child experiences disorientation and anxiety while facing a new environment or unfamiliar culture.

The Cost of Adjusting to a New Environment/Culture

The whole family was excited when we moved to the U.S. While my husband, our oldest daughter, and I were classmates in clinical psychology at a university in North Carolina, Judith attended high school by herself. The three of us adults were always together and had visited the U.S. several times before. Hence, adopting a new culture was not an issue for us. In fact, it was fun! However, we soon realized that a teenager's feelings and perspectives differ from an adult's.

Stepping into the unknown was uncomfortable for Judith. Anxiety hit her as she thought about being in a new school, making new friends, not knowing anyone in the classroom, and sitting alone in the cafeteria. Additionally, learning a third language (note that Malagasy is her first language and French her second) along with intense cultural differences brought significant distress to Judith.

The Adolescent Brain

Adolescence is the most difficult period in one's life due to significant changes, including physical, hormonal, emotional, and cognitive shifts. The brain is still maturing, making adolescents more sensitive to stress and change, which likely intensifies their anxiety responses. Adults may not recognize this sensitivity and vulnerability when adolescents leave their friends behind and move into unfamiliar environments.

Research on adolescents navigating acculturation suggests that early adolescence is the phase when they begin to build their cultural values, which encompass beliefs, emotional expression, peer interactions, and self-understanding as individuals and members of society. Consequently, a sudden change can lead to real disorientation.

Listen More, Talk Less

Let's revisit the evenings when Judith would constantly sob, pouring her heart out to me. My first instinct was to provide a rationale: "Your whole family is here. You can't go back home by yourself and stay there alone ..."

However, these phrases did not help Judith at all. She still came home from school in tears. I was overwhelmed too, unsure of how to support her. I prayed and gave myself grace. In the following evenings, I became more aware that my rationales and solutions were not what Judith needed. I decided to sit with her, wrapping my arms around her, and listening to her concerns. In fact, I refrained from speaking, allowing her to decompress and cry. I would then empathize with her: "That's tough! It must be difficult to leave your friends back home and make new ones here! Plus, the language is new to you, and I can see your struggles and frustrations!" Things began to improve although there were still ups and downs.

Empathy is more effective than logic or suggestions when emotions are heightened during stress because cortisol impacts the prefrontal cortex, decreasing its functionality. When individuals feel heard in a safe space through someone's unconditional positive regard, empathy, or validation, their intense feelings will calm down. Thus, emotional regulation occurs, and the prefrontal cortex is reactivated, allowing for rational thinking and a readiness to welcome any advice. While active listening, empathy, and validation may yield success, your child is still likely to revert to overwhelming feelings when feeling anxious. Therefore, continuously implementing empathetic listening skills can help alleviate their emotional distress.

One enemy you should not allow space for when experiencing setbacks is guilt and self-condemnation.

Challenges Turning into Opportunities

In addition to listening and empathy, taking Judith to visit her new school before it started helped her familiarize herself with the environment. We also arranged for her to meet her teachers and introduce herself to them. As homesickness subsided, she enrolled in extracurricular activities, particularly music and choir, which were essential for building friendships.

The choir performed at various venues in North Carolina, providing her with opportunities to make friends who shared common interests. I encouraged her, as a daily practice, to approach other kids and say "hi" to initiate conversations and show interest in them. The more she practiced this, the more confident she became in socializing.

You Can't Pour from an Empty Cup

When your children are facing long-term challenges in adjusting to a new environment, they need parental support. This connection is vital for both the child and the parent. However, prolonged crises can lead to compassion fatigue for parents. As a therapist, I discovered that providing emotional support to one's child for an extended period can be more taxing than seeing a long-term client in therapy sessions. At times, I felt emotionally exhausted witnessing my daughter's pain and overwhelm.

Here are some self-care strategies that reinforced my coping mechanisms, which may benefit you as well:

- **Engaging with family and friends** who are not directly involved in Judith's crisis; talking with them helped relieve my burdens.
- **Praying** individually and with family, along with meditation.
- **Journaling** my feelings and thoughts daily.
- Coming from a collectivistic culture, our family would often **go for walks together, play** basketball, or sing with a guitar.

In working with families, couples, and parents, I have noted that people are quick to speak but seldom take the time to listen. In day-to-day life, it is easy to attempt to fix our children's problems by giving advice when they approach us with intense feelings.

Active listening, empathy, and emotional validation are skills that every parent—including me—needs to master. These skills are not only for mental health professionals but are essential for every parent to help support their children and teenagers, whose emotions tend to be more intense and frequent than those of adults. This aligns with the statement by Alfred Adler: "Empathy is seeing with the eyes of another, listening with the ears of another, and feeling with the heart of another."

Faramalala Ravaoarimanga is a Licensed Professional Counselor Resident offering therapy services in Virginia. She is a doctoral candidate in Clinical Pastoral Counseling. Ravaoarimanga has taught over 1,000 parents in Madagascar to hug and positively affirm their children daily—behaviors not traditionally part of the culture. This led to improved school grades and a decrease in bed-wetting among the children. Additionally, she has helped thousands of individuals, both abroad and in the United States, facilitate self-discovery and develop self-worth. Her approach combines cognitive behavioral therapy, dialectical behavior therapy, and person-centered therapy. With a deep understanding of integrating Christianity into clinical practice,

Ravaoarimanga lives in Virginia with her husband and has two daughters, a son-in-law, and two grandchildren. Download the 10 steps to follow when you empathize with your child at https://www.ny-balsama.com/10tipstoempathizewithyourchild.

55

PIVOT TURN

Pamela Ladas

——

At 41, I had to choose between the love of my life and having children. He didn't want any, and I couldn't wait any longer. You may have two questions.

First: Why did I wait so long?

Answer: I always thought I had time, as all the women in my family had babies in their forties.

Second: If he was the love of my life, why didn't he agree to have children?

Answer: Good point.

My biggest question was: What do I do now? I wanted to pursue my dream of becoming a mother. I still had time, right?

Sadly, I found myself again with another man who seemed on board but was not. But being without a partner didn't have to mean being childless, right?

This was my pivot turn: I had to re-envision my path toward motherhood.

Inspired by the Single Mothers by Choice organization, I decided it was time to make my dream come true. I applied to adopt, created an album for birth parents to get to know me, and conducted extensive research on where I could adopt a newborn as a single parent.

I landed in Mexico with a lawyer who handled private adoptions and began my long wait for a birth mother to choose me. The waiting. The suspense. The disappointment.

Part of my work was to start creating my reality by living as if the adoption had already taken place. I prepared a room for my baby, pictured us together, wrote her songs and poems, drew her pictures, and even dreamed about her magically looking just like I imagined.

My soul stretched out over the sea to connect with hers. I knew in my heart my baby would be Mexican. I even passed up adoption opportunities in the U.S. because I was so certain. We were already connected.

We have come together, you and me, wing tips touching across the sea. The flight of our souls brought your heart to mine. I have waited for you for the longest time.

One hot day in August, I got the call! A birth mother had chosen me! Miraculously, I was able to talk to her on the phone and even meet her in Tijuana. The moment she saw me, she knew I was the one. I looked just like her Godmother, and she was sure.

Six long months, five court dates, ten airplane rides, ten different beds, and a thousand boiled bottles later, we arrived in the United States. The flower of my heart was now a U.S. citizen, and I was devoted to her for a lifetime.

Fast forward four years, and I find myself eager for another child. This time, I thought I'd try to conceive. And yet ... how did I become 48 years old? But hey, I can still do this, right? Unfortunately, my fallopian tubes disagreed, as they were blocked. My doctors declared I was too old.

That's when I decided to pivot toward what might bring me success again. Not the conventional route. Not what I always thought would be my path. But the one I now choose to pursue.

I decided to go all out with IVF and a donor egg. Should I do it? Will it still feel like my baby? You bet! I have an adopted daughter, and she is mine as much as any daughter could ever be. Call it wholehearted, pig-headed, determined, or guided, but I went for it. Thirty-five weeks later, my youngest was born, healthy and strong.

Not of my blood nor of my seed, but from my love you were conceived. It was not biology, but boundless grace brought you to me.

And now, the truly heroic work began.

Learning to Pivot as a Mother

I spent so much time figuring out how to become a mother but hadn't learned how to BE a mother. So, I read dozens of books, attended seminars and webinars, and joined several parenting communities. I learned and grew, realizing that the very qualities it took to become a mother could also help me be the best version of a mother: dedication and perseverance, of course; never giving up on my girls or my journey to parent them well; and the ability to pivot. The capacity to reimagine and reinvent outside-the-box solutions, to rewire long-ingrained responses, and turn toward a more successful version of myself who allows imagination, passion, and creativity to inspire a path forward—even when there seem to be insurmountable walls in the way.

But what to pivot from and toward? Here are some strategies that have worked for me—not immediately, not easily, but undoubtedly successfully:

1. From blame to apology

This can be so hard! But when I set aside my pride and acknowledge my part in a disagreement, it creates space for my daughters to respond in kind. Not readily, but over time. I was floored recently when my daughter said, "You know, Mom, none of that was really about you; I'm sorry."

2. From anger to calm

This is certainly one of the hardest transitions. Anger is an all-consuming beast, with clutches so strong it's hard to let go. What has worked best for me is what I learned from *Calm the Chaos*: practicing out of the moment. I can't remember what to do when I'm in fight or flight and totally flooded! My anchor is, "This is not the time; I can return to this." I anticipate when I might get triggered and practice beforehand. Thank you, Dayna Abraham!

3. From telling to asking

I have Cecilia Hilkey of Happily Family to thank for encouraging me to move from criticism and judgment to questions. When I feel the urge to evaluate and insert my opinion, I pivot to ask my daughters what they think and whether they want my feedback.

4. From demand to fun

I'm continually working on engaging my girls to find creative, mutually satisfying, and even fun solutions. During a recent homework skirmish, I asked, "Can you think of a way that learning these spelling words can be fun?" My daughter came up with a brilliant game: "Whenever I get a word right, we search for a song with that word as its title." We found outrageous songs and got through the list between fits of laughter.

5. From perfection to peace

How can I accept my imperfections and regressions and be at peace making progress, one (sometimes messy) step at a time?

None of this means I ignore the feelings involved. Feelings often intensify when dismissed and dissipate when acknowledged, accepted, and heard. However, it means turning to another path, even when I might not know how. Sometimes, the pivot is not the polar opposite but a variation on the theme.

There are many ways to create a family and unlimited definitions of what makes a family. There are numerous paths toward success as a parent. The key is to find strategies that work for each of us; to forgive ourselves for mistakes and take gradual but diligent steps toward the parent we want to be, to introspect and make internal changes that will reflect externally. When things aren't working, we can always make a pivot turn.

Pamela Ladas is a proud mother of two powerful, dynamic, and inspiring daughters: Coriandra, age 17, and Kailina, age 12. She has dedicated her adult life to helping others, first through her work as a fitness trainer and massage therapist, and then as a doctor of Oriental medicine and teacher. For the last 20 years, she has been an enthusiastic dance instructor for the National Dance Institute of New Mexico, where she teaches children determination, self-confidence, teamwork, and fortitude through dance and performance. Pamela is an avid athlete and health enthusiast, particularly enjoying outdoor athletic adventures. Her greatest accomplishment is creating her family and being a mother to her girls. She will forever be grateful to the birth mother and egg donor who helped make this dream come true. Her greatest wish for her daughters is that they have the inspiration, courage, and resilience to follow their hearts and unique paths.

56

NAVIGATING THE PATH TO SUPPORTING INDIGENOUS CHILDREN

Jean LaFauci Schutt, Ph.D.

As an Italian American counselor trained in and centering multiculturalism and social justice, I am aware of the needs of children from cultures different from mine. However, through parenting multi-ethnic children via adoption, I have learned more about the systems in which I was raised, the inaccuracies in education, the harmful effects of cultural appropriation, and the need for ongoing advocacy.

Indigenous peoples and Native Americans, especially where we live, are somewhat of an invisible minority group. In my experience, Native Americans are often treated as a group from the past, while they represent a thriving and resilient community of many nations (currently 574 federally recognized tribes) within our country; this does not include Indigenous peoples throughout the world. I share my learning, which is an ongoing work in progress, to assist adoptive parents from different backgrounds who are raising Indigenous children, as well as all individuals who care about children, in empowering advocacy and connecting with and changing our systems. This is critical for positive mental health, identity development, and creating welcoming, safe spaces for all.

I am a mother through adoption to two children of multiple cultural backgrounds, including Northern Arapaho and Cheyenne River Sioux (Lakota). Our younger child qualified for tribal membership and is an enrolled citizen of his nation. Despite living in a multicultural area, we are addressing issues of racism and discrimination for our children's marginalized identities, as well as insensitive and stereotypical portrayals of Indigenous peoples and inaccuracies that are ingrained in American culture.

First, what we learned in school about Native Americans was likely inaccurate, missing information, and informed by a White-European American colonialist viewpoint. You don't know what you don't know, so there is a need to educate oneself about Tribal Nations and general Native American issues and to re-examine—from Indigenous viewpoints—what we learned.

An example of not knowing about something and not being respectful happened to us following the birth of our second son. While we were in South Dakota for his birth, we felt that we needed to visit Mount Rushmore. Later, we learned that this national monument is on sacred land, "The Six Grandfathers," stolen from the Lakota Sioux. At the time, we did not think about the fact that it celebrates individuals who endorsed the killing of Native Americans, trying to eliminate their culture and land rights. In retrospect, I wish we had been more cognizant of the history when visiting and could have approached it with greater understanding. The Crazy Horse Memorial, honoring Tasunke Witco of the Oglala Lakota, who protected his people, was on our list of places to visit; however, we never made it there—something I wish we had prioritized.

When educating oneself, learning from Indigenous sources or Indigenous-endorsed sources is best. One starting resource to learn more is *An Indigenous Peoples' History of the United States* by Roxanne Dunbar-Ortiz. It is also important to recognize that holidays you grew up celebrating, such as Columbus Day, Thanksgiving, and Independence Day, may cause pain to—or not be celebrated by—Indigenous individuals, and to educate others about this. What we have found is that these holidays are often presented in schools with false narratives and culturally appropriated, uninformed ways that are hurtful to Indigenous peoples. There are resources available on Columbus and Thanksgiving to help include Native voices and shed light on the inaccuracies. For some Native Americans, Independence Day represents colonialism, and since their ancestors have been living on Turtle Island before it became the United States, it is not always a celebratory day. As a family, we try to use it to honor what is good about our country while also acknowledging the past and needed changes. Additional acknowledgment and action—knowing and honoring the Indigenous presence and land you live on and engaging with and committing to action and changes (e.g., education about sovereignty, Indigenous reparations)—is also a critical practice.

If you are not Indigenous and are raising or supporting an Indigenous child, it is important to connect them to their Tribal Nation(s) and Indigenous individuals as much as possible. As in all transracial adoptions, we incorporate books, music, objects, food, etc., from our children's cultures into our family culture. With social media and websites, it is also becoming somewhat easier to connect with Tribal Nations, at least for basic information.

Additionally, it is critical to be aware of your privileges and how they may play out in terms of cultural appropriation. I have seen instances where individuals or institutions take pieces of Indigenous cultures without having a connection to them or truly understanding them. Examples include a farm putting up teepees for a "photo op" area, having children make dream catchers without explaining the history and purpose, wearing "mohawk" hairstyles without considering that the style was created for individuals who protected their nation, and individuals "dressing up" as Native Americans in regalia-like attire. In Indigenous cultures, for anyone to wear their traditional dress/regalia as a costume is disrespectful. Furthermore, native phrases and terms have been misused and appropriated into American culture; this likely unintended incivility should be avoided and advocated against. Examples of this include having a "pow-wow," "find your tribe," "this is my spirit animal," "went on the warpath," and "too many chiefs."

Another place where I see privilege and disrespect play out is in the use of Native mascots and related imagery. Research (e.g., Davis-Delano, Gone, and Fryberg 2020) has shown that Native American mascots harm both Indigenous (e.g., lowers self-esteem) and non-Indigenous (e.g., promotes stereotypes) people. This cultural appropriation continues the power imbalance and reinforces stereotypes, perpetuating the idea that Indigenous cultures are in the past while alienating minority cultures.[25]

It is important to also be aware that Indigenous as well as Black children and children of color are often viewed as older than their actual age or threatening. Research (e.g., Priest, et al. 2018) has found substantial racial stereotyping and negative attitudes towards young children of color among white adults who work with them; we have unfortunately found this to be true. It is critical to explore and be aware of our own biases, educate those working with children, and advocate when noticing unjust treatment.[26]

Finally, as a Catholic, I struggle with the Church's history with Indigenous peoples, especially the Doctrine of Discovery and the trauma and cultural erasure at boarding schools. Fortunately, our government has started to acknowledge this. I hope we can continue to address the pains and wrongs of the past as we work toward reconciliation and healing.

There are many resources (books, websites, and organizations) available to help support Indigenous children, educate others, and advocate for change. I invite you to conduct your own research to locate resources specific to Tribal Nations and to connect with and listen to Native voices to learn about their diversity. I have learned much and will continue to learn on my parenting journey.

Jean M. LaFauci Schutt, a doctoral-level licensed and nationally certified professional counselor and supervisor, has over twenty years of experience in the counseling field, specializing in disaster mental health, traumatic stress, multiculturalism, supervision, and training. She has worked as a counselor, clinical supervisor, professor, researcher, and consultant in educational, social service, clinical, and community settings. Dr. LaFauci has conducted training and presentations for in-service staff, as well as national and international audiences, and has published in peer-reviewed journals and newsletters. She currently serves as an associate editor for *Trauma Counseling and Resilience*, the journal of the International Association for Resilience and Trauma Counseling, a division of the American Counseling Association. Dr. LaFauci is a mother of two children through adoption and has been part of a research team that explored adoption as a diversity issue in the preparation of counselors and teachers. Her current focus is on education and advocacy for paradigm shifts in schools and other settings to promote trauma-informed, relational, and positive neuroscience-backed approaches to supporting all children. Dr. LaFauci has learned and grown tremendously through her parenting journey, as much as, or even more than, through her years of education.

57

THRIVING PAST THE DISABILITY DIAGNOSIS

Jessica Wayt

W hile sipping hot tea from a mug that urges me to "Seize the Day," I reminisce about a day I didn't want to seize or even accept. It was my daughter Chloe's routine well-check visit. Chloe had survived a traumatic full-term birth three years earlier, arriving blue and not breathing. That story alone could fill a book, but that's for another time. After spending a few harrowing weeks in a children's hospital, where doctors recommended that we take her off life support, Chloe's unwavering will to live shone through. She proved her resilience, defying the odds, and was sent home with oxygen and a nasal feeding tube. Not long after, she yanked out both the oxygen and the feeding tube. With the nurse's permission, we decided to temporarily leave the tubes out, and Chloe continued to breathe steadily on her own and even began to take a bottle and nurse a little.

Chloe was a determined little girl and a true fighter. Although progress was neither easy nor swift, she made strides bit by bit. Even so, she remained significantly delayed, and in those early years, the pediatrician, case managers, and therapists frequently said, "She has developmental delays." As parents, we initially found that phrase harmless enough—after all, if they were "developmental" delays, wouldn't she eventually develop those needed skills and abilities? However, with each passing well-check visit, it became discouragingly clear that Chloe was not meeting many milestones "on time."

Reflecting on that life-altering well-check visit when Chloe was three, the kindly, grandfatherly pediatrician we had come to know well over the years conducted some examinations and basic preschooler assessments before leaving the room to do some research. When he returned, he informed me that Chloe's developmental disabilities likely fell under the category of cerebral palsy. I had no idea what that meant, and I remember very little of what was said beyond that point, other than him saying, "But it's okay, things are changing, and children now typically continue to live with their parents rather than going to an institution." I was in shock and probably speechless, although my mind was swirling with thoughts like a brewing hurricane.

Telling my husband that night brought us both to tears, although we didn't fully understand what we were crying about at the time. The fear of the unknown diagnosis and the grief over losing the dream of a "normal" life for our daughter and ourselves was raw and brutal. If you've been there, you know it is a true grieving process that must be navigated. However, while the diagnosis brought uncertainty and shattered dreams, it also provided the faintest silver lining that we couldn't see in that dark valley—because of the diagnosis that tore our hearts in half, Chloe could begin receiving the assistance needed to help her gain more abilities, skills, and independence.

Before the official diagnosis, Chloe had already shown her determination to move around. One of her grandpas made her a tiny wooden cube chair, and she would scoot it all around our little house. Seeing her determination, her other grandpa came up with the idea to make a similar-style chair with casters on it. Once she had that, she started zooming around the house with the biggest smile and giggle. Unfortunately, the preschool wouldn't let her use her custom-made chair at school, deeming it unsafe and too much of a liability.

As we navigated the next steps following Chloe's diagnosis, the process seemed daunting, but we found ourselves grateful for the support that began to come our way. Chloe received her first real manual wheelchair, which allowed her to ride the bus to public preschool. She also got a specialized walker and tiny custom-fitted braces for her feet and ankles. She qualified for more therapies than she had previously received. These services and adaptive equipment were incredibly expensive and beyond our means, given that we lived in an expensive area and relied solely on Chloe's dad's bus driving and teaching salaries. The blessing of having insurance cover these costs made all the difference. This crucial support was only possible because of the official diagnosis, which ensured that these essential items were correctly coded for insurance coverage.

Chloe's journey over the past 20 years has been nothing short of remarkable. She has surpassed milestones we never dared to dream of, proving time and again that she will not be limited. Would you look at Chloe and think she is a typical young lady? No, the wheelchair and iPad communication device she carries with her everywhere signal that she's not "typical." However, with the direct support she has received from countless individuals—speech, occupational, and physical therapists, doctors, counselors, psychologists, and psychiatrists, equipment specialists, teachers, professors, dedicated one-on-one aides, classmates, friends, ARC advocates, family members, and more—Chloe has not only made significant strides toward independence but also thrives with cerebral palsy. She is currently attending a local community college and working towards a degree in digital filmography, with hopes of becoming a movie director one day. Her determination and resilience continue to inspire everyone around her.

My hope in sharing Chloe's story is to offer encouragement and hope to other parents who might feel overwhelmed by a lifetime diagnosis for their child. If you find yourself stopped in your tracks by such news and overwhelmed by the next steps in the process of receiving a diagnosis, I want you to know that embracing that label or diagnosis can be a gateway to the support and resources your child needs. Embracing the diagnosis can provide access to essential services and assistance that will help your child develop skills and abilities they may not have otherwise achieved. Rather than seeing it as the end of the world, allow it to open doors that can aid in your child's journey toward greater independence. Reach out to your local community service board for help or your local chapter of The ARC. Ask other parents of children with needs where they are getting services. These case managers, advocates, and other parents will become your new tribe. And there is no stronger tribe than a circle of dedicated people helping a child with special needs. Remember, the diagnosis is not the end—it's the beginning of a new journey filled with possibilities for growth and triumph.

Jessica Wayt embraces life in Colorado with her husband, Ryan, of 25 years. Navigating the complexities of raising their three unique children includes chasing dreams of stardom with their 12-year-old film actor son, attending the many musical performances of their neurodivergent gifted 17-year-old daughter, and supporting Chloe, who has cerebral palsy, in her daily life, college classes, and budding career as a film director. Beyond their busy home life, Jessica serves her community as the chair of the board of directors for her local chapter of The Arc, focusing on providing resources and advocacy for individuals with disabilities. She also volunteers year-round on her local community connections team for Operation Christmas Child.

Dedicated to her aspirations as an author, she is currently working on a full-length biography of her daughter Chloe's life, with Chloe co-authoring the book and adding excerpts from her perspective.

You can connect with Jessica and learn more about a documentary film being made about Chloe's life by using the provided QR code.

ENDNOTES

Section One

1. Maté, G. (2022). The Myth of Normal: Trauma, Illness, and Healing in a Toxic Culture. Avery.

2. McKenna, J. J. (2020). Safe Infant Sleep: Expert Answers to Your Cosleeping Questions. Platypus Media.

3. See Maté

4. Correa-Chávez, M., Mejía-Arauz, R., & Rogoff, B. (Eds.). (2015). Children Learn by Observing and Contributing to Family and Community Endeavors: A Cultural Paradigm (Volume 49). Elsevier.

5. See Maté

6. Judith E. Glaser, *Conversational Intelligence: How Great Leaders Build Trust and Get Extraordinary Results* (New York: Bibliomotion, 2016).

7. Some prominent researchers in this field include Michael Meaney (whose work on maternal care in rats showed epigenetic effects), Moshe Szyf, and Rachel Yehuda (whose research examined trauma effects across generations).

Section Two

8. American Psychological Association (APA) conducts annual "Stress in America" surveys that often include parental stress statistics as does Pew Research Center and the CDC.

9. U.S. Department of Health and Human Services, "Parents Under Pressure: The U.S. Surgeon General's Advisory on the Mental Health and Well-Being of Parents," 2024, https://www.hhs.gov/parents-under-pressure-the-us-surgeon-generals-advisory-on-the-mental-health-and-well-being-of-parents.

10. See U.S. Department of Health and Human Services

Section Three

11. Alex Lloyd, Amy Broadbent, Edmund Brooks, Karen Bulsara, Kim Donoghue, Rouhma Saijaf, Katie N. Sampson, Abigail Thomson, Pasco Fearon, and Peter J. Lawrence, "The Impact of Family Interventions on Communication in the Context of Anxiety and Depression in Those Aged 14–24 Years: Systematic Review of Randomised Control Trials," BJPsych Open 9, no. 5 (August 29, 2023): e161, https://doi.org/10.1192/bjo.2023.545.

12. Purtell, K., Jiang, H., Justice, L. M., Lin, T.-J., Logan, J., (2020). "It's a struggle: Transitioning children into kindergarten." Columbus, Ohio: Crane Center for Early Childhood Research and Policy & The Ohio State University.

13. Roben, CK, Cole PM, Armstrong LM. "Longitudinal relations among language skills, anger expression, and regulatory

strategies in early childhood." Child Dev. 2013 May-June, 84(3):891-905

14. Rachel Minkin and Juliana Horowitz, "Parenting in America Today," Pew Research Center, January 24, 2023.

15. Jennifer J. Harman, Sadie Leder-Elder, and Zeynep Biringen, "Prevalence of Adults Who Are the Targets of Parental Alienating Behaviors and Their Impact," Children and Youth Services Review 106 (November 2019): 104471, https://doi.org/10.1016/j.childyouth.2019.104471.

16. Richard A. Gardner, "The Parental Alienation Syndrome: Past, Present, and Future," Richard A. Gardner, M.D., accessed March 5, 2025, https://richardagardner.com/the-parental-alienation-syndrome-past-present-and-future/.

17. Richard A. Warshak, "Developmental Psychology and the Scientific Status of Parental Alienation," Warshak.com, accessed March 5, 2025, https://www.warshak.com/e-libe/developmental-psychology-and-the-scientific-status-of-parental-alienation/

18. Maggi LeDuc, "Why Sex Education Matters," Power to Decide, February 27, 2023, https://powertodecide.org/why-sex-education-matters.

Section Four

19. American Psychological Association. "Stress in America: Parents and Adults Who Are Caregivers to Children Report Higher Levels of Stress than Adults Without Children."

American Psychological Association, 2023. https://www.apa. org/news/press/releases/stress/2023/infographics/infograph- ic-parents-other-adults.

Section Five

20. youtube.com/watch?v=ZIcmudAKF4M

21. Elaine Aron, "The Highly Sensitive Person," accessed March 15, 2025, https://hsperson.com/.

22. The study was published in *The Journal of Clinical Child & Adolescent Psychiatry* in 2020.

Section Seven

23. Brenan, M. "K-12 Education Satisfaction in U.S. Ties Record Low." Gallup, August 31, 2023. https://news.gallup.com/ poll/510401/education-satisfaction-tiesrecord-low.aspx.

24. Cash, T. N., and D. M. Oppenheimer. "Parental Rights or Parental Wrongs: Parents' Metacognitive Knowledge of the Factors That Influence Their School Choice Decisions." PLoS One 19, no. 4 (2024): e0301768. https://doi.org/10.1371/journal. pone.0301768.

25. Davis-Delano, L.R., Gone, J.P., & Fryberg, S.A. (2020). The psy- chosocial effects of Native American mascots: A comprehen- sive review of empirical research findings. Race, Ethnicity and Education. https://doi.org/10.1080/13613324.2020.1772221

26. Priest, N., Slopen, N., Woolford, S., Philip, J.T., Singer, D., Kauffman, A.D., et al. (2018). Stereotyping across intersections of race and age: Racial stereotyping among White adults working with children. PLoS ONE, 13(9): e0201696. https://doi.org/10.1371/journal.pone.0201696

BIBLIOGRAPHY

American Psychological Association. Annual "Stress in America" surveys.

Aron, Elaine. "The Highly Sensitive Person." Accessed March 15, 2025. https://hsperson.com/.

Brenan, M. "K-12 Education Satisfaction in U.S. Ties Record Low." Gallup, August 31, 2023. https://news.gallup.com/poll/510401/education-satisfaction-tiesrecord-low.aspx.

Cash, T. N., and D. M. Oppenheimer. "Parental Rights or Parental Wrongs: Parents' Metacognitive Knowledge of the Factors That Influence Their School Choice Decisions." PLoS One 19, no. 4 (2024): e0301768. https://doi.org/10.1371/journal.pone.0301768.

Correa-Chávez, M., R. Mejía-Arauz, and B. Rogoff, eds. Children Learn by Observing and Contributing to Family and Community Endeavors: A Cultural Paradigm (Volume 49). Elsevier, 2015.

Davis-Delano, L. R., J. P. Gone, and S. A. Fryberg. "The Psychosocial Effects of Native American Mascots: A Comprehensive Review of Empirical Research Findings." Race, Ethnicity and Education (2020). https://doi.org/10.1080/13613324.2020.1772221.

Gardner, Richard A. "The Parental Alienation Syndrome: Past, Present, and Future." Accessed March 5, 2025. https://richardagardner.com/the-parental-alienation-syndrome-past-present-and-future/.

Glaser, Judith E. Conversational Intelligence: How Great Leaders Build Trust and Get Extraordinary Results. New York: Bibliomotion, 2016.

Harman, Jennifer J., Sadie Leder-Elder, and Zeynep Biringen. "Prevalence of Adults Who Are the Targets of Parental Alienating Behaviors and Their Impact." Children and Youth Services Review 106 (November 2019): 104471. https://doi.org/10.1016/j.childyouth.2019.104471.

LeDuc, Maggi. "Why Sex Education Matters." Power to Decide, February 27, 2023. https://powertodecide.org/why-sex-education-matters.

Lloyd, Alex, Amy Broadbent, Edmund Brooks, Karen Bulsara, Kim Donoghue, Rouhma Saijaf, Katie N. Sampson, Abigail Thomson, Pasco Fearon, and Peter J. Lawrence. "The Impact of Family Interventions on Communication in the Context of Anxiety and Depression in Those Aged 14–24 Years: Systematic Review of Randomised Control Trials." BJPsych Open 9, no. 5 (August 29, 2023): e161. https://doi.org/10.1192/bjo.2023.545.

Maté, G. The Myth of Normal: Trauma, Illness, and Healing in a Toxic Culture. Avery, 2022.

McKenna, J. J. Safe Infant Sleep: Expert Answers to Your Cosleeping Questions. Platypus Media, 2020.

Minkin, Rachel, and Juliana Horowitz. "Parenting in America Today." Pew Research Center, January 24, 2023.

Priest, N., N. Slopen, S. Woolford, J. T. Philip, D. Singer, A. D. Kauffman, et al. "Stereotyping Across Intersections of Race and Age: Racial Stereotyping Among White Adults Working With Children." PLoS ONE 13, no. 9 (2018): e0201696. https://doi.org/10.1371/journal. pone.0201696.

Purtell, K., H. Jiang, L. M. Justice, T.-J. Lin, and J. Logan. "It's a Struggle: Transitioning Children into Kindergarten." Columbus, Ohio: Crane Center for Early Childhood Research and Policy & The Ohio State University, 2020.

Roben, C. K., P. M. Cole, and L. M. Armstrong. "Longitudinal Relations Among Language Skills, Anger Expression, and Regulatory Strategies in Early Childhood." Child Development 84, no. 3 (May-June 2013): 891-905.

U.S. Department of Health and Human Services. "Parents Under Pressure: The U.S. Surgeon General's Advisory on the Mental Health and Well-Being of Parents." 2024. https://www.hhs.gov/ parents-under-pressure-the-us-surgeon-generals-advisory-on-the-mental-health-and-well-being-of-parents.

Warshak, Richard A. "Developmental Psychology and the Scientific Status of Parental Alienation." Accessed March 5, 2025. https://www.warshak.com/e-libe/developmental-psychology-and-the-scientific-status-of-parental-alienation/.

YOU'VE FINISHED THE BOOK, BUT THE JOURNEY DOESN'T HAVE TO END.

Want more connection in your family? As a reader of *The Perfectly Imperfect Family*, you get a FREE invitation to join us for...

THE HAPPILY FAMILY ONLINE CONFERENCE

Connect with therapists, authors, psychologists, and parent coaches in this supportive online event at no cost. Gain deeper insights into your family and join a community of parents committed to growth.

- Hear from leading experts in child behavior, conscious parenting, and brain science
- Practical workshops on emotional regulation, healthy boundaries, and connection
- Get answers to your specific family challenges
- Gain digital tools and resources from top presenters

"I feel so encouraged and empowered. You and all the presenters made all the content accessible, easy to understand, easy to implement, and it was fun. I love how you and so many presenters used personal experiences and made it so relatable. It's very powerful."
—Ingrid M., previous attendee

JOIN US!

Visit: HappilyFamily.com/BookBonus

Join over 100k parents worldwide who are creating more connected, peaceful families—one imperfect step at a time.

QUESTIONS? EMAIL SUPPORT@HAPPILYFAMILY.COM

Made in the USA
Monee, IL
14 May 2025